JUSTICE SOCIETY OF AMERICA

BLACK ADAM AND ISIS

JUSTICE SOCIETY of AMERICA

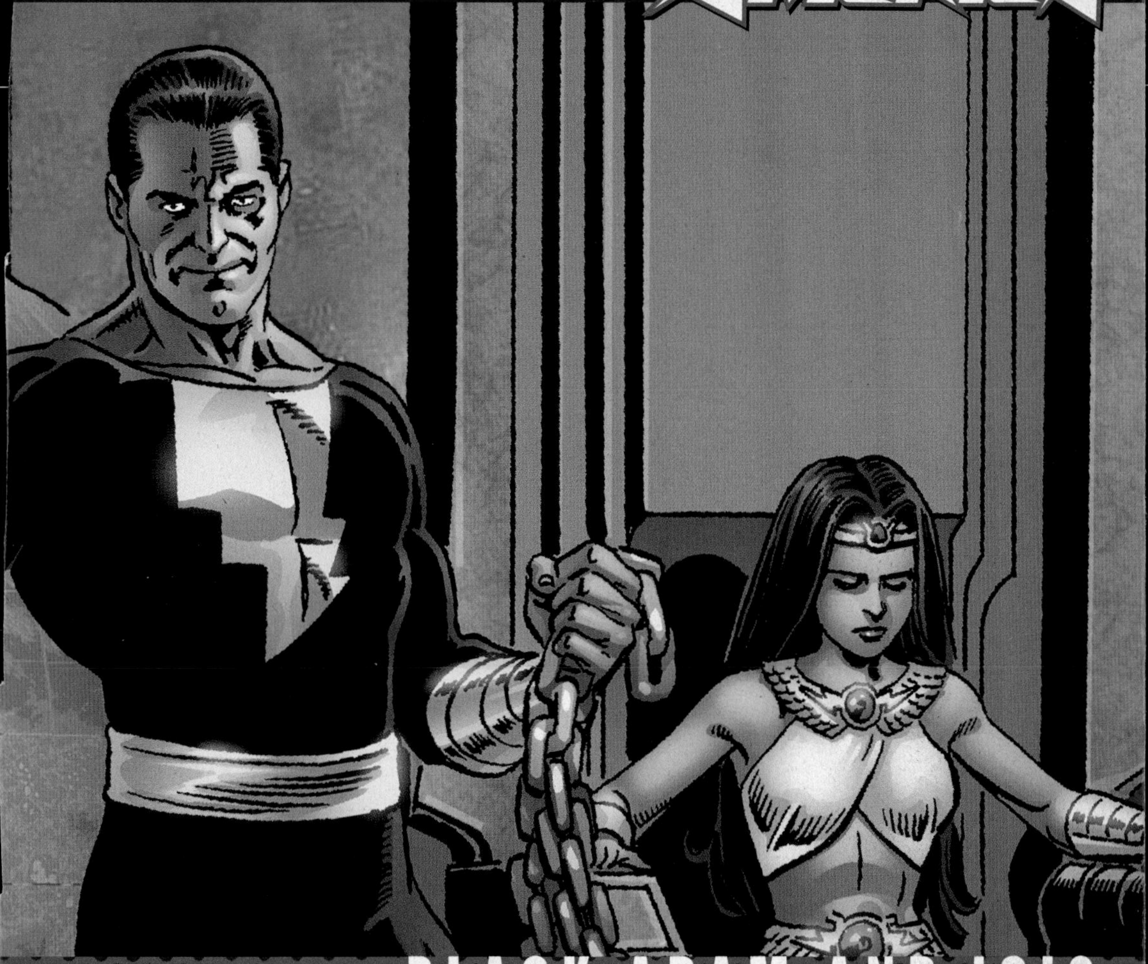

BLACK ADAM AND ISIS

JSA #23-25
STORY BY **GEOFF JOHNS & JERRY ORDWAY** PENCILS **JERRY ORDWAY**
INKS **BOB WIACEK** WITH **JERRY ORDWAY**

JSA #26
WRITER **GEOFF JOHNS** PENCILS **DALE EAGLESHAM** INKS **NATHAN MASSENGILL**

JSA #27 & 28
WRITER AND PENCILS **JERRY ORDWAY** INKER **BOB WIACEK**

ORIGINS & OMENS
WRITER **MATTHEW STURGES** ART **FERNANDO PASARIN**

COLORIST **HI-FI**
LETTERER **ROB LEIGH**

DAN DIDIO SVP – EXECUTIVE EDITOR MICHAEL SIGLAIN MIKE CARLIN EDITORS – ORIGINAL SERIES
GEORG BREWER VP – DESIGN & DC DIRECT CREATIVE BOB HARRAS GROUP EDITOR – COLLECTED EDITIONS
ANTON KAWASAKI EDITOR ROBBIN BROSTERMAN DESIGN DIRECTOR – BOOKS

DC COMICS
PAUL LEVITZ PRESIDENT & PUBLISHER RICHARD BRUNING SVP – CREATIVE DIRECTOR
PATRICK CALDON EVP – FINANCE & OPERATIONS AMY GENKINS SVP – BUSINESS & LEGAL AFFAIRS
JIM LEE EDITORIAL DIRECTOR – WILDSTORM GREGORY NOVECK SVP – CREATIVE AFFAIRS
STEVE ROTTERDAM SVP – SALES & MARKETING CHERYL RUBIN SVP – BRAND MANAGEMENT

COVER BY ALEX ROSS
PUBLICATION DESIGN BY ROBBIE BIEDERMAN

JUSTICE SOCIETY OF AMERICA: BLACK ADAM AND ISIS

DC COMICS, 1700 BROADWAY, NEW YORK, NY 10019. A WARNER BROS. ENTERTAINMENT COMPANY. PRINTED BY RR DONNELLY, SALEM, VA, USA. 8/25/10 FIRST PRINTING.
ISBN: 978-1-4012-2531-5

SUSTAINABLE FORESTRY INITIATIVE
Certified Chain of Custody
Promoting Sustainable Forest Management
www.sfiprogram.org

Fiber used in this product line meets the sourcing requirements of the SFI program www.sfiprogram.org NFS-SPICOC-C000180

GREEN LANTERN Engineer Alan Scott found a lantern carved from a meteorite known as the Starheart. Fulfilling the lamp's prophecy to grant astonishing power, Scott tapped into the emerald energy and fought injustice as the Green Lantern. His ring can generate a variety of effects and energy constructs, sustained purely by his will.

THE FLASH The first in a long line of super-speedsters, Jay Garrick is capable of running at velocities near the speed of light. A scientist, Garrick has also served as mentor to other speedsters, and to many heroes over several generations.

WILDCAT A former heavyweight boxing champ, Ted Grant, a.k.a. Wildcat, prowls the mean streets defending the helpless. One of the world's foremost hand-to-hand combatants, he has trained many of today's best fighters — including Black Canary, Catwoman, and the Batman himself.

HAWKMAN Originally Prince Khufu of ancient Egypt, the hero who would become known as Hawkman discovered an alien spacecraft from the planet Thanagar, powered by a mysterious antigravity element called Nth metal. The unearthly energies of the metal transformed his soul, and he and his love Princess Chay-Ara were reincarnated over and over for centuries. Currently he is Carter Hall, archaeologist and adventurer.

POWER GIRL Once confused about her origins, Karen Starr now knows she is the cousin of an alternate-Earth Superman — who gave his life in the Infinite Crisis. Her enhanced strength and powers of flight and invulnerability are matched only by her self-confidence in action, which sometimes borders on arrogance.

MR. TERRIFIC Haunted by the death of his wife, Olympic gold medal-winning decathlete Michael Holt was ready to take his own life. Instead, inspired by the Spectre's story of the original Mr. Terrific, he rededicated himself to ensuring fair play among the street youth, using his wealth and technical skills to become the living embodiment of those ideals. He now divides his time between the JSA and the government agency known as Checkmate.

HOURMAN Rick Tyler struggled for a while before accepting his role as the son of the original Hourman. It hasn't been an easy road — he's endured addiction to the Miraclo drug that increases his strength and endurance, and nearly died from a strange disease. Now, after mastering the drug, he uses a special hourglass that enables him to see one hour into the future.

LIBERTY BELLE Jesse Chambers is the daughter of the Golden Age Johnny Quick and Liberty Belle. Originally adopting her father's speed formula, Jesse became the superhero known as Jesse Quick. After a brief period without powers, Jesse has returned — now taking over her mother's role. As the new Liberty Belle, Jesse is an

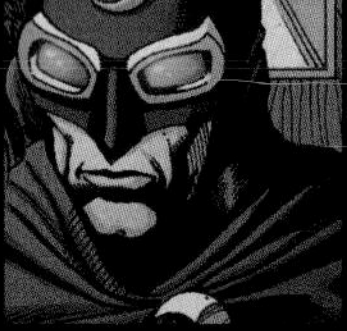

DR. MID-NITE A medical prodigy, Pieter Anton Cross refused to work within the limits of the system. Treating people on his own, he came into contact with a dangerous drug that altered his body chemistry, enabling him to see light in the infrared spectrum. Although he lost his normal sight in a murder attempt disguised as a car accident, his uncanny night vision allows him to protect the weak under the assumed identity of Dr. Mid-Nite.

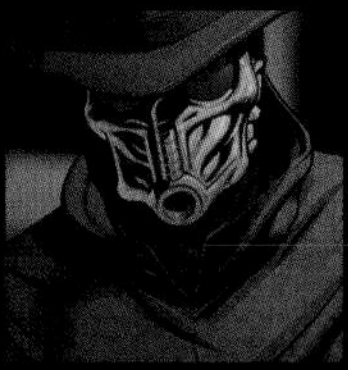

SANDMAN Sandy Hawkins was the ward of original Sandman Wesley Dodds, and he is the nephew of Dodds's lifelong partner, Dian Belmont. After a bizarre accident, Hawkins was able to transform himself into a pure silicon or sand form. Recently, he has been experiencing prophetic dreams. He also carries a gas mask, gas guns and other equipment.

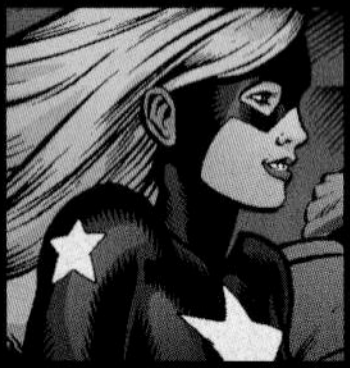

STARGIRL When Courtney Whitmore discovered the cosmic converter belt that had been worn by the JSA's original Star-Spangled Kid (her stepfather, Pat Dugan, was the Kid's sidekick Stripesy), she saw it as an opportunity to cut class and kick some butt. Now called Stargirl, she divides her time between her adventures with the JSA and bickering/teaming up with Pat — who sometimes monitors Courtney from his S.T.R.I.P.E. robot.

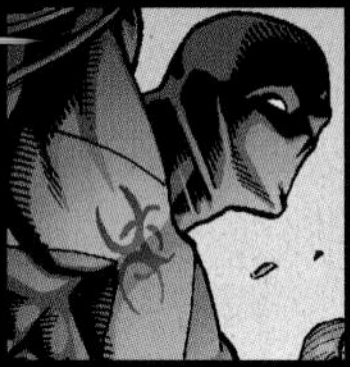

DAMAGE Grant Emerson has had a difficult life. Growing up, he was the victim of an abusive foster father. Then later, after discovering his explosive powers, he accidentally blew up half of downtown Atlanta. Last year, he was almost beaten to death by the super-speed villain known as Zoom. Grant has worn a full-face mask as Damage ever since.

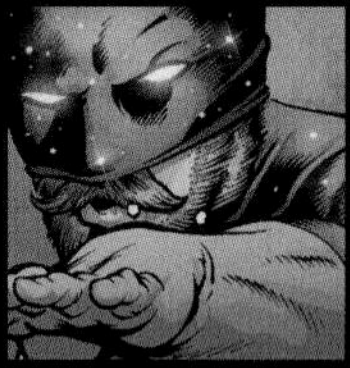

STARMAN A mysterious new Starman recently appeared in Opal City, saving its citizens numerous times. He apparently suffers from some form of schizophrenia, and hears voices in his head. Voluntarily residing in the Sunshine Sanitarium, Starman will occasionally leave and use his gravity-altering powers to fight crime.

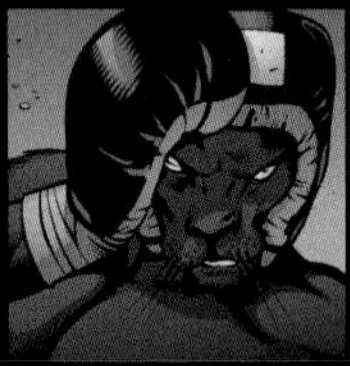

WILDCAT II Tommy Bronson is the newly discovered son of original Wildcat Ted Grant. But it's not quite "like father, like son" here. For one thing, Tom doesn't want to be a fighter like his dad. And second, this new Wildcat has the ability to turn into a feral creature, with enhanced agility and animalistic senses.

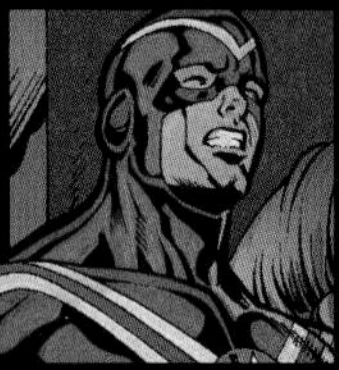

CITIZEN STEEL The grandson of the original Steel, Nathan Heywood is a former football hero who has suffered numerous tragedies. First, an injury and infection required his leg to be amputated. Then, a vicious attack by the Fourth Reich wiped out most of his family. But during the attack, a bizarre incident left him with metal-like skin and superhuman strength.

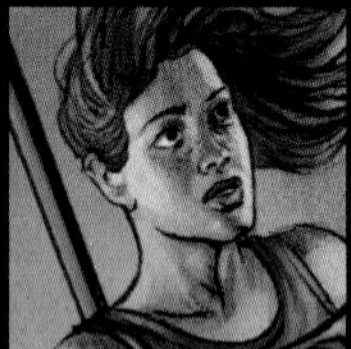

CYCLONE Maxine Hunkel is the granddaughter of the original Red Tornado, Abigail Mathilda "Ma" Hunkel (who is the current custodian of the Justice Society Museum). Maxine grew up idolizing her grandmother's allies in the JSA and still can't believe she's now part of the team. Maxine has the power of wind manipulation and can summon up cyclones and whirlwinds while gliding through the air.

JUSTICE SOCIETY OF AMERICA #23 cover by Alex Ross
Interior art by Jerry Ordway & Bob Wiacek

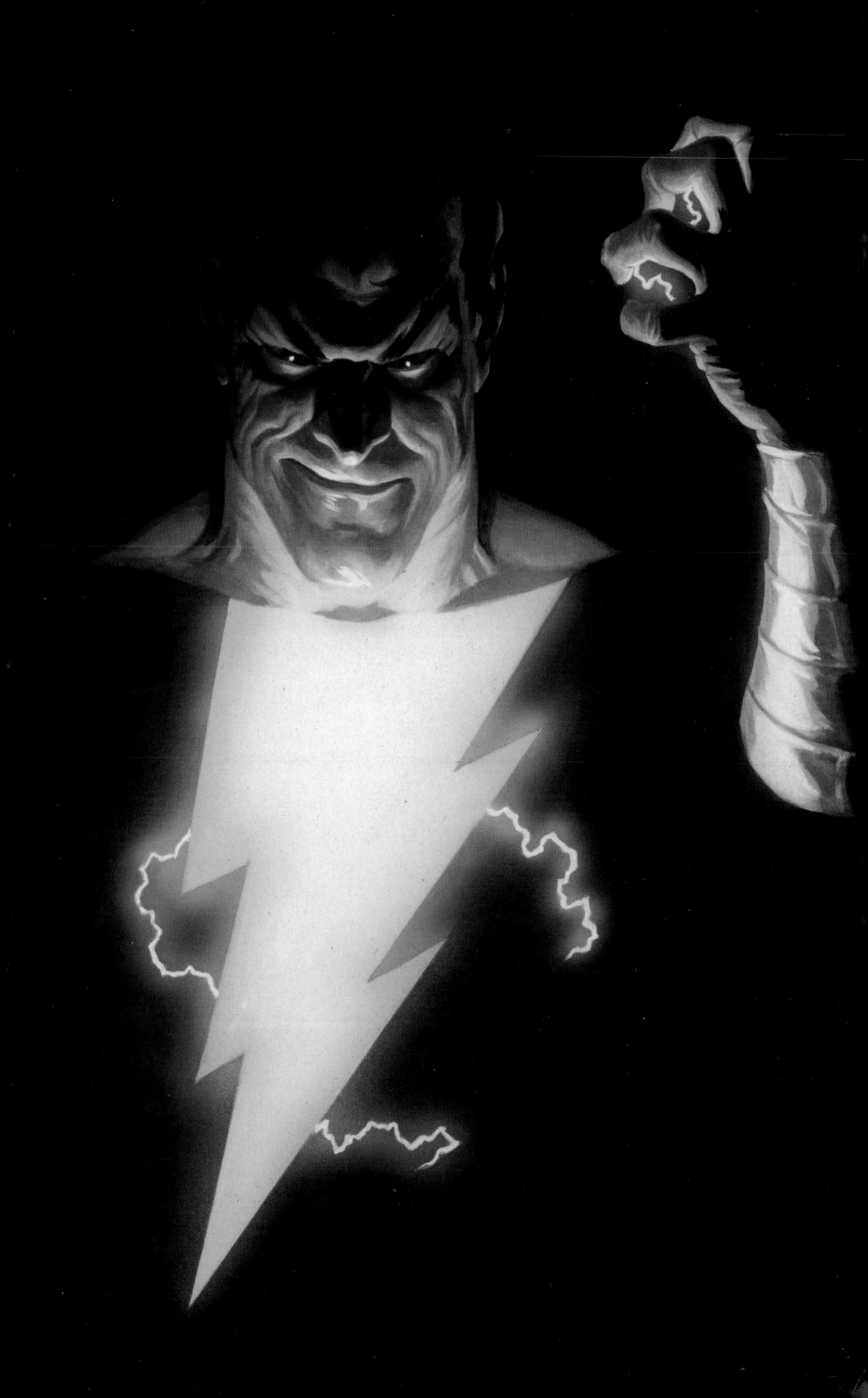

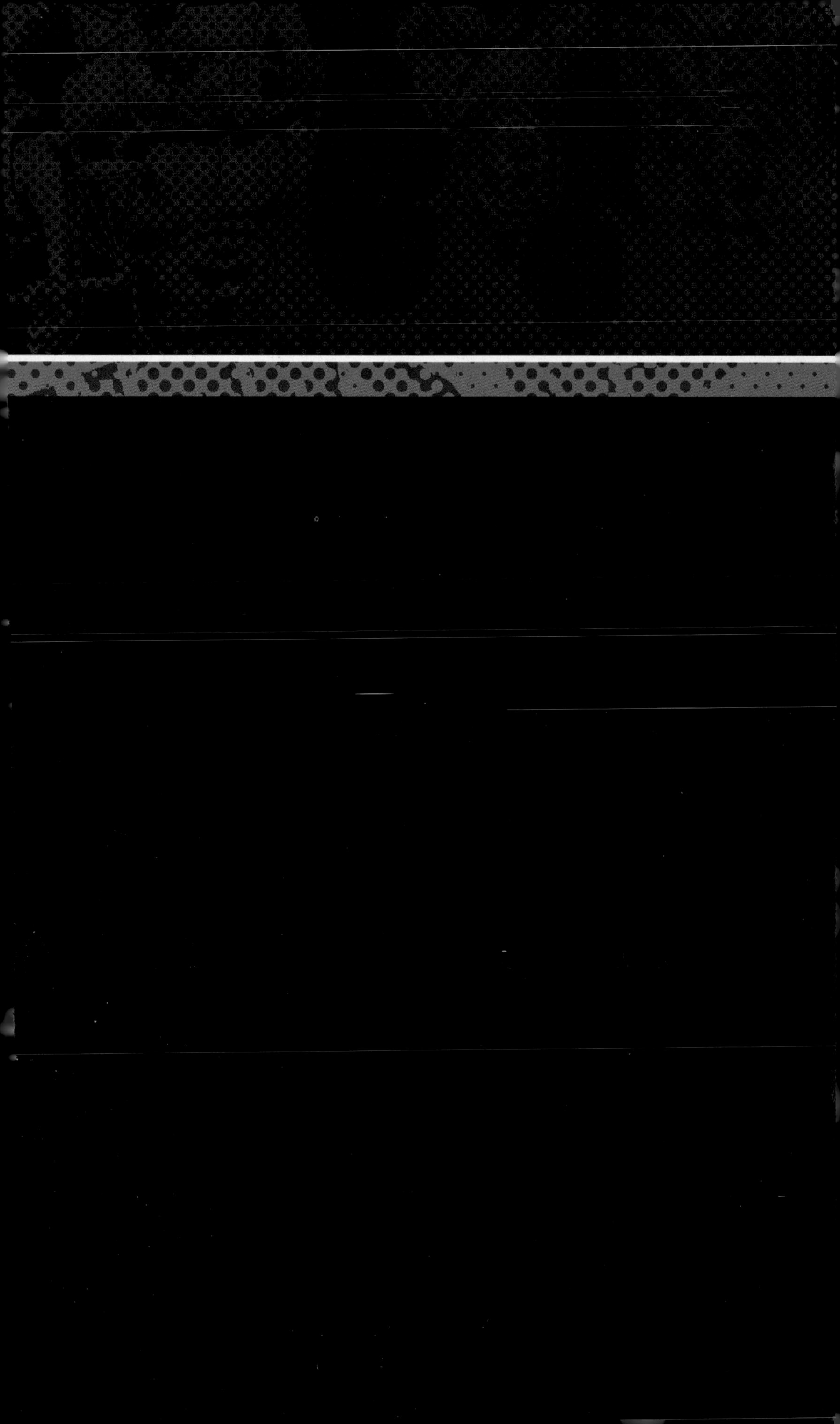

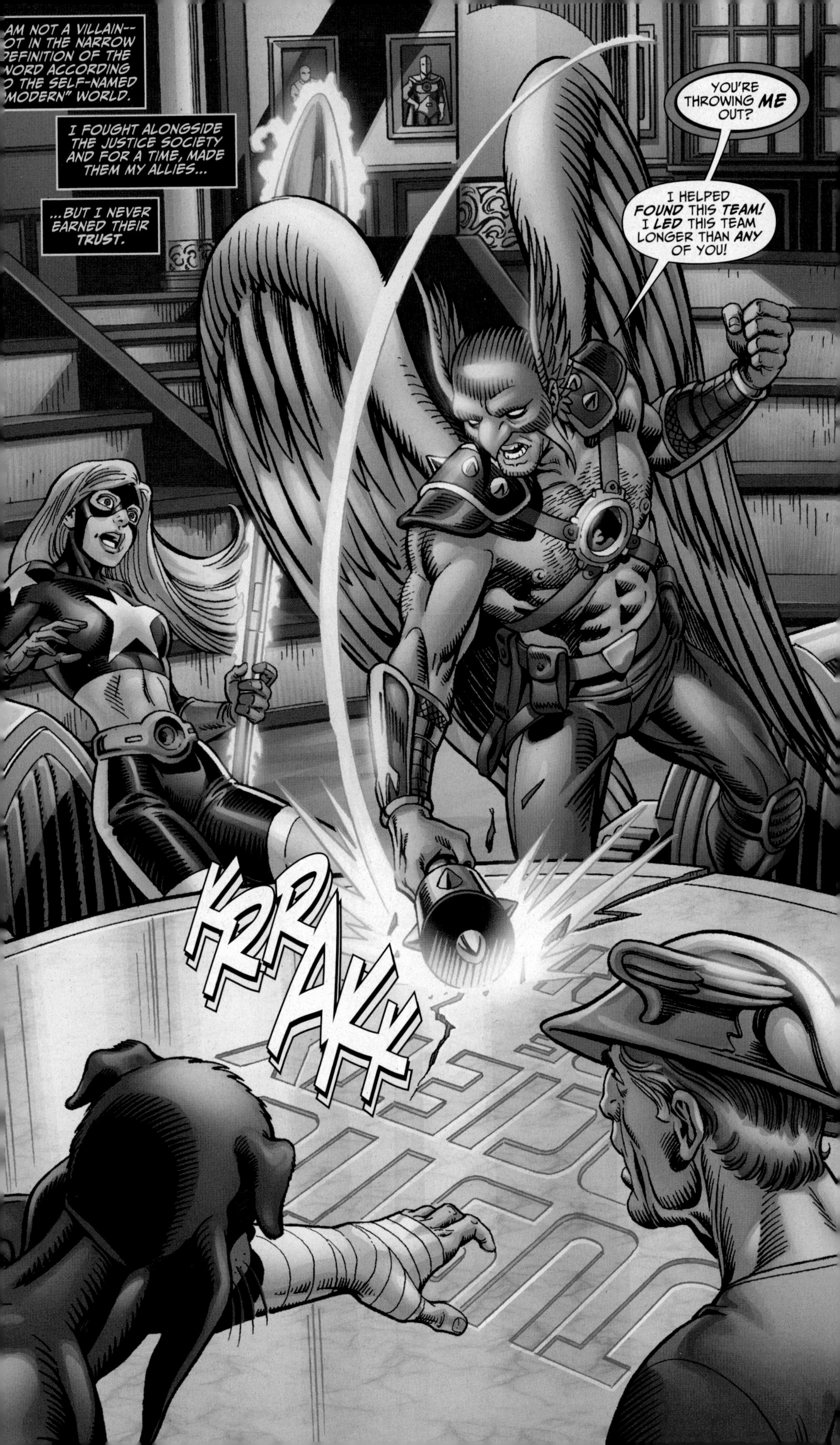
AM NOT A VILLAIN-- OT IN THE NARROW DEFINITION OF THE WORD ACCORDING O THE SELF-NAMED "MODERN" WORLD.
I FOUGHT ALONGSIDE THE JUSTICE SOCIETY AND FOR A TIME, MADE THEM MY ALLIES...
...BUT I NEVER EARNED THEIR TRUST.
YOU'RE THROWING **ME** OUT?
I HELPED **FOUND** THIS **TEAM!** I **LED** THIS TEAM LONGER THAN **ANY** OF YOU!
KRRAKK

THAT TABLE IS HANDMADE, YOU KNOW.
I *KNOW*. I *MADE* IT.
NO ONE IS SUGGESTING A *PERMANENT* LEAVE, CARTER.
THINK OF IT AS A COOLING-O PERIOD.
EACH ONE OF US HAD OUR *FAITH* TESTED BY GOG.
TRUE, MID-NITE, BUT HAWKMAN *DIVIDED* THE TEAM.
THOSE KIDS WHO SIDED WITH ME ARE THE *FUTURE*, ALAN.
THEY'RE AS TIRED AS I AM OF CODDLING CRIMINALS, AND WAITING ON YOU TO TELL THEM WHEN IT'S RIGHT TO FOLLOW THEIR *"MORAL COMPASS."*
YOU CAN PUNISH *THEM* A "TIME-OUT" NOT *ME*. I'M D
CARTER--! JAY, LET GO OF ME!
LET GO OF *HIM*, ALAN. HE'LL BE BACK.
HAWKMAN *ALWAYS* RETURNS.

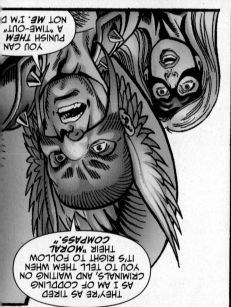

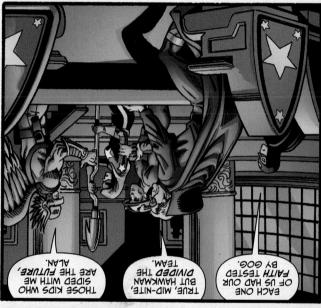

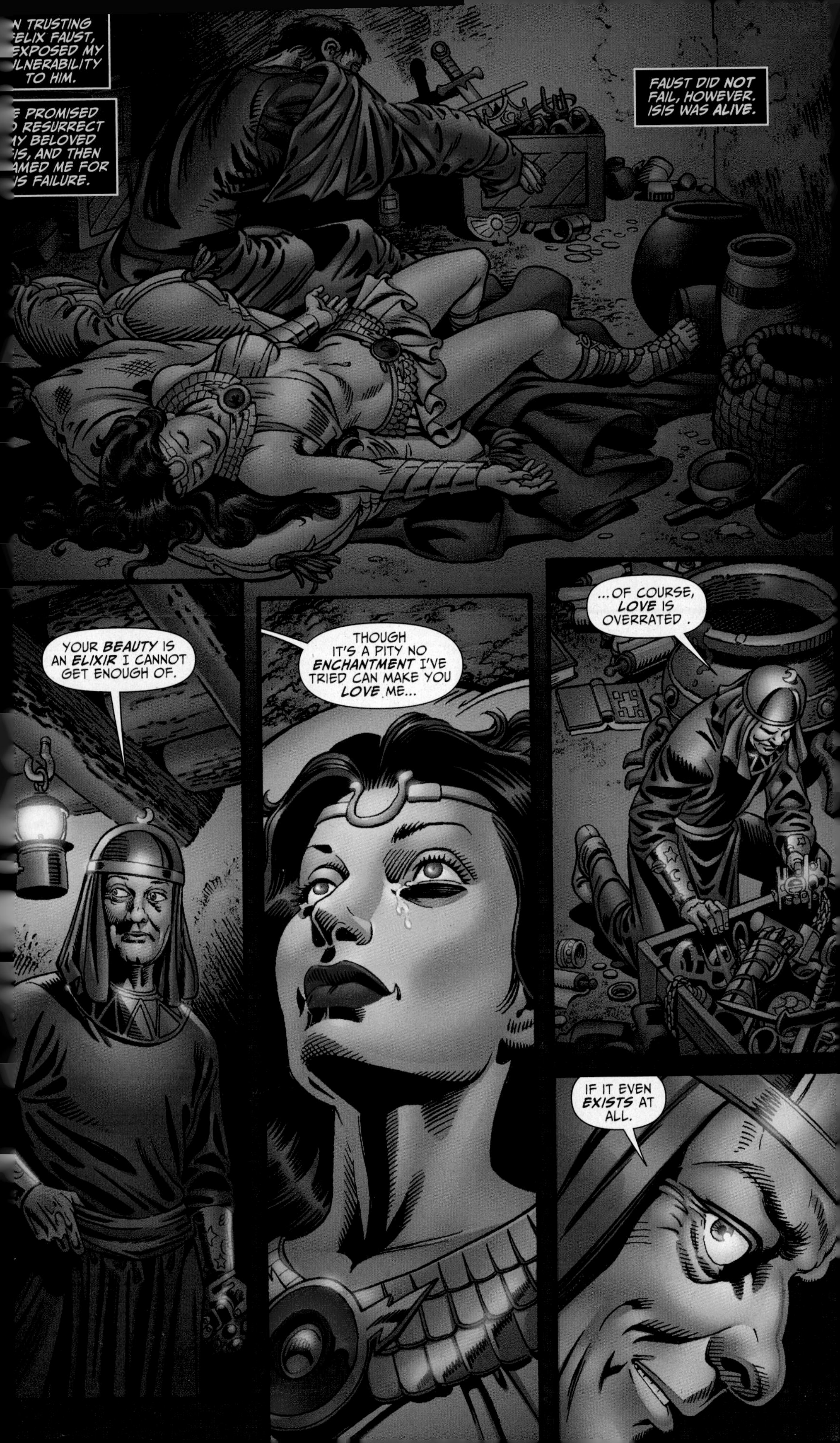
N TRUSTING FELIX FAUST, EXPOSED MY ULNERABILITY TO HIM.
E PROMISED O RESURRECT MY BELOVED SIS, AND THEN AMED ME FOR IS FAILURE.
FAUST DID NOT FAIL, HOWEVER. ISIS WAS ALIVE.
YOUR BEAUTY IS AN ELIXIR I CANNOT GET ENOUGH OF.
THOUGH IT'S A PITY NO ENCHANTMENT I'VE TRIED CAN MAKE YOU LOVE ME...
...OF COURSE, LOVE IS OVERRATED.
IF IT EVEN EXISTS AT ALL.

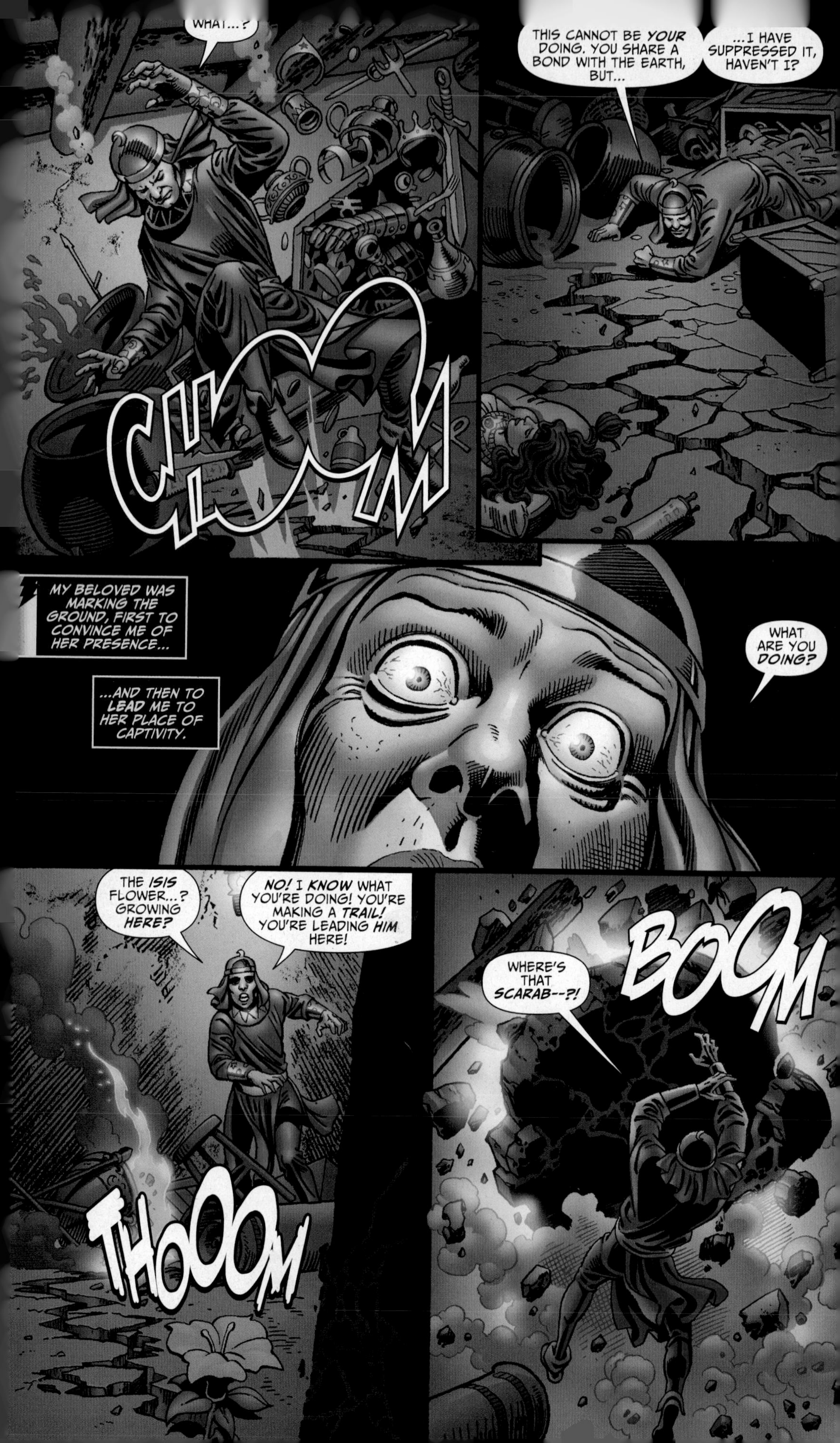
WHAT...?
CHOOM
THIS CANNOT BE *YOUR* DOING. YOU SHARE A BOND WITH THE EARTH, BUT...
...I HAVE SUPPRESSED IT, HAVEN'T I?
MY BELOVED WAS MARKING THE GROUND, FIRST TO CONVINCE ME OF HER PRESENCE...
...AND THEN TO *LEAD* ME TO HER PLACE OF CAPTIVITY.
WHAT ARE YOU *DOING?*
THE *ISIS* FLOWER...? GROWING *HERE?*
NO! I *KNOW* WHAT YOU'RE DOING! YOU'RE MAKING A *TRAIL!* YOU'RE LEADING *HIM* HERE!
THOOOM
WHERE'S THAT *SCARAB--?!*
BOOM

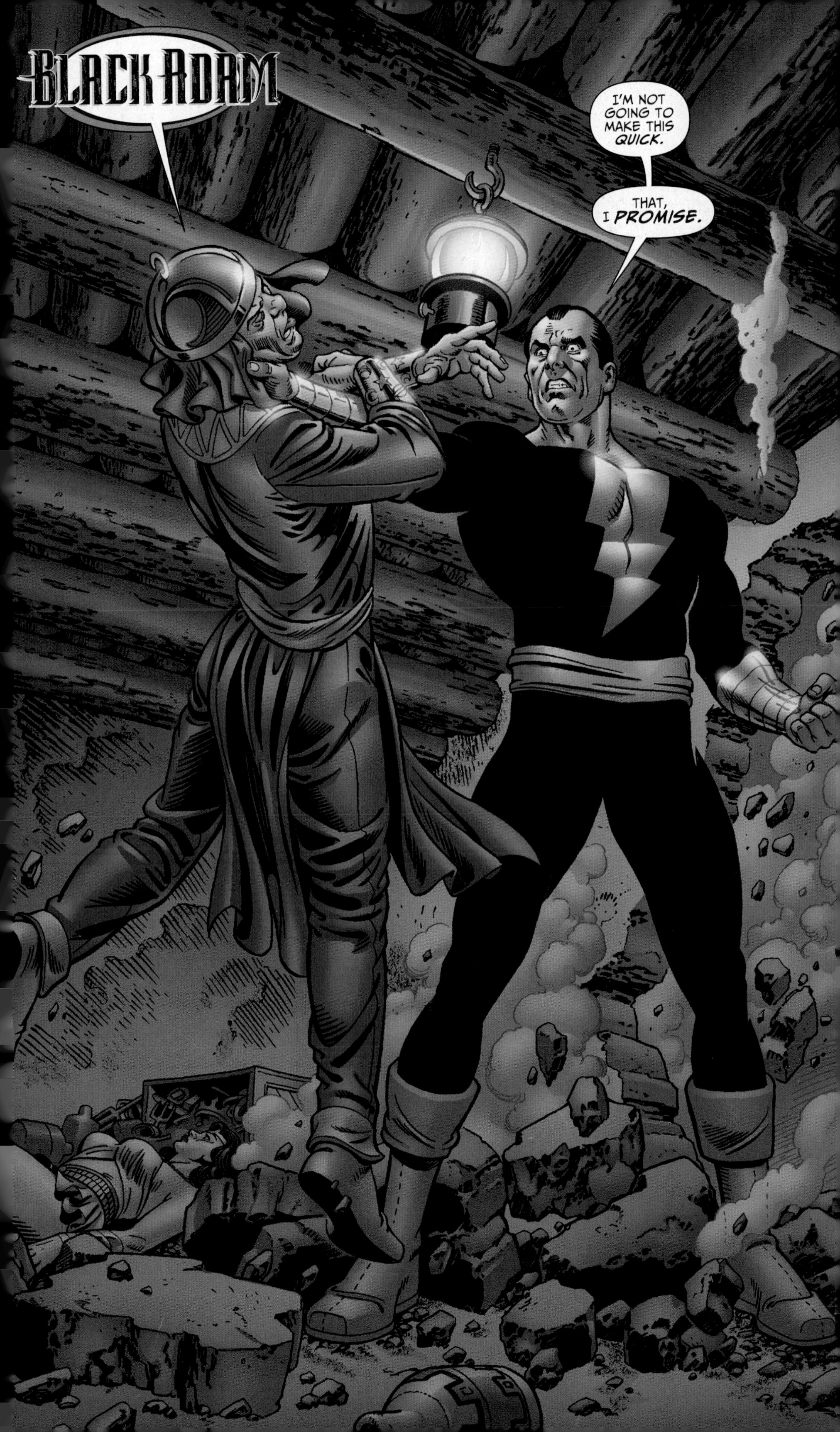
BLACK ADAM
I'M NOT GOING TO MAKE THIS QUICK.
THAT, I PROMISE.

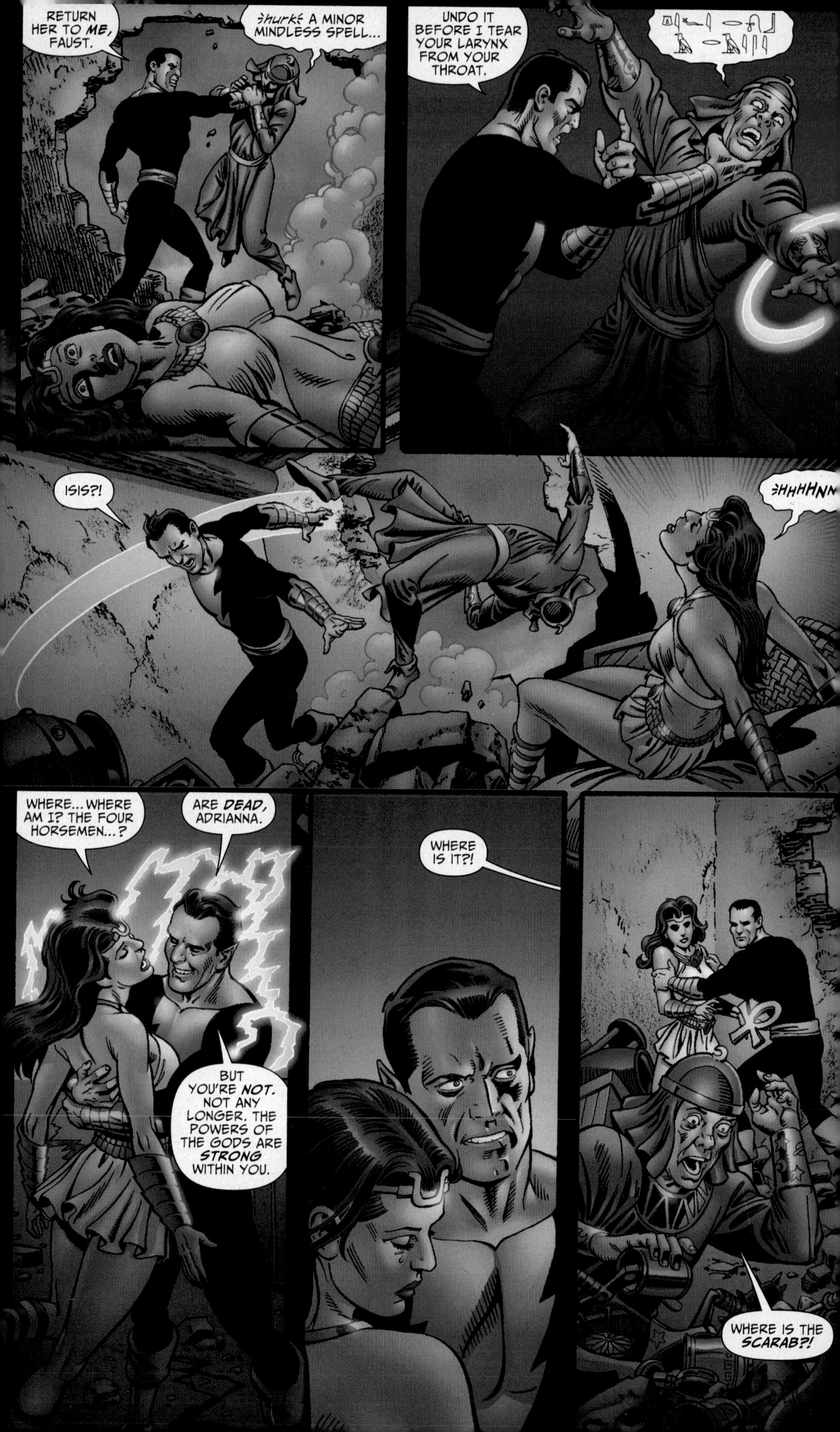
RETURN HER TO *ME*, FAUST.
≷hurk≶ A MINOR MINDLESS SPELL...
UNDO IT BEFORE I TEAR YOUR LARYNX FROM YOUR THROAT.
ISIS?!
≷HHHHNN
WHERE... WHERE AM I? THE FOUR HORSEMEN...?
ARE *DEAD*, ADRIANNA.
BUT YOU'RE *NOT*. NOT ANY LONGER. THE POWERS OF THE GODS ARE *STRONG* WITHIN YOU.
WHERE IS IT?!
WHERE IS THE *SCARAB?!*

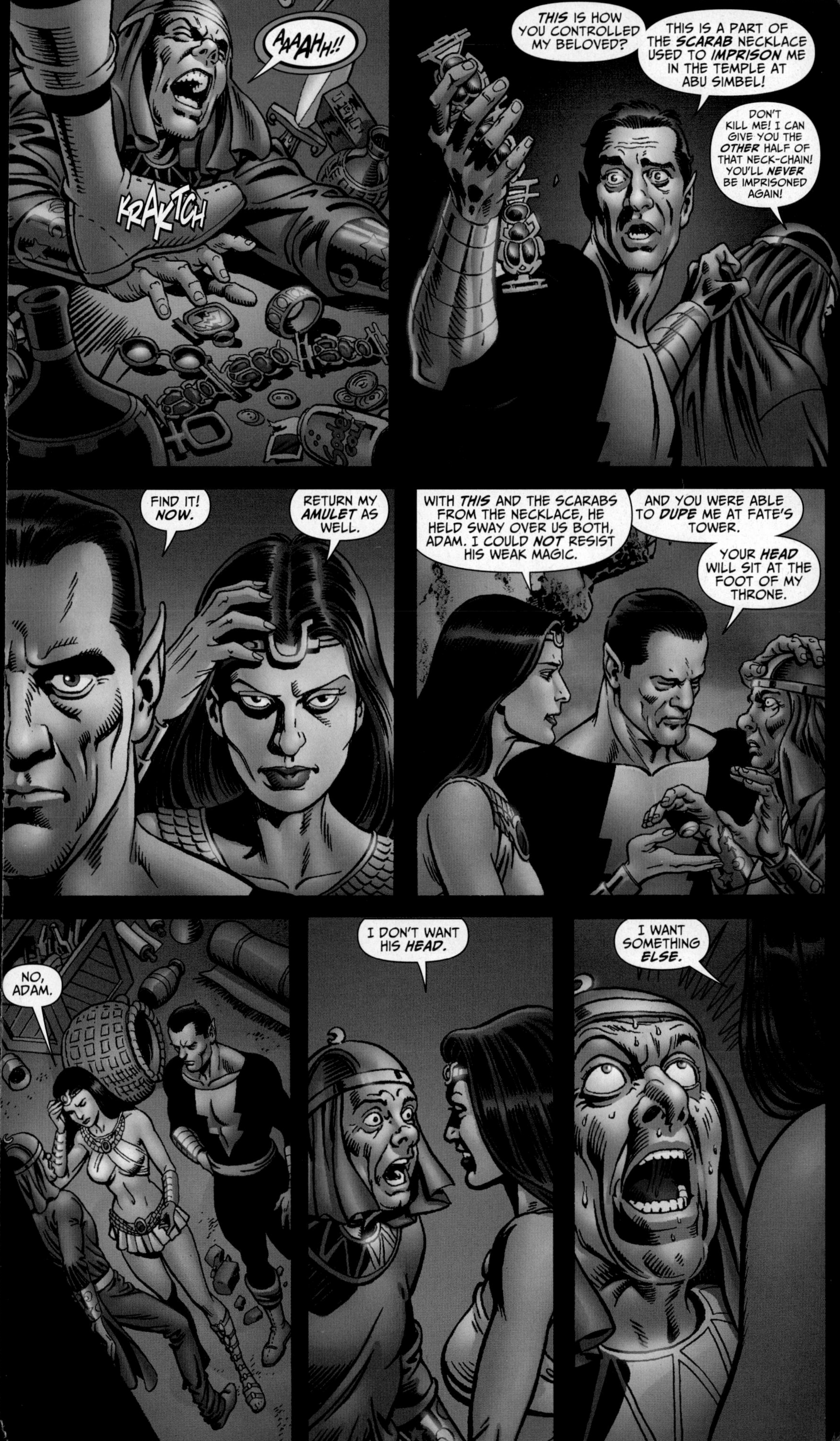
AAAAHH!!
KRAKTCH
THIS IS HOW YOU CONTROLLED MY BELOVED?
THIS IS A PART OF THE SCARAB NECKLACE USED TO IMPRISON ME IN THE TEMPLE AT ABU SIMBEL!
DON'T KILL ME! I CAN GIVE YOU THE OTHER HALF OF THAT NECK-CHAIN! YOU'LL NEVER BE IMPRISONED AGAIN!
FIND IT! NOW.
RETURN MY AMULET AS WELL.
WITH THIS AND THE SCARABS FROM THE NECKLACE, HE HELD SWAY OVER US BOTH, ADAM. I COULD NOT RESIST HIS WEAK MAGIC.
AND YOU WERE ABLE TO DUPE ME AT FATE'S TOWER.
YOUR HEAD WILL SIT AT THE FOOT OF MY THRONE.
NO, ADAM.
I DON'T WANT HIS HEAD.
I WANT SOMETHING ELSE.

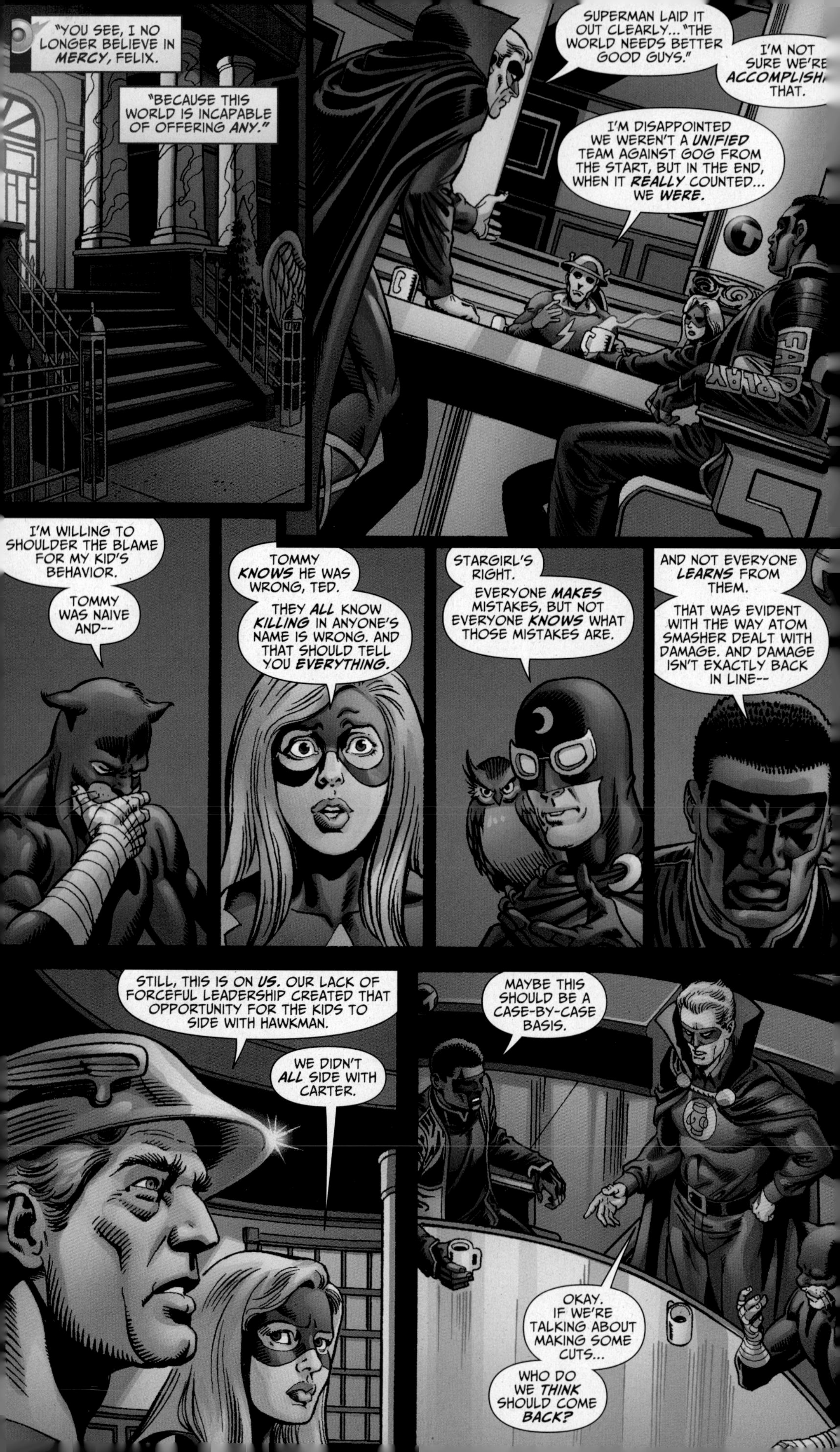
"YOU SEE, I NO LONGER BELIEVE IN *MERCY*, FELIX.
"BECAUSE THIS WORLD IS INCAPABLE OF OFFERING *ANY*."
SUPERMAN LAID IT OUT CLEARLY... "THE WORLD NEEDS BETTER GOOD GUYS."
I'M NOT SURE WE'RE *ACCOMPLISH* THAT.
I'M DISAPPOINTED WE WEREN'T A *UNIFIED* TEAM AGAINST GOG FROM THE START, BUT IN THE END, WHEN IT *REALLY* COUNTED... WE *WERE*.
I'M WILLING TO SHOULDER THE BLAME FOR MY KID'S BEHAVIOR.
TOMMY WAS NAIVE AND--
TOMMY *KNOWS* HE WAS WRONG, TED.
THEY *ALL* KNOW *KILLING* IN ANYONE'S NAME IS WRONG. AND THAT SHOULD TELL YOU *EVERYTHING*.
STARGIRL'S RIGHT.
EVERYONE *MAKES* MISTAKES, BUT NOT EVERYONE *KNOWS* WHAT THOSE MISTAKES ARE.
AND NOT EVERYONE *LEARNS* FROM THEM.
THAT WAS EVIDENT WITH THE WAY ATOM SMASHER DEALT WITH DAMAGE. AND DAMAGE ISN'T EXACTLY BACK IN LINE--
STILL, THIS IS ON *US*. OUR LACK OF FORCEFUL LEADERSHIP CREATED THAT OPPORTUNITY FOR THE KIDS TO SIDE WITH HAWKMAN.
WE DIDN'T *ALL* SIDE WITH CARTER.
MAYBE THIS SHOULD BE A CASE-BY-CASE BASIS.
OKAY. IF WE'RE TALKING ABOUT MAKING SOME CUTS...
WHO DO WE *THINK* SHOULD COME *BACK?*

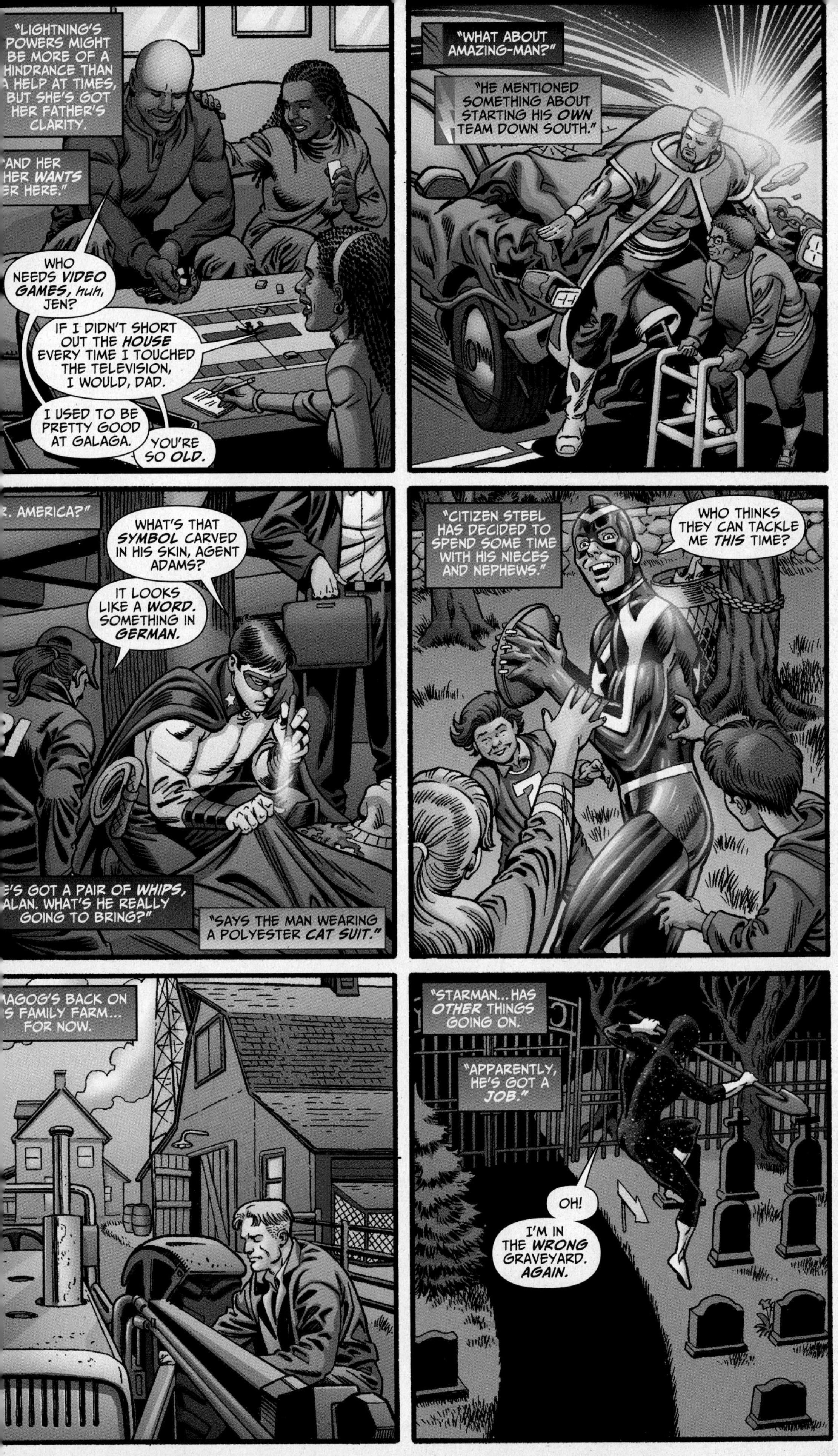
"LIGHTNING'S POWERS MIGHT BE MORE OF A HINDRANCE THAN A HELP AT TIMES, BUT SHE'S GOT HER FATHER'S CLARITY.
"AND HER HER WANTS ER HERE."
WHO NEEDS VIDEO GAMES, huh, JEN?
IF I DIDN'T SHORT OUT THE HOUSE EVERY TIME I TOUCHED THE TELEVISION, I WOULD, DAD.
I USED TO BE PRETTY GOOD AT GALAGA.
YOU'RE SO OLD.
"WHAT ABOUT AMAZING-MAN?"
"HE MENTIONED SOMETHING ABOUT STARTING HIS OWN TEAM DOWN SOUTH."
. AMERICA?"
WHAT'S THAT SYMBOL CARVED IN HIS SKIN, AGENT ADAMS?
IT LOOKS LIKE A WORD. SOMETHING IN GERMAN.
E'S GOT A PAIR OF WHIPS, ALAN. WHAT'S HE REALLY GOING TO BRING?"
"SAYS THE MAN WEARING A POLYESTER CAT SUIT."
"CITIZEN STEEL HAS DECIDED TO SPEND SOME TIME WITH HIS NIECES AND NEPHEWS."
WHO THINKS THEY CAN TACKLE ME THIS TIME?
AGOG'S BACK ON S FAMILY FARM... FOR NOW.
"STARMAN... HAS OTHER THINGS GOING ON.
"APPARENTLY, HE'S GOT A JOB."
OH!
I'M IN THE WRONG GRAVEYARD. AGAIN.

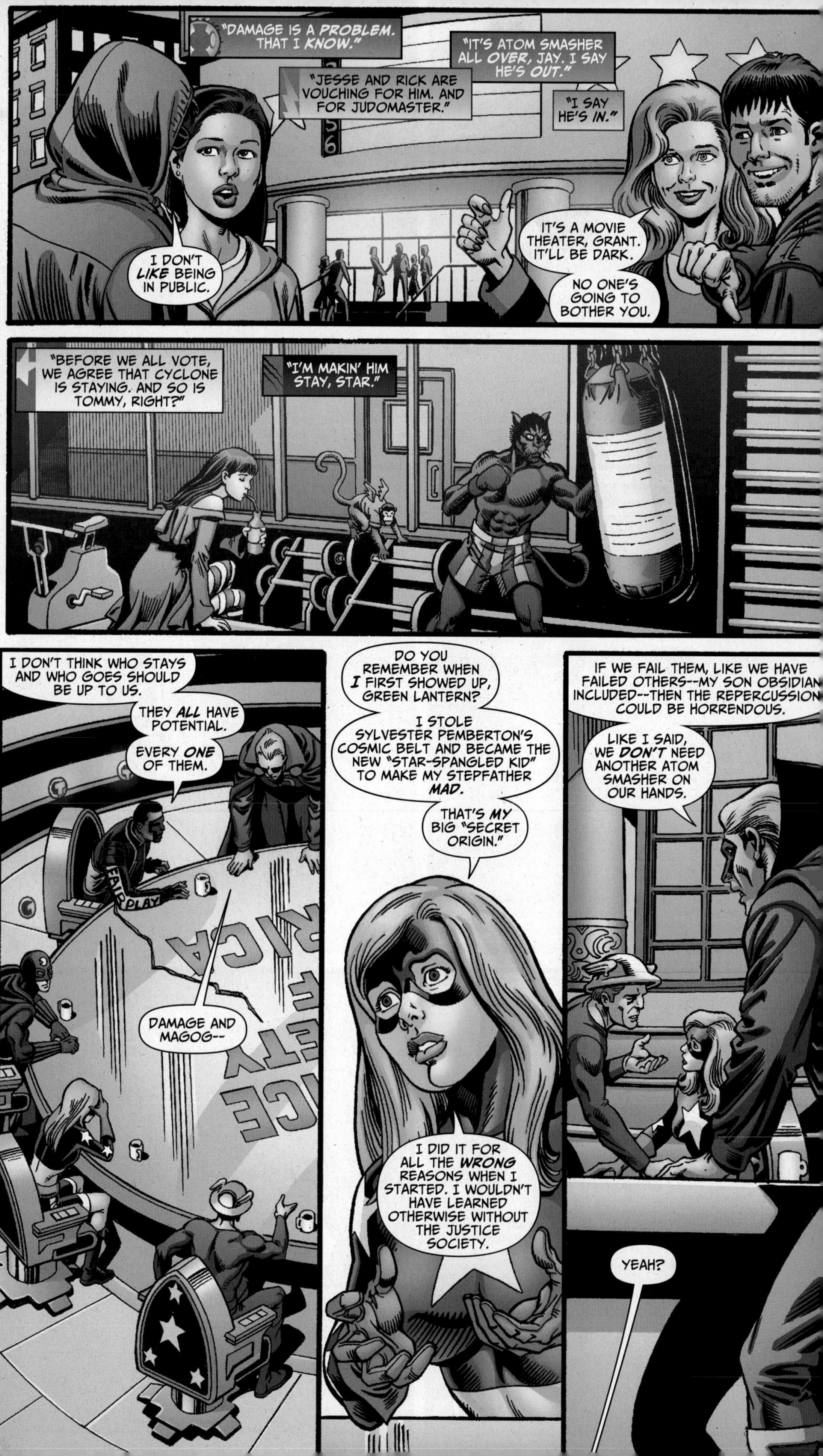
"DAMAGE IS A *PROBLEM*. THAT I *KNOW*."
"JESSE AND RICK ARE VOUCHING FOR HIM. AND FOR JUDOMASTER."
"IT'S ATOM SMASHER ALL *OVER*, JAY. I SAY HE'S *OUT*."
"I SAY HE'S *IN*."
I DON'T *LIKE* BEING IN PUBLIC.
IT'S A MOVIE THEATER, GRANT. IT'LL BE DARK.
NO ONE'S GOING TO BOTHER YOU.
"BEFORE WE ALL VOTE, WE AGREE THAT CYCLONE IS STAYING. AND SO IS TOMMY, RIGHT?"
"I'M MAKIN' HIM STAY, STAR."
I DON'T THINK WHO STAYS AND WHO GOES SHOULD BE UP TO US.
THEY *ALL* HAVE POTENTIAL.
EVERY *ONE* OF THEM.
DAMAGE AND MAGOG--
DO YOU REMEMBER WHEN *I* FIRST SHOWED UP, GREEN LANTERN?
I STOLE SYLVESTER PEMBERTON'S COSMIC BELT AND BECAME THE NEW "STAR-SPANGLED KID" TO MAKE MY STEPFATHER *MAD*.
THAT'S *MY* BIG "SECRET ORIGIN."
I DID IT FOR ALL THE *WRONG* REASONS WHEN I STARTED. I WOULDN'T HAVE LEARNED OTHERWISE WITHOUT THE JUSTICE SOCIETY.
IF WE FAIL THEM, LIKE WE HAVE FAILED OTHERS--MY SON OBSIDIAN INCLUDED--THEN THE REPERCUSSION COULD BE HORRENDOUS.
LIKE I SAID, WE *DON'T* NEED ANOTHER ATOM SMASHER ON OUR HANDS.
YEAH?

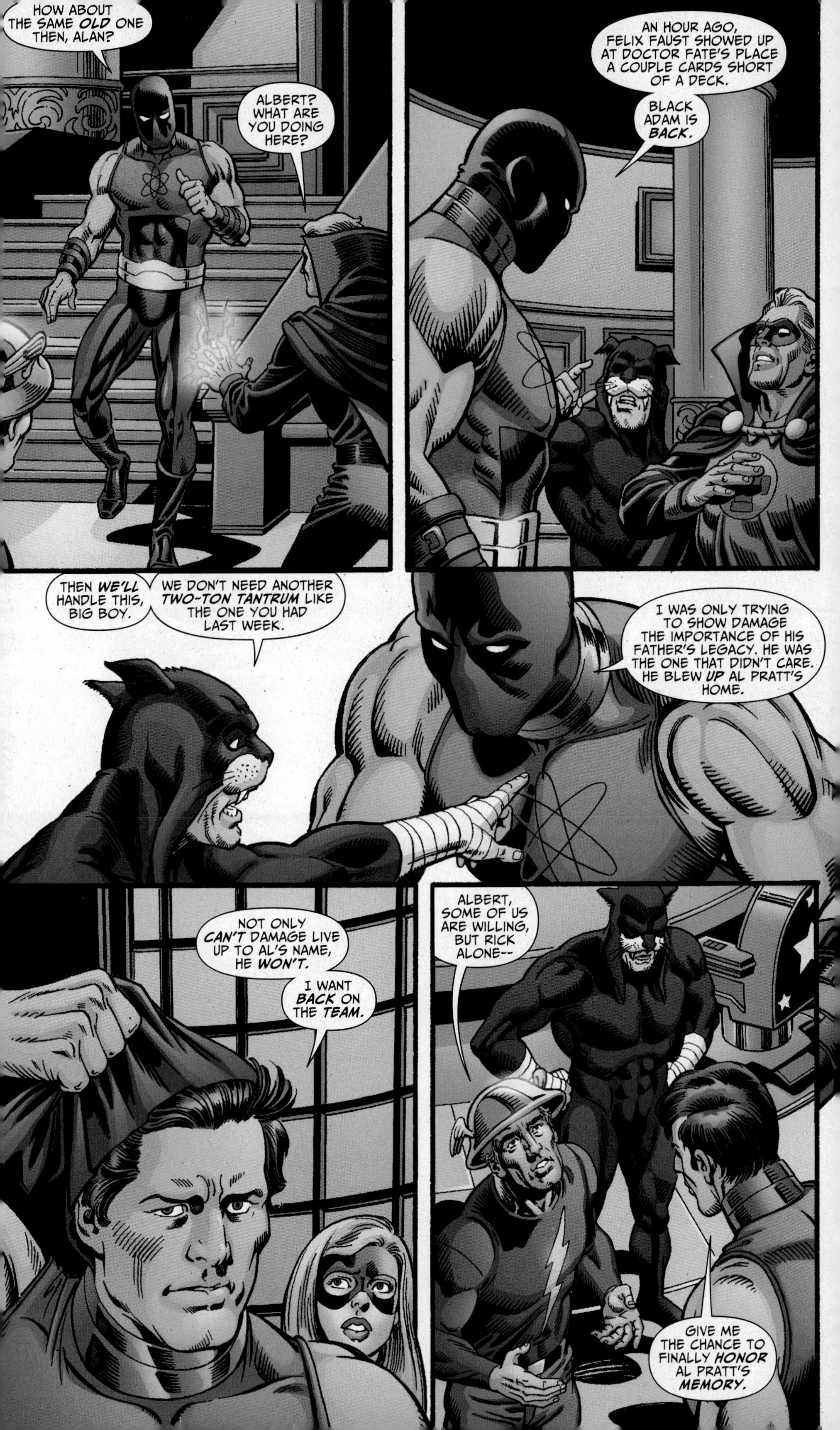
HOW ABOUT THE SAME OLD ONE THEN, ALAN?
ALBERT? WHAT ARE YOU DOING HERE?
AN HOUR AGO, FELIX FAUST SHOWED UP AT DOCTOR FATE'S PLACE A COUPLE CARDS SHORT OF A DECK.
BLACK ADAM IS BACK.
THEN WE'LL HANDLE THIS, BIG BOY.
WE DON'T NEED ANOTHER TWO-TON TANTRUM LIKE THE ONE YOU HAD LAST WEEK.
I WAS ONLY TRYING TO SHOW DAMAGE THE IMPORTANCE OF HIS FATHER'S LEGACY. HE WAS THE ONE THAT DIDN'T CARE. HE BLEW UP AL PRATT'S HOME.
NOT ONLY CAN'T DAMAGE LIVE UP TO AL'S NAME, HE WON'T.
I WANT BACK ON THE TEAM.
ALBERT, SOME OF US ARE WILLING, BUT RICK ALONE--
GIVE ME THE CHANCE TO FINALLY HONOR AL PRATT'S MEMORY.

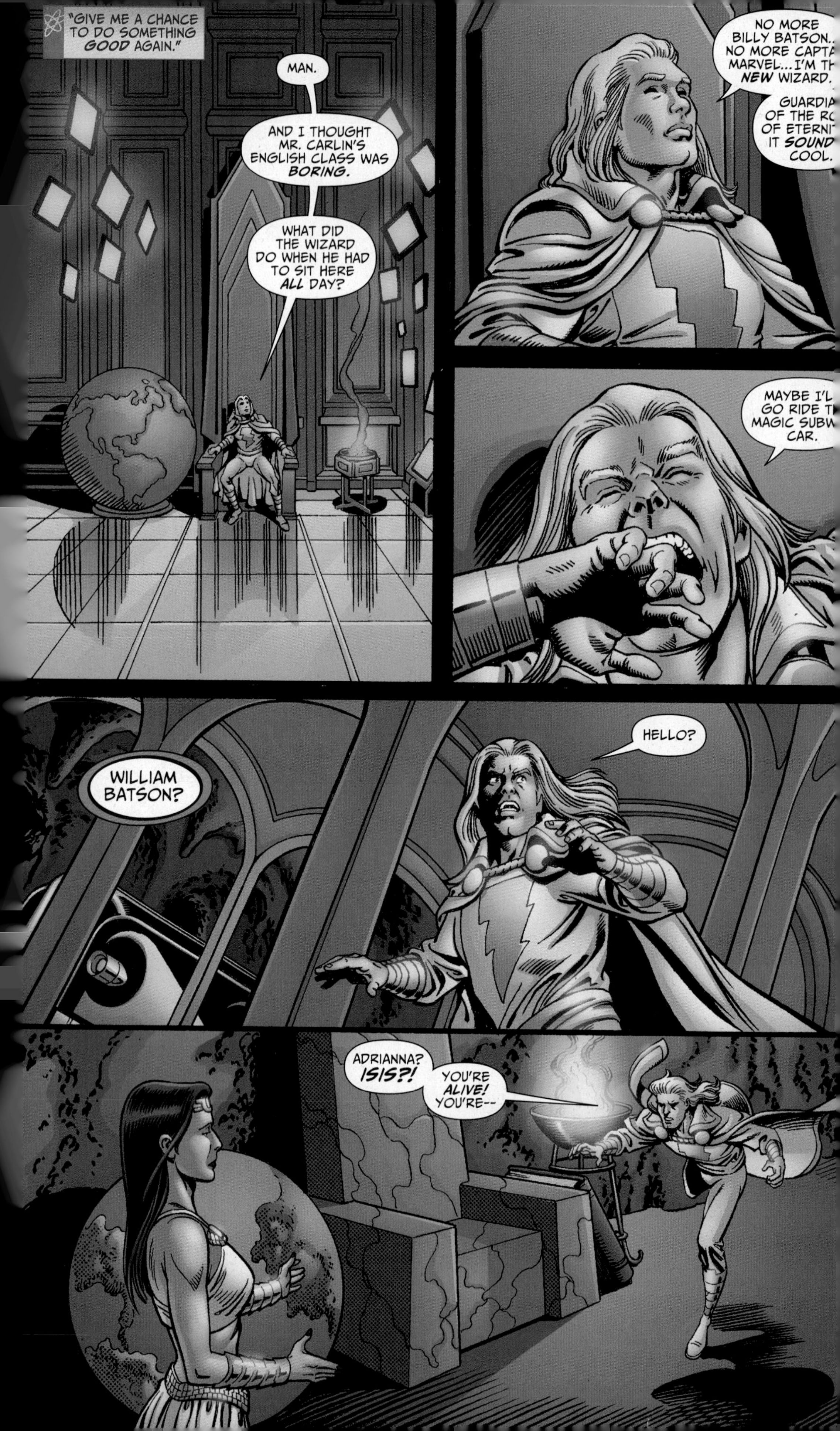
"GIVE ME A CHANCE TO DO SOMETHING GOOD AGAIN."
MAN.
AND I THOUGHT MR. CARLIN'S ENGLISH CLASS WAS BORING.
WHAT DID THE WIZARD DO WHEN HE HAD TO SIT HERE ALL DAY?
NO MORE BILLY BATSON... NO MORE CAPTA MARVEL... I'M TH NEW WIZARD.
GUARDIA OF THE RO OF ETERNIT IT SOUND COOL.
MAYBE I'L GO RIDE T MAGIC SUBW CAR.
HELLO?
WILLIAM BATSON?
ADRIANNA? ISIS?!
YOU'RE ALIVE! YOU'RE--

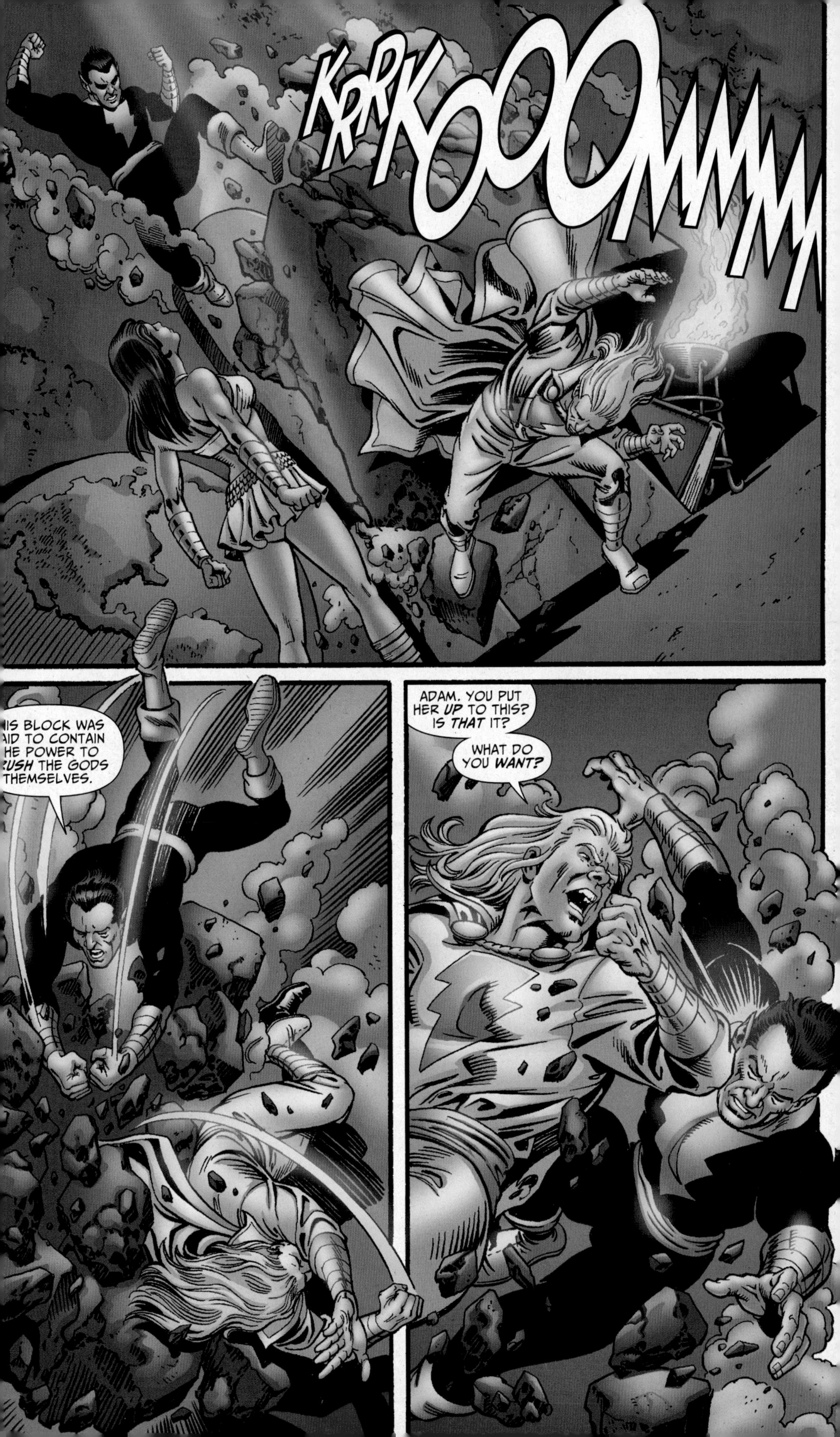
KRRKOOOMMMMM
IS BLOCK WAS
AID TO CONTAIN
HE POWER TO
RUSH THE GODS
THEMSELVES.
ADAM. YOU PUT HER UP TO THIS? IS THAT IT?
WHAT DO YOU WANT?

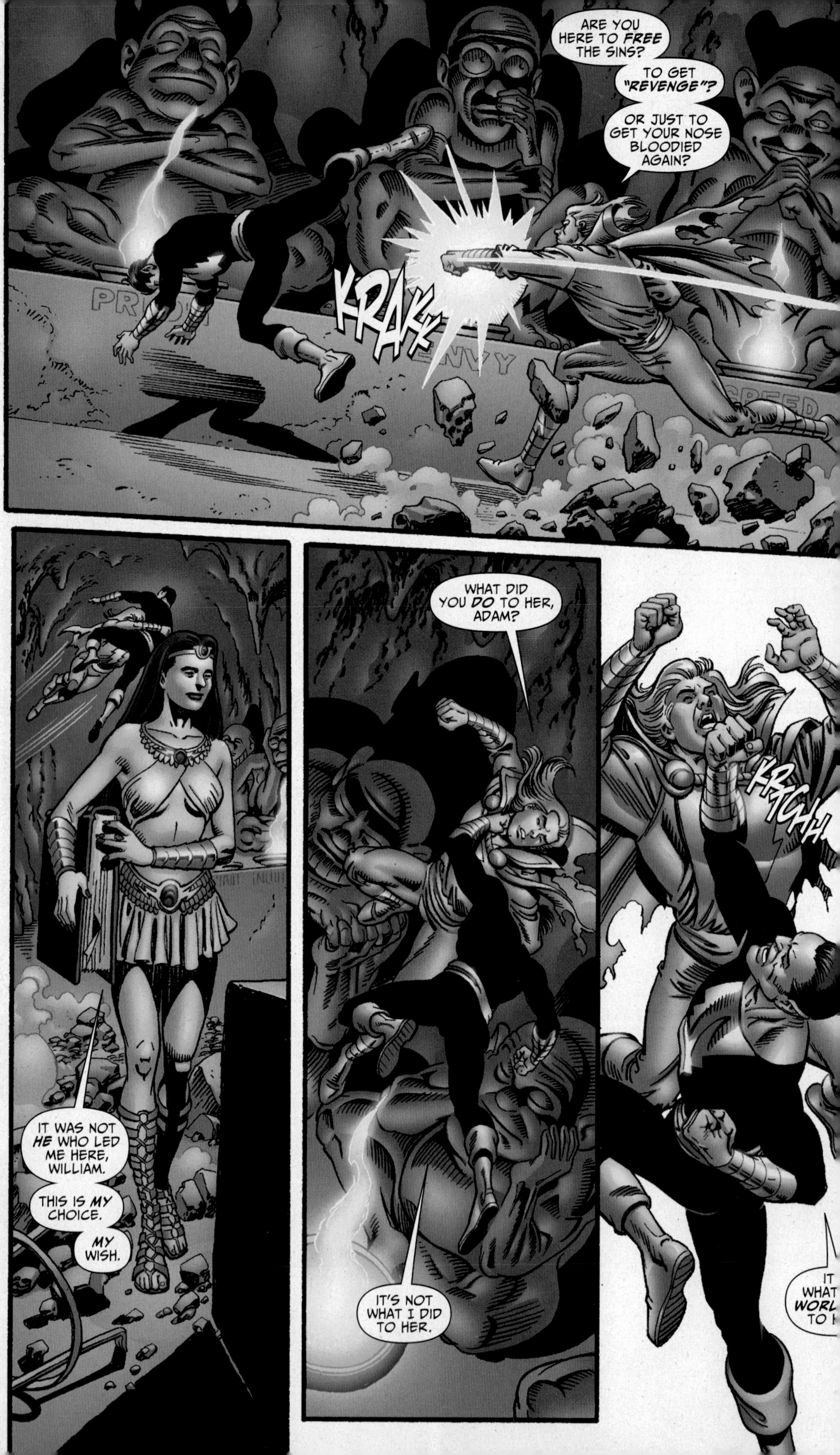
ARE YOU HERE TO FREE THE SINS?
TO GET "REVENGE"?
OR JUST TO GET YOUR NOSE BLOODIED AGAIN?
KRAKK
ENVY
IT WAS NOT HE WHO LED ME HERE, WILLIAM.
THIS IS MY CHOICE.
MY WISH.
WHAT DID YOU DO TO HER, ADAM?
IT'S NOT WHAT I DID TO HER.
KRTCHH

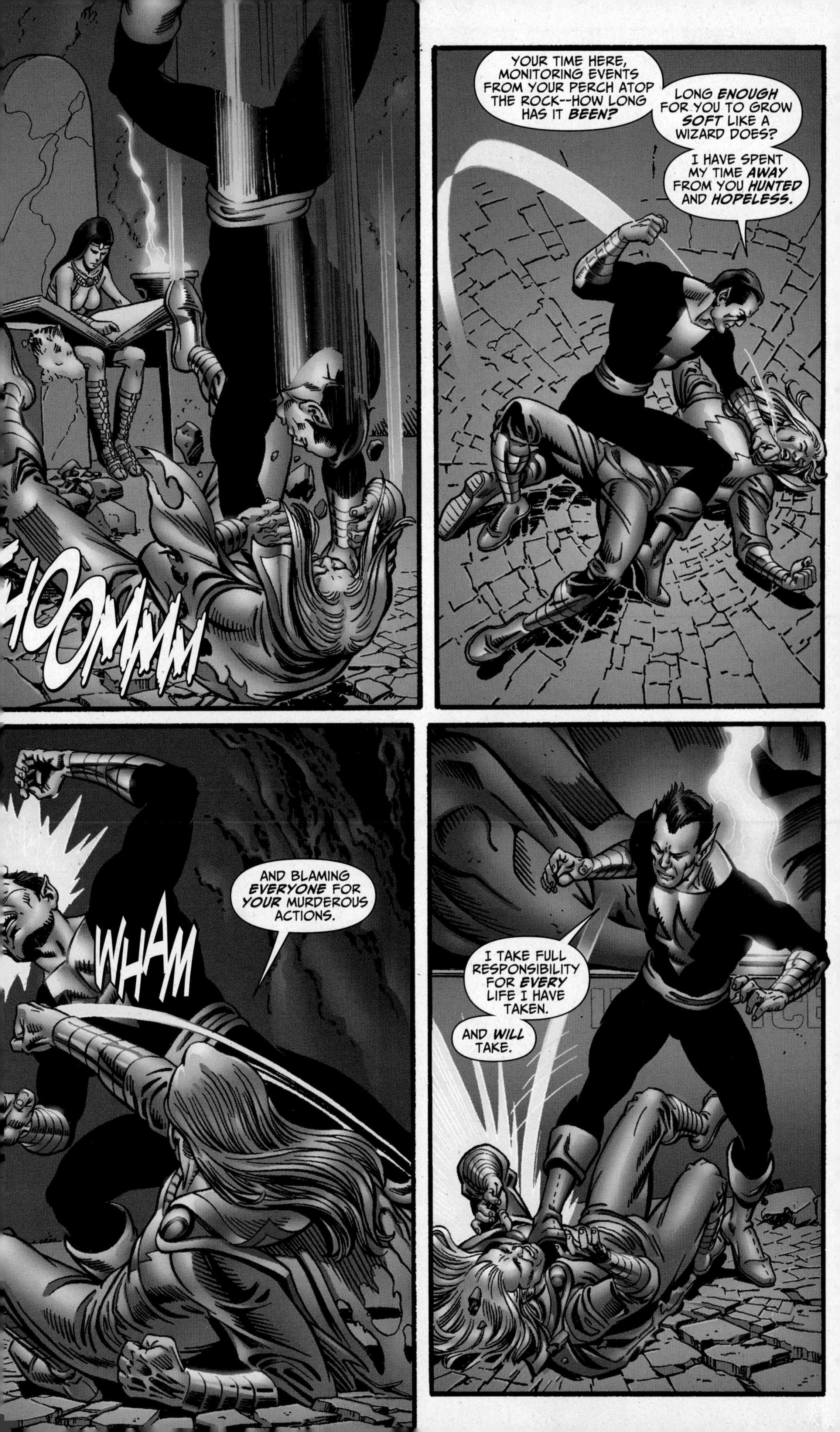
YOUR TIME HERE, MONITORING EVENTS FROM YOUR PERCH ATOP THE ROCK--HOW LONG HAS IT *BEEN?*
LONG *ENOUGH* FOR YOU TO GROW *SOFT* LIKE A WIZARD DOES?
I HAVE SPENT MY TIME *AWAY* FROM YOU *HUNTED* AND *HOPELESS.*
WHAM
AND BLAMING *EVERYONE* FOR *YOUR* MURDEROUS ACTIONS.
I TAKE FULL RESPONSIBILITY FOR *EVERY* LIFE I HAVE TAKEN.
AND *WILL* TAKE.

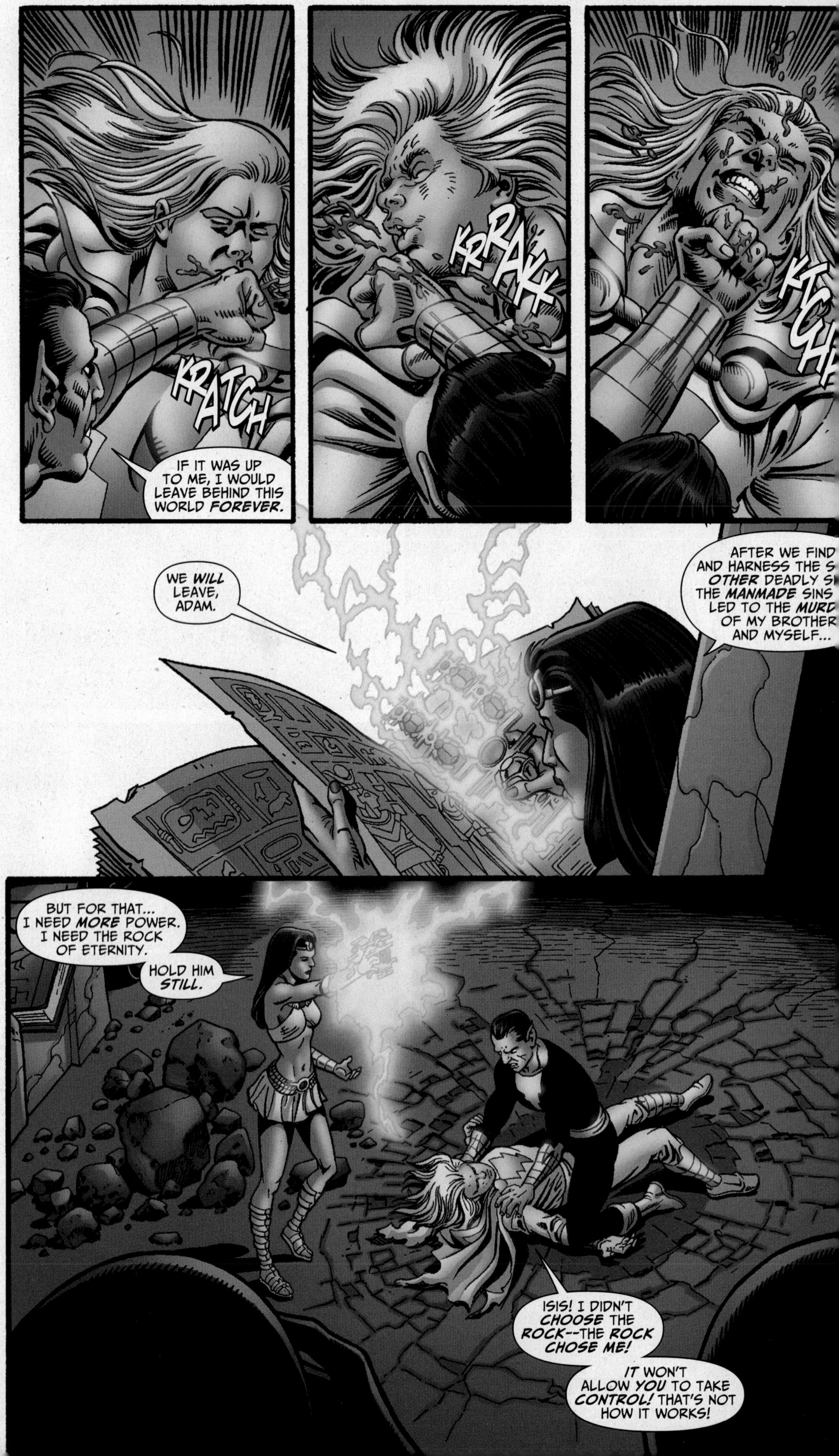
KRATCH
IF IT WAS UP TO ME, I WOULD LEAVE BEHIND THIS WORLD FOREVER.
KRRAKK
WE WILL LEAVE, ADAM.
AFTER WE FIND AND HARNESS THE
THE MANMADE SINS
OF MY BROTHER AND MYSELF...
BUT FOR THAT... I NEED MORE POWER. I NEED THE ROCK OF ETERNITY.
HOLD HIM STILL.
ISIS! I DIDN'T CHOOSE THE ROCK--THE ROCK CHOSE ME!
IT WON'T ALLOW YOU TO TAKE CONTROL! THAT'S NOT HOW IT WORKS!

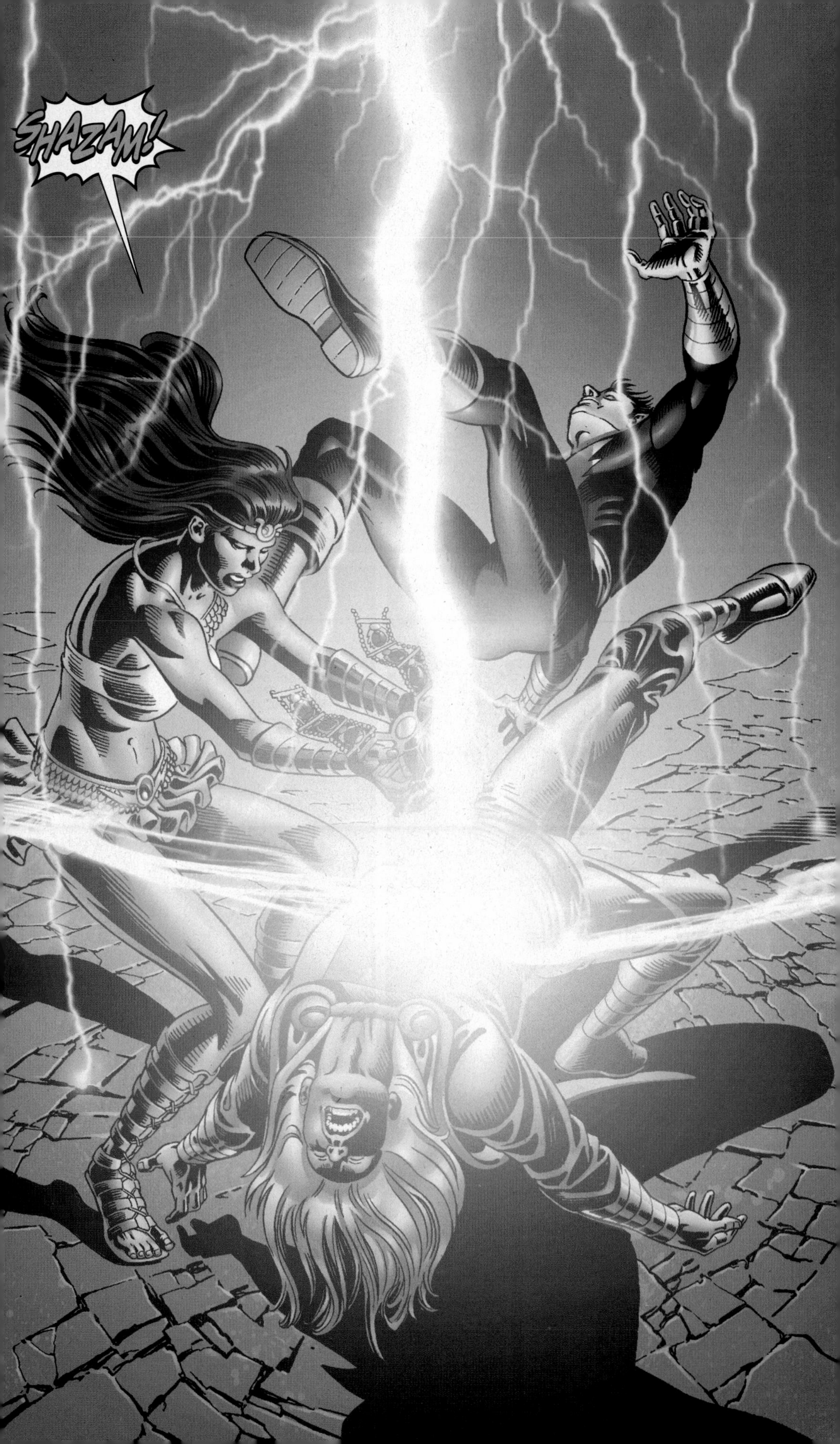
SHAZAM!

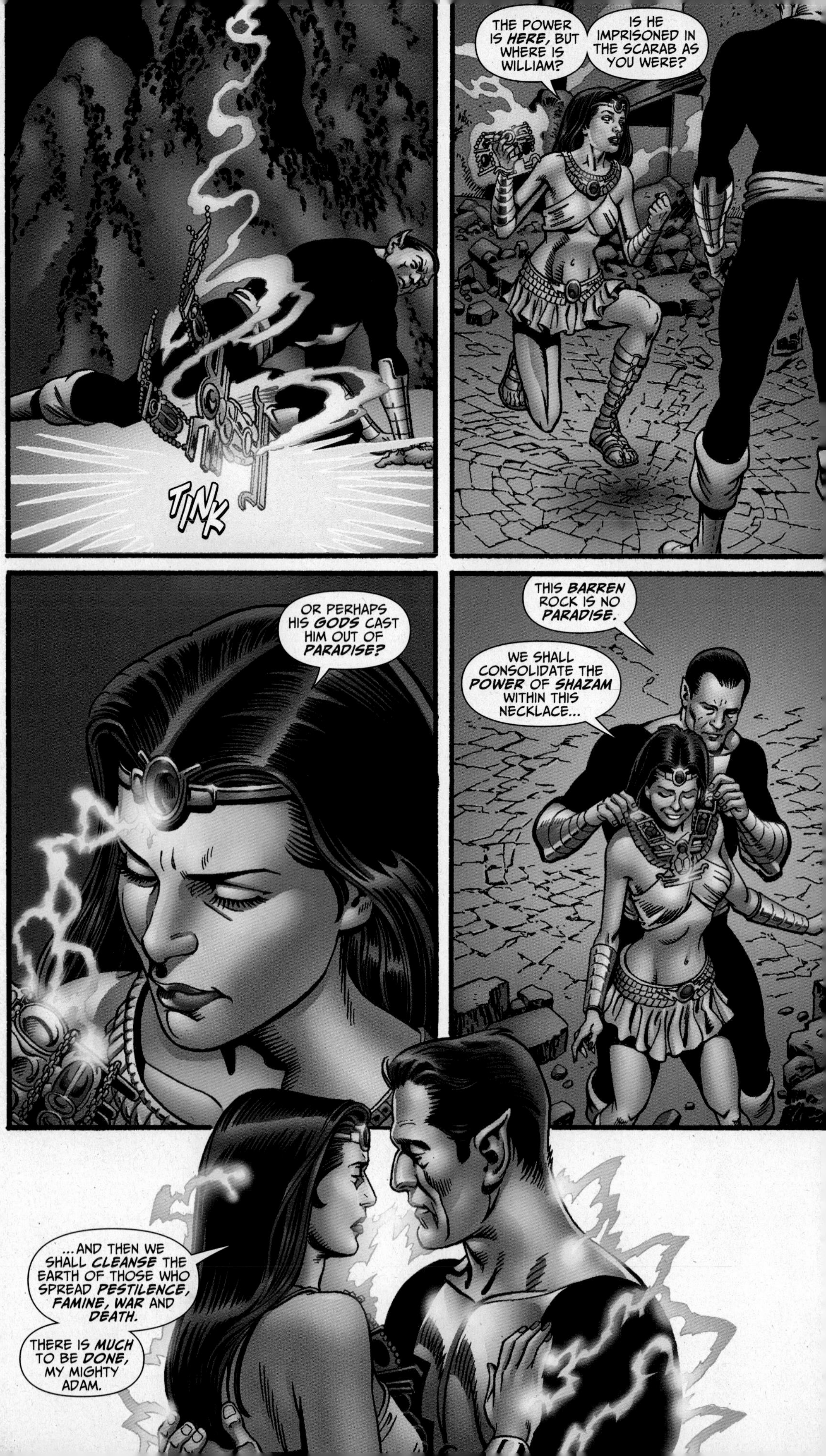
TINK
THE POWER IS HERE, BUT WHERE IS WILLIAM?
IS HE IMPRISONED IN THE SCARAB AS YOU WERE?
OR PERHAPS HIS GODS CAST HIM OUT OF PARADISE?
THIS BARREN ROCK IS NO PARADISE.
WE SHALL CONSOLIDATE THE POWER OF SHAZAM WITHIN THIS NECKLACE...
...AND THEN WE SHALL CLEANSE THE EARTH OF THOSE WHO SPREAD PESTILENCE, FAMINE, WAR AND DEATH.
THERE IS MUCH TO BE DONE, MY MIGHTY ADAM.

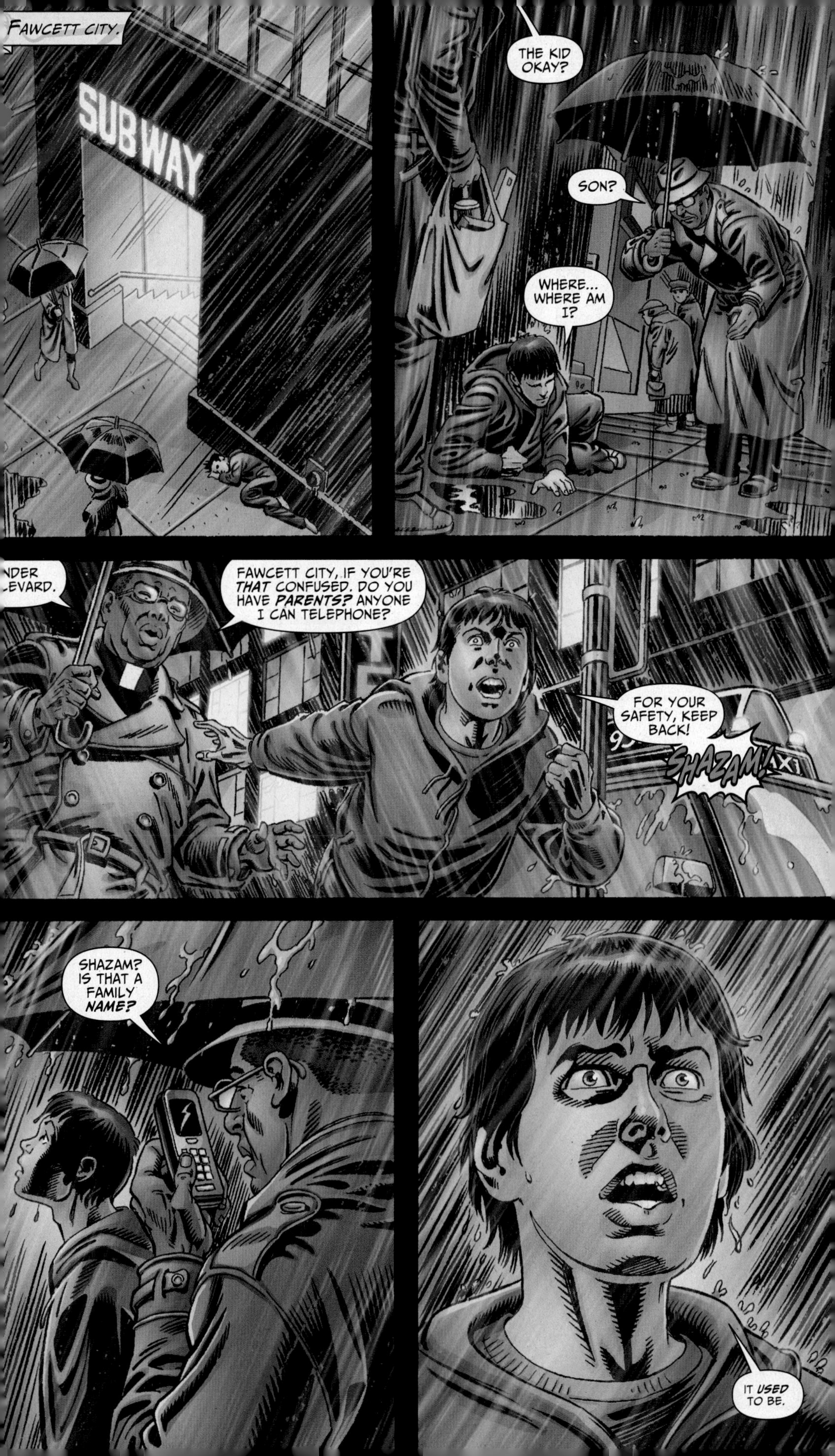
FAWCETT CITY.
SUBWAY
THE KID OKAY?
SON?
WHERE... WHERE AM I?
FAWCETT CITY, IF YOU'RE *THAT* CONFUSED. DO YOU HAVE *PARENTS?* ANYONE I CAN TELEPHONE?
FOR YOUR SAFETY, KEEP BACK!
SHAZAM!
SHAZAM? IS THAT A FAMILY *NAME?*
IT *USED* TO BE.

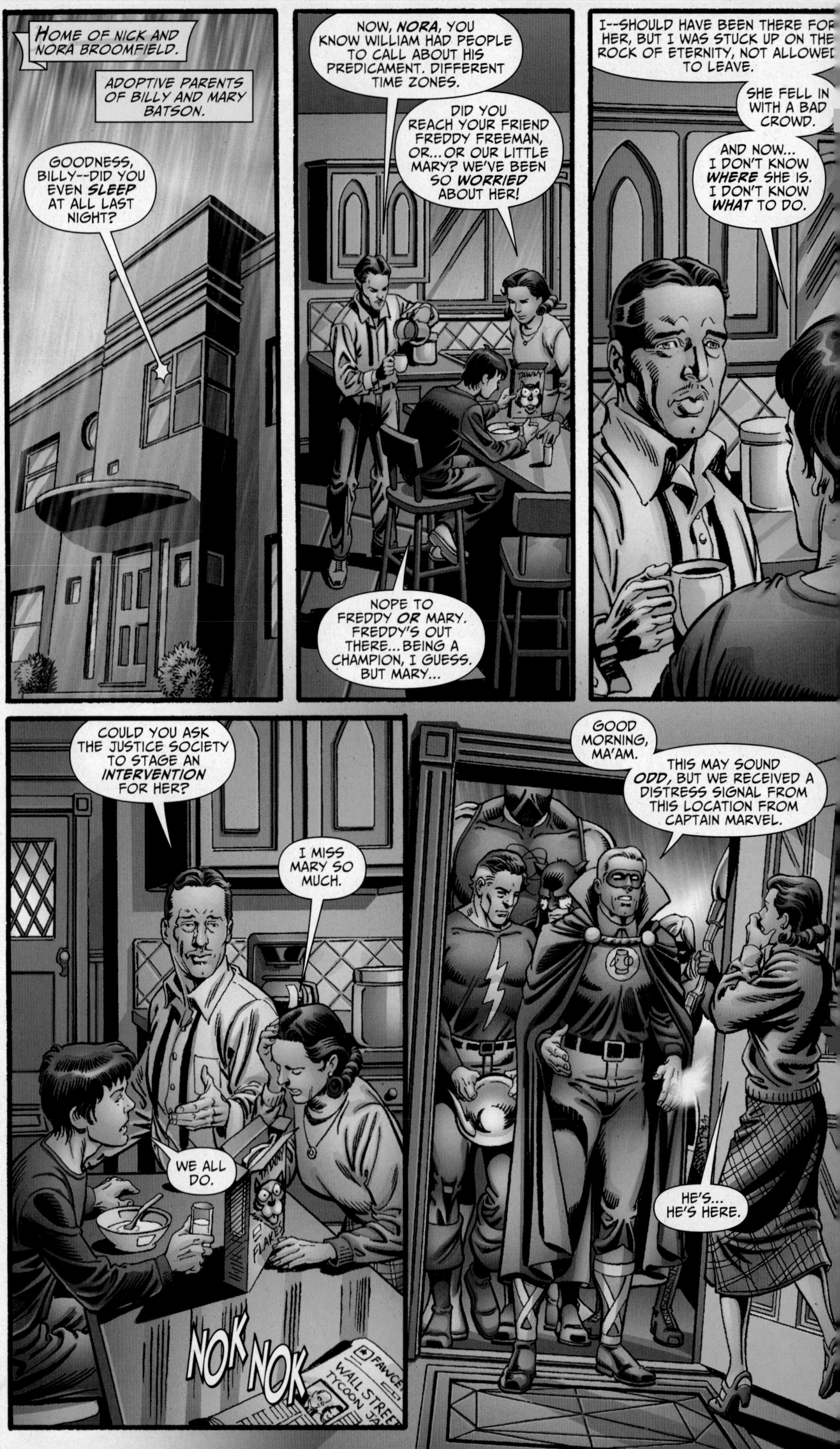
HOME OF NICK AND NORA BROOMFIELD.
ADOPTIVE PARENTS OF BILLY AND MARY BATSON.
GOODNESS, BILLY--DID YOU EVEN SLEEP AT ALL LAST NIGHT?
NOW, NORA, YOU KNOW WILLIAM HAD PEOPLE TO CALL ABOUT HIS PREDICAMENT. DIFFERENT TIME ZONES.
DID YOU REACH YOUR FRIEND FREDDY FREEMAN, OR...OR OUR LITTLE MARY? WE'VE BEEN SO WORRIED ABOUT HER!
TAWNY
NOPE TO FREDDY OR MARY. FREDDY'S OUT THERE...BEING A CHAMPION, I GUESS. BUT MARY...
I--SHOULD HAVE BEEN THERE FOR HER, BUT I WAS STUCK UP ON THE ROCK OF ETERNITY, NOT ALLOWED TO LEAVE.
SHE FELL IN WITH A BAD CROWD.
AND NOW... I DON'T KNOW WHERE SHE IS. I DON'T KNOW WHAT TO DO.
COULD YOU ASK THE JUSTICE SOCIETY TO STAGE AN INTERVENTION FOR HER?
I MISS MARY SO MUCH.
WE ALL DO.
FLAKES
NOK NOK
FAWCE
WALL STREET TYCOON
GOOD MORNING, MA'AM.
THIS MAY SOUND ODD, BUT WE RECEIVED A DISTRESS SIGNAL FROM THIS LOCATION FROM CAPTAIN MARVEL.
HE'S... HE'S HERE.

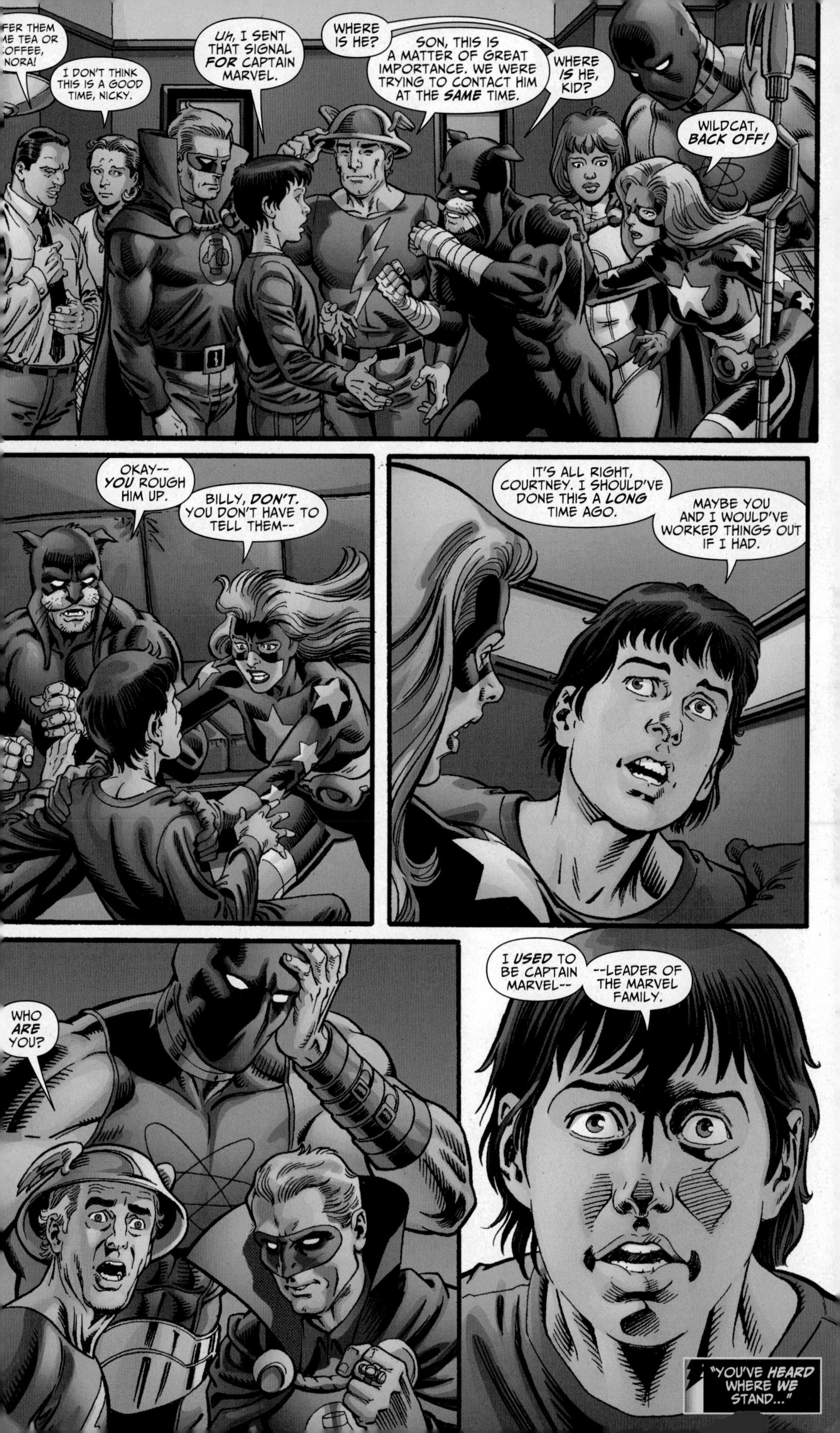
FER THEM ME TEA OR COFFEE, NORA!
I DON'T THINK THIS IS A GOOD TIME, NICKY.
UH, I SENT THAT SIGNAL FOR CAPTAIN MARVEL.
WHERE IS HE?
SON, THIS IS A MATTER OF GREAT IMPORTANCE. WE WERE TRYING TO CONTACT HIM AT THE SAME TIME.
WHERE IS HE, KID?
WILDCAT, BACK OFF!
OKAY-- YOU ROUGH HIM UP.
BILLY, DON'T. YOU DON'T HAVE TO TELL THEM--
IT'S ALL RIGHT, COURTNEY. I SHOULD'VE DONE THIS A LONG TIME AGO.
MAYBE YOU AND I WOULD'VE WORKED THINGS OUT IF I HAD.
WHO ARE YOU?
I USED TO BE CAPTAIN MARVEL--
--LEADER OF THE MARVEL FAMILY.
"YOU'VE HEARD WHERE WE STAND..."

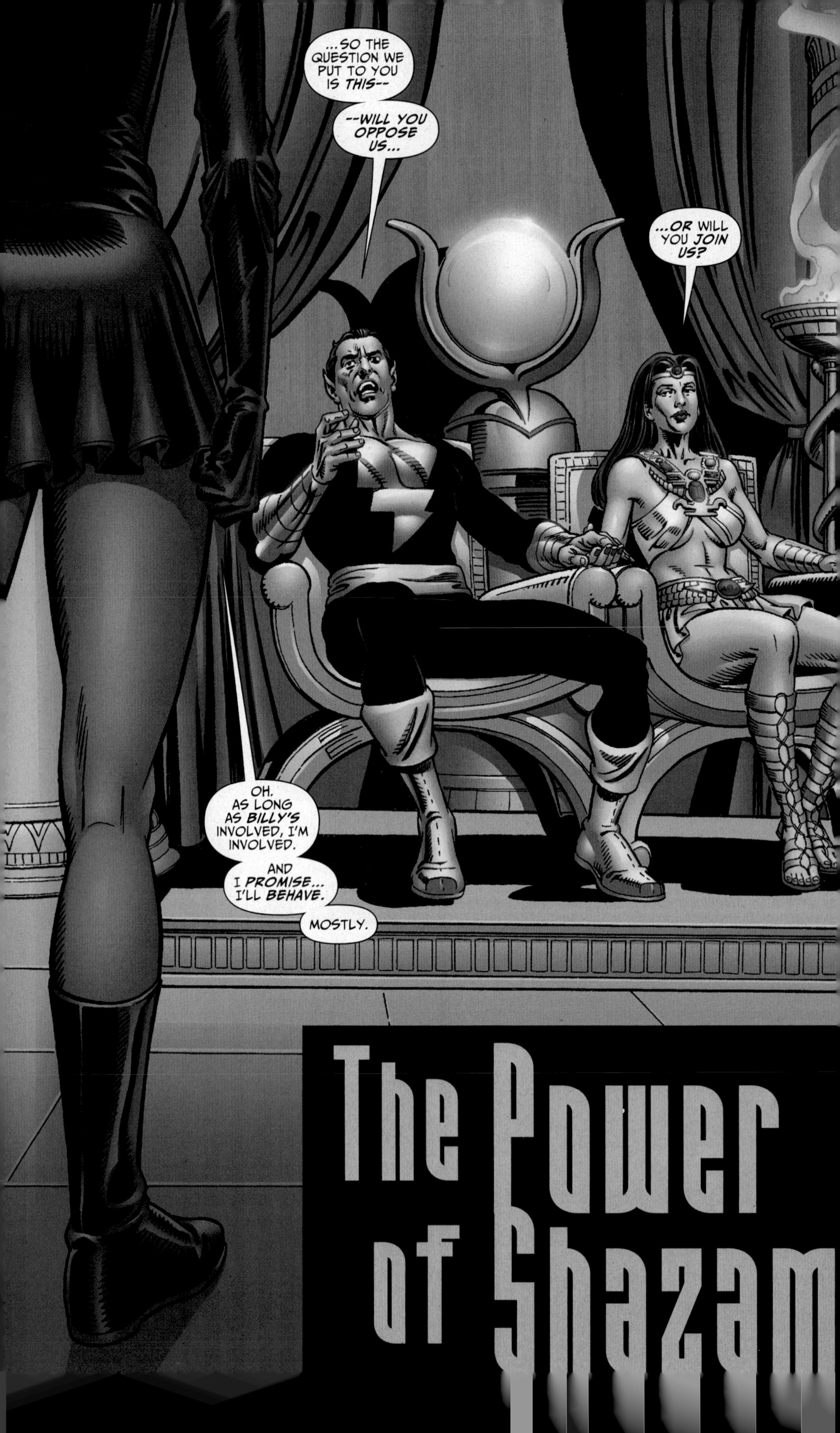
...SO THE QUESTION WE PUT TO YOU IS THIS--
--WILL YOU OPPOSE US...
...OR WILL YOU JOIN US?
OH. AS LONG AS BILLY'S INVOLVED, I'M INVOLVED.
AND I PROMISE... I'LL BEHAVE.
MOSTLY.
The Power of Shazam

USTICE SOCIETY OF AMERICA #24 cover A by Alex Ross
nterior art by Jerry Ordway & Bob Wiacek, with Flashback sequence by Ordway

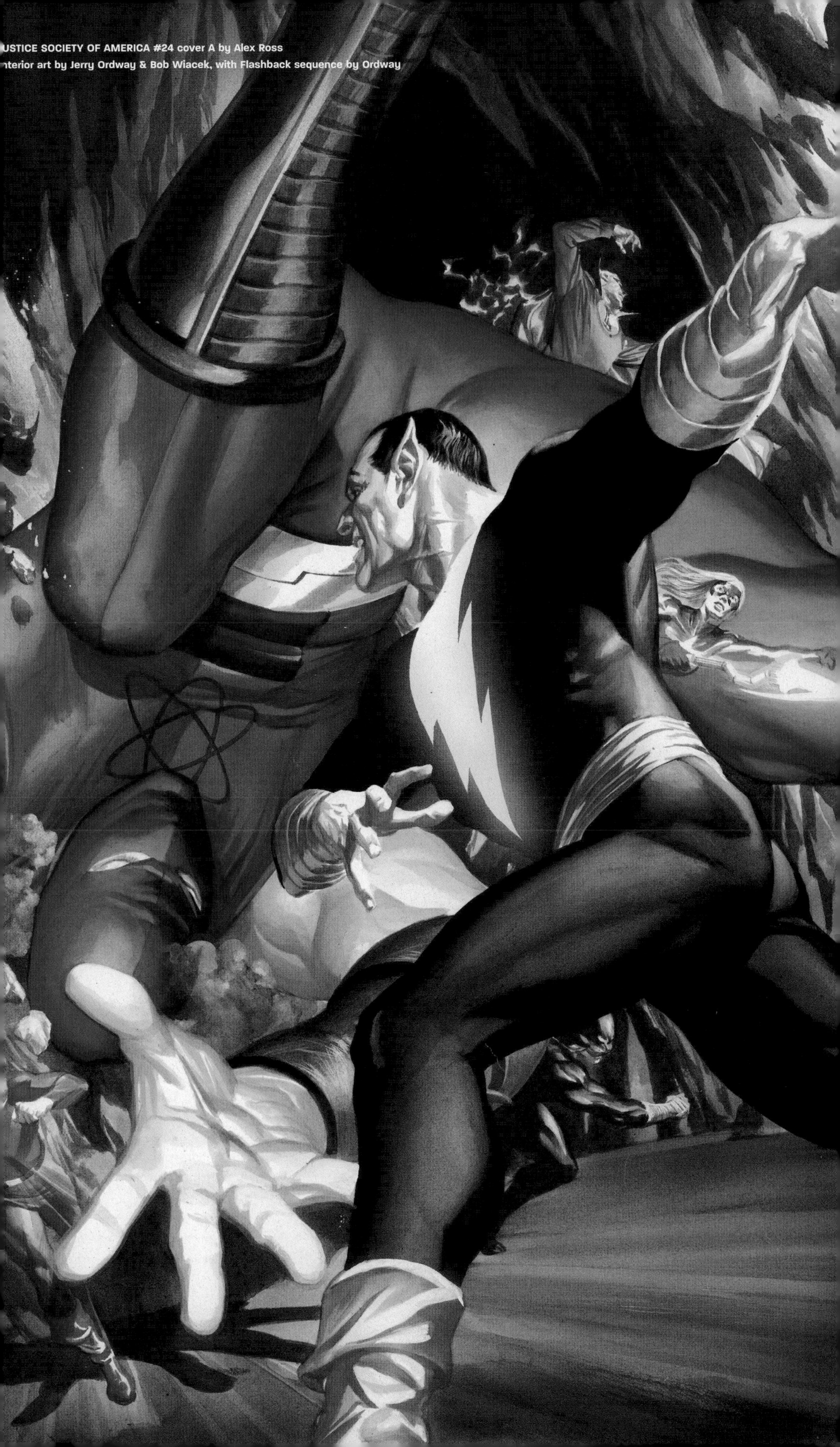

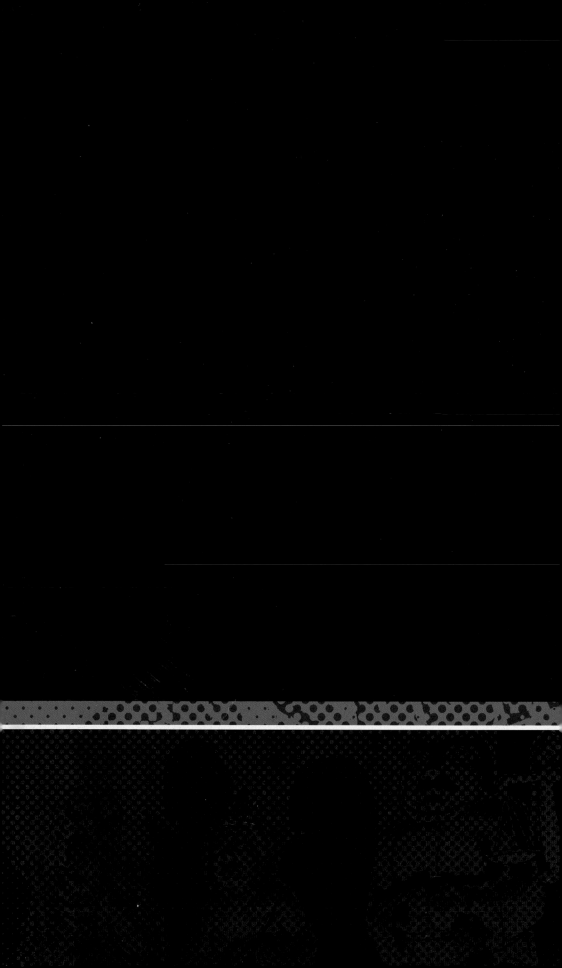

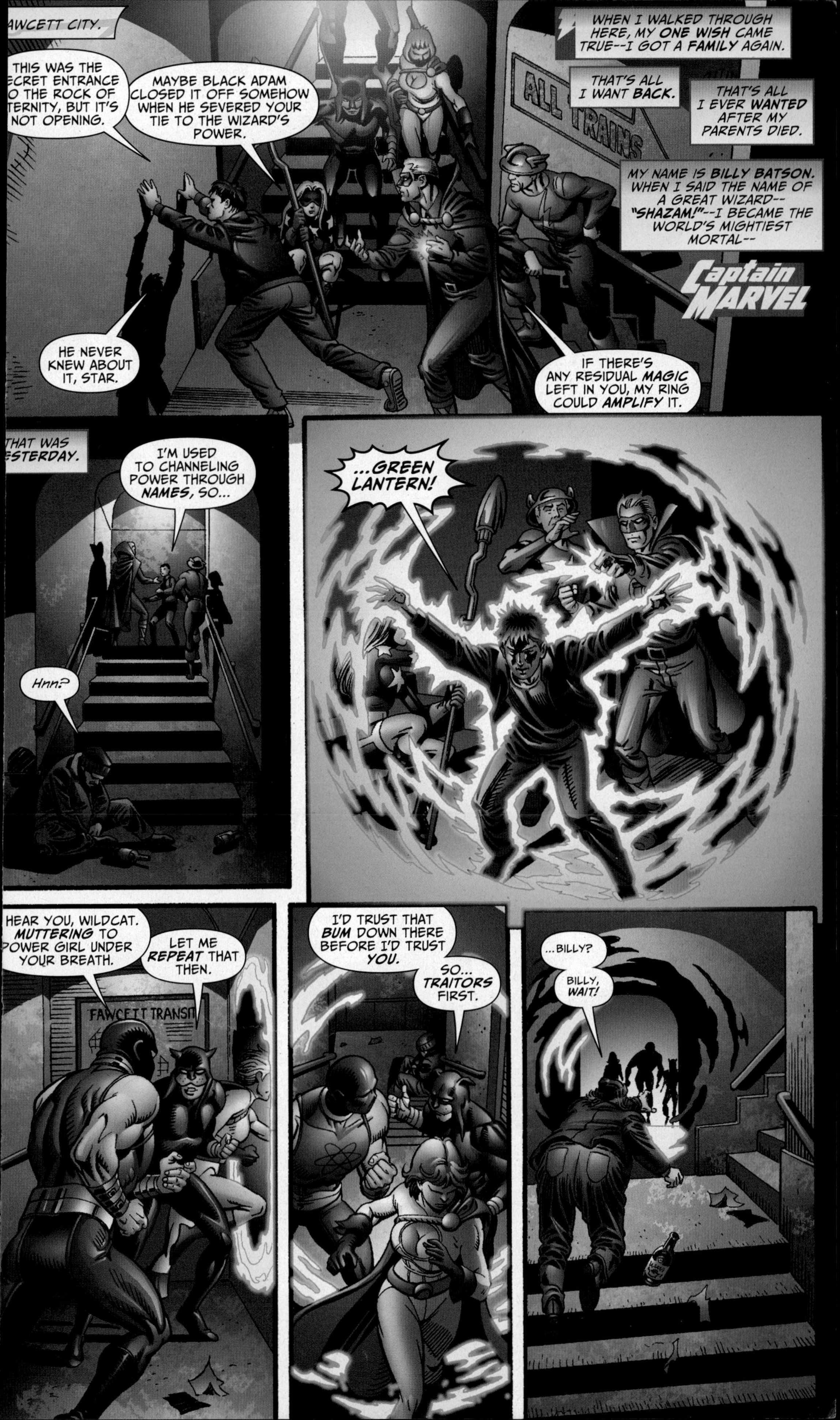

AWCETT CITY.
THIS WAS THE ECRET ENTRANCE O THE ROCK OF TERNITY, BUT IT'S NOT OPENING.
MAYBE BLACK ADAM CLOSED IT OFF SOMEHOW WHEN HE SEVERED YOUR TIE TO THE WIZARD'S POWER.
WHEN I WALKED THROUGH HERE, MY ONE WISH CAME TRUE--I GOT A FAMILY AGAIN.
THAT'S ALL I WANT BACK.
THAT'S ALL I EVER WANTED AFTER MY PARENTS DIED.
MY NAME IS BILLY BATSON. WHEN I SAID THE NAME OF A GREAT WIZARD--"SHAZAM!"--I BECAME THE WORLD'S MIGHTIEST MORTAL--
Captain MARVEL
ALL TRAINS
HE NEVER KNEW ABOUT IT, STAR.
IF THERE'S ANY RESIDUAL MAGIC LEFT IN YOU, MY RING COULD AMPLIFY IT.
THAT WAS ESTERDAY.
I'M USED TO CHANNELING POWER THROUGH NAMES, SO...
Hnn?
...GREEN LANTERN!
HEAR YOU, WILDCAT. MUTTERING TO POWER GIRL UNDER YOUR BREATH.
LET ME REPEAT THAT THEN.
FAWCETT TRANSIT
I'D TRUST THAT BUM DOWN THERE BEFORE I'D TRUST YOU.
SO... TRAITORS FIRST.
...BILLY?
BILLY, WAIT!

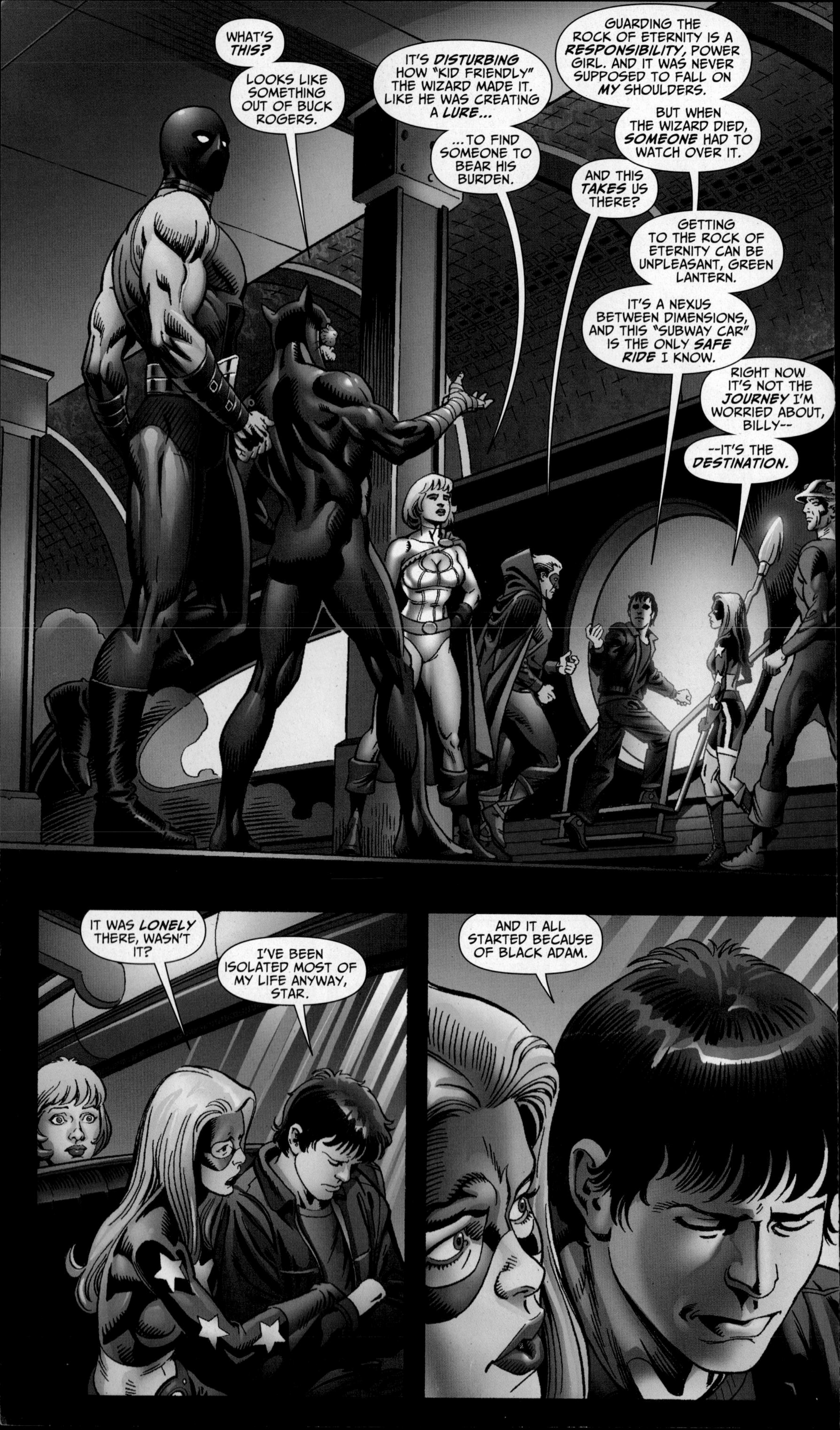
WHAT'S *THIS?*
LOOKS LIKE SOMETHING OUT OF BUCK ROGERS.
IT'S *DISTURBING* HOW "KID FRIENDLY" THE WIZARD MADE IT. LIKE HE WAS CREATING A *LURE...*
...TO FIND SOMEONE TO BEAR HIS BURDEN.
GUARDING THE ROCK OF ETERNITY IS A *RESPONSIBILITY,* POWER GIRL. AND IT WAS NEVER SUPPOSED TO FALL ON *MY* SHOULDERS.
BUT WHEN THE WIZARD DIED, *SOMEONE* HAD TO WATCH OVER IT.
AND THIS *TAKES* US THERE?
GETTING TO THE ROCK OF ETERNITY CAN BE UNPLEASANT, GREEN LANTERN.
IT'S A NEXUS BETWEEN DIMENSIONS, AND THIS "SUBWAY CAR" IS THE ONLY *SAFE RIDE* I KNOW.
RIGHT NOW IT'S NOT THE *JOURNEY* I'M WORRIED ABOUT, BILLY--
--IT'S THE *DESTINATION.*
IT WAS *LONELY* THERE, WASN'T IT?
I'VE BEEN ISOLATED MOST OF MY LIFE ANYWAY, STAR.
AND IT ALL STARTED BECAUSE OF BLACK ADAM.

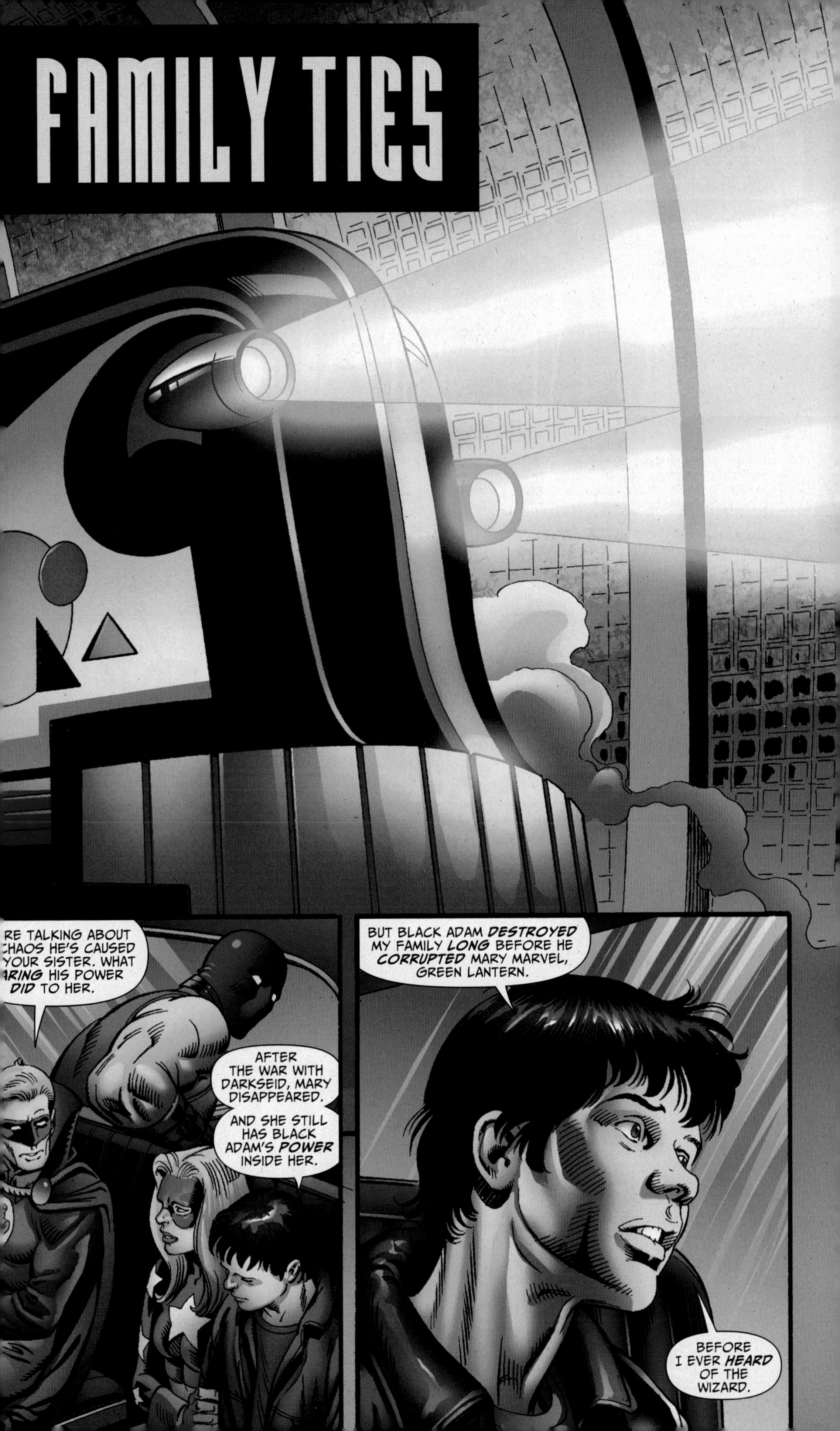

FAMILY TIES
RE TALKING ABOUT
CHAOS HE'S CAUSED
YOUR SISTER. WHAT
ARING HIS POWER
DID TO HER.
AFTER THE WAR WITH DARKSEID, MARY DISAPPEARED.
AND SHE STILL HAS BLACK ADAM'S POWER INSIDE HER.
BUT BLACK ADAM DESTROYED MY FAMILY LONG BEFORE HE CORRUPTED MARY MARVEL, GREEN LANTERN.
BEFORE I EVER HEARD OF THE WIZARD.

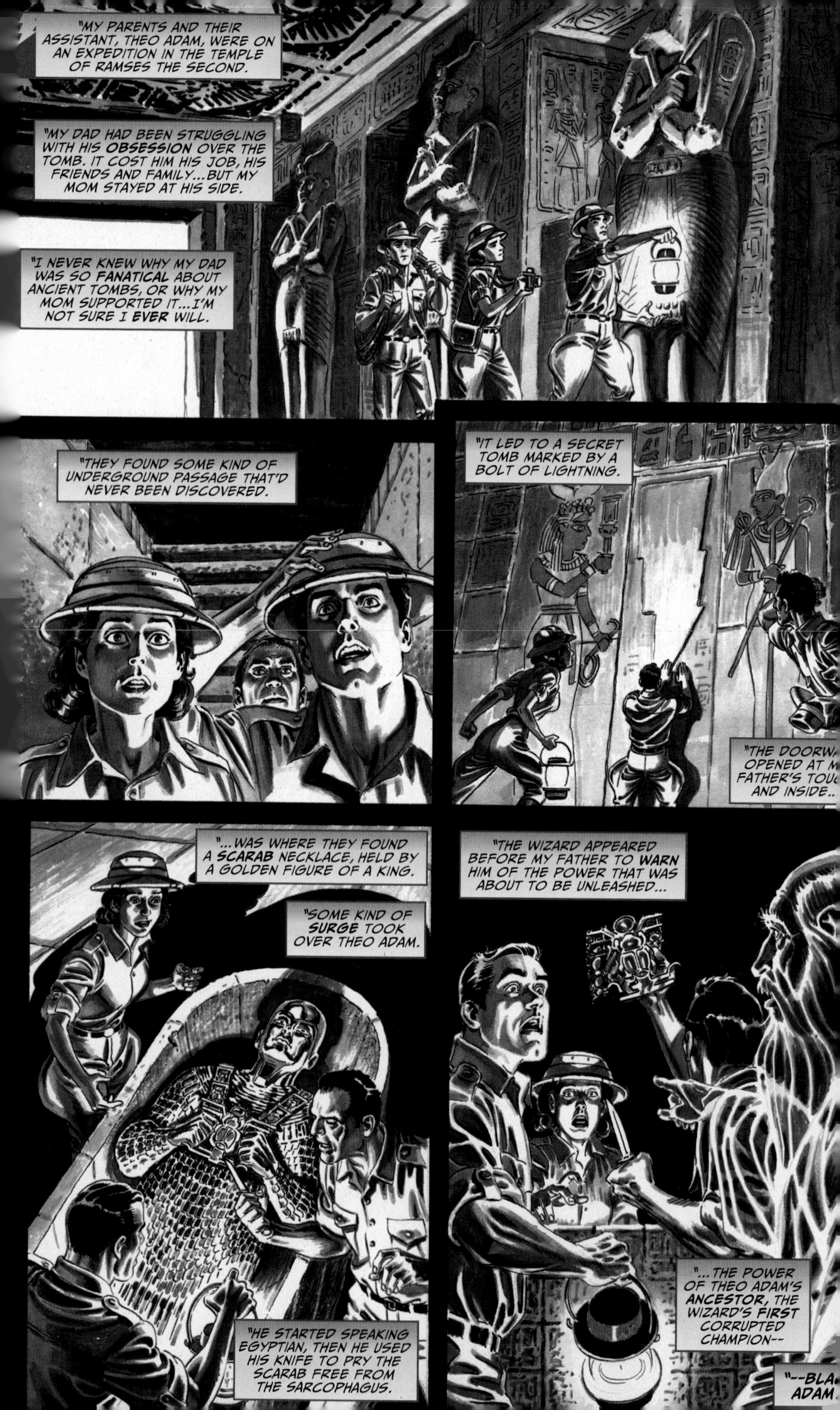
"MY PARENTS AND THEIR ASSISTANT, THEO ADAM, WERE ON AN EXPEDITION IN THE TEMPLE OF RAMSES THE SECOND.
"MY DAD HAD BEEN STRUGGLING WITH HIS OBSESSION OVER THE TOMB. IT COST HIM HIS JOB, HIS FRIENDS AND FAMILY...BUT MY MOM STAYED AT HIS SIDE.
"I NEVER KNEW WHY MY DAD WAS SO FANATICAL ABOUT ANCIENT TOMBS, OR WHY MY MOM SUPPORTED IT...I'M NOT SURE I EVER WILL.
"THEY FOUND SOME KIND OF UNDERGROUND PASSAGE THAT'D NEVER BEEN DISCOVERED.
"IT LED TO A SECRET TOMB MARKED BY A BOLT OF LIGHTNING.
"THE DOORW OPENED AT M FATHER'S TOU AND INSIDE..
"...WAS WHERE THEY FOUND A SCARAB NECKLACE, HELD BY A GOLDEN FIGURE OF A KING.
"SOME KIND OF SURGE TOOK OVER THEO ADAM.
"HE STARTED SPEAKING EGYPTIAN, THEN HE USED HIS KNIFE TO PRY THE SCARAB FREE FROM THE SARCOPHAGUS.
"THE WIZARD APPEARED BEFORE MY FATHER TO WARN HIM OF THE POWER THAT WAS ABOUT TO BE UNLEASHED...
"...THE POWER OF THEO ADAM'S ANCESTOR, THE WIZARD'S FIRST CORRUPTED CHAMPION--
"--BLA ADAM.

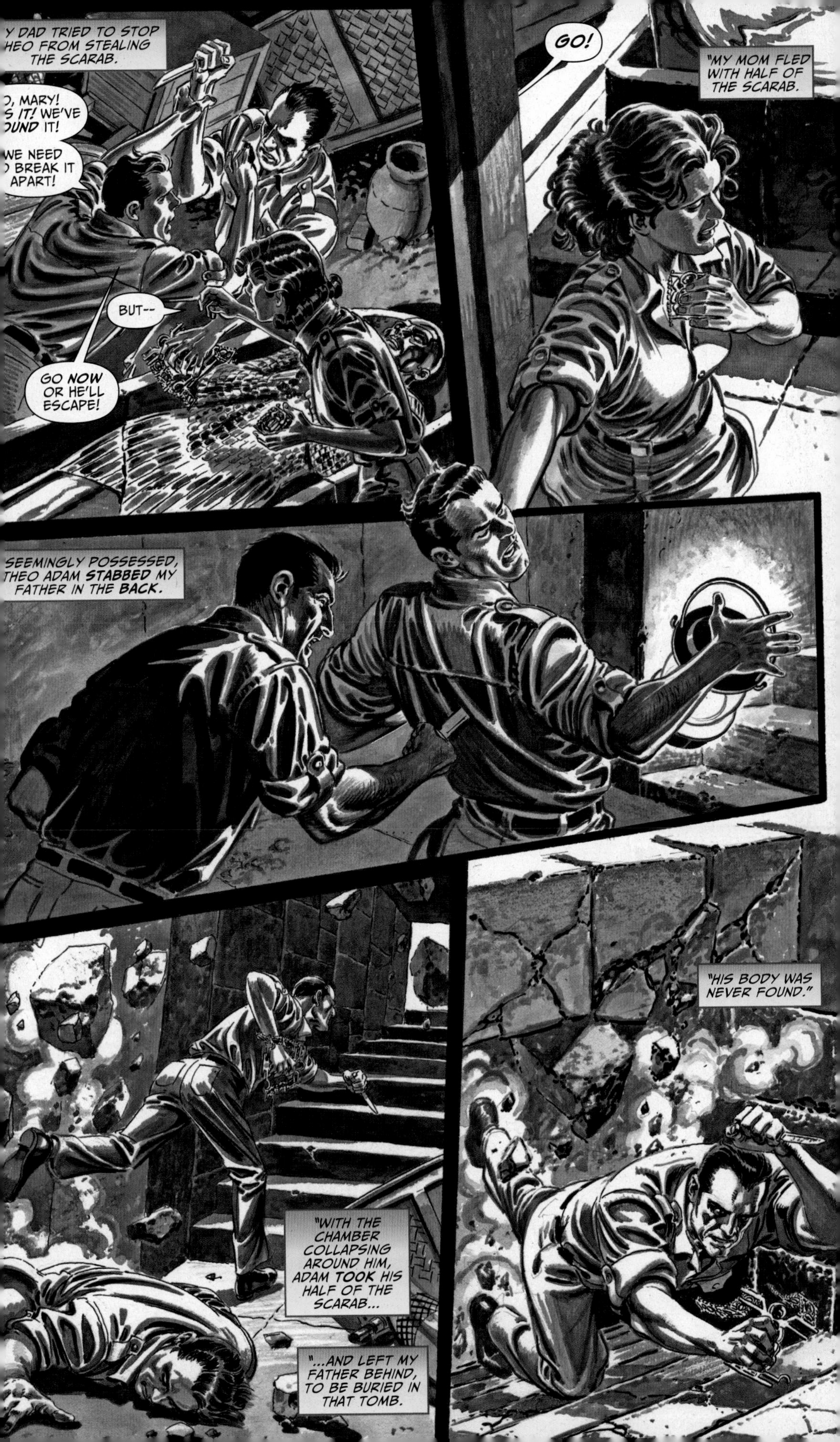
Y DAD TRIED TO STOP HEO FROM STEALING THE SCARAB.
O, MARY! S IT! WE'VE OUND IT!
WE NEED O BREAK IT APART!
BUT--
GO NOW OR HE'LL ESCAPE!
GO!
"MY MOM FLED WITH HALF OF THE SCARAB.
SEEMINGLY POSSESSED, THEO ADAM STABBED MY FATHER IN THE BACK.
"WITH THE CHAMBER COLLAPSING AROUND HIM, ADAM TOOK HIS HALF OF THE SCARAB...
"...AND LEFT MY FATHER BEHIND, TO BE BURIED IN THAT TOMB.
"HIS BODY WAS NEVER FOUND."

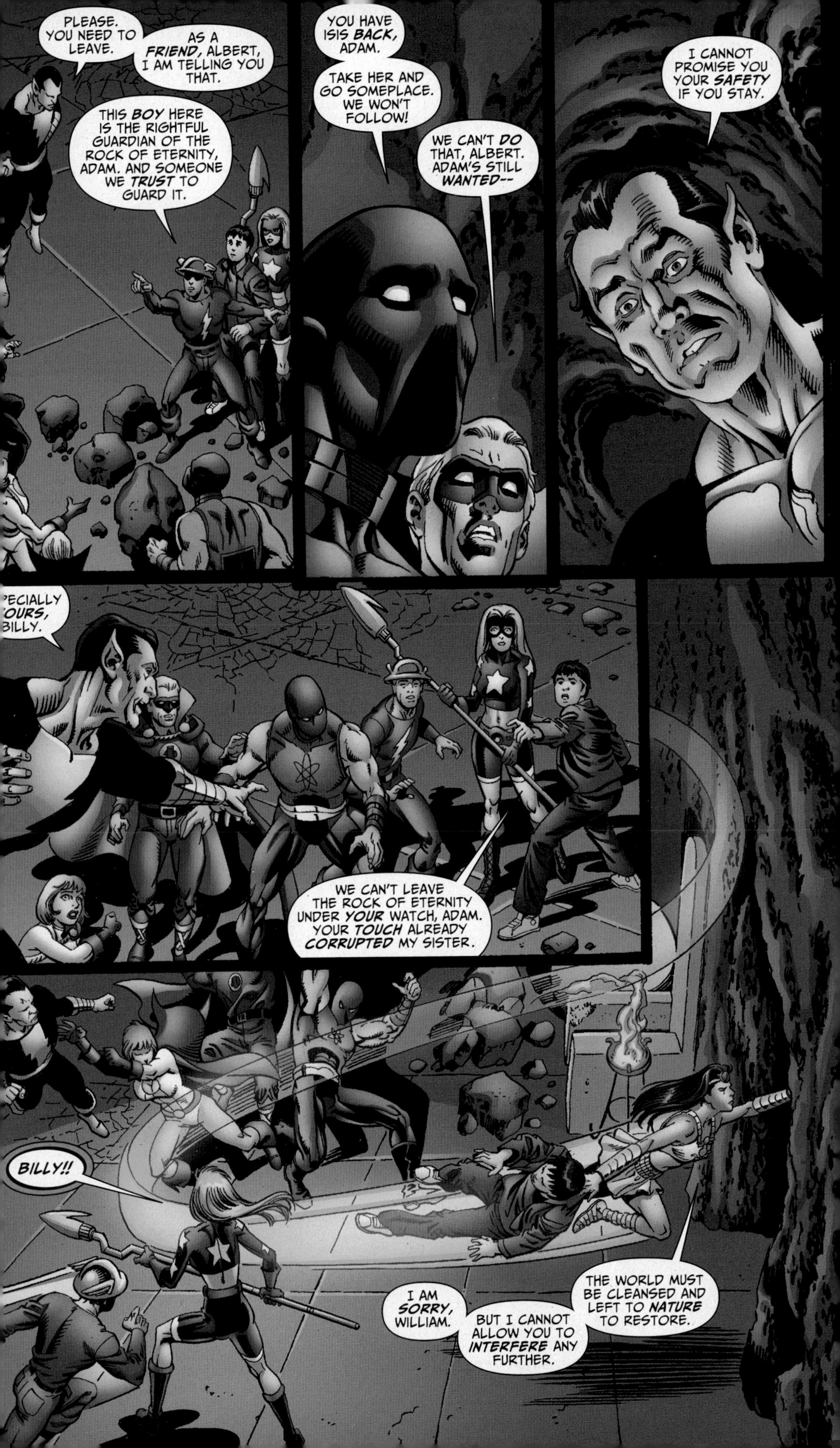
PLEASE. YOU NEED TO LEAVE.
AS A FRIEND, ALBERT, I AM TELLING YOU THAT.
THIS BOY HERE IS THE RIGHTFUL GUARDIAN OF THE ROCK OF ETERNITY, ADAM. AND SOMEONE WE TRUST TO GUARD IT.
YOU HAVE ISIS BACK, ADAM.
TAKE HER AND GO SOMEPLACE. WE WON'T FOLLOW!
WE CAN'T DO THAT, ALBERT. ADAM'S STILL WANTED--
I CANNOT PROMISE YOU YOUR SAFETY IF YOU STAY.
PECIALLY OURS, BILLY.
WE CAN'T LEAVE THE ROCK OF ETERNITY UNDER YOUR WATCH, ADAM. YOUR TOUCH ALREADY CORRUPTED MY SISTER.
BILLY!!
THE WORLD MUST BE CLEANSED AND LEFT TO NATURE TO RESTORE.
I AM SORRY, WILLIAM.
BUT I CANNOT ALLOW YOU TO INTERFERE ANY FURTHER.

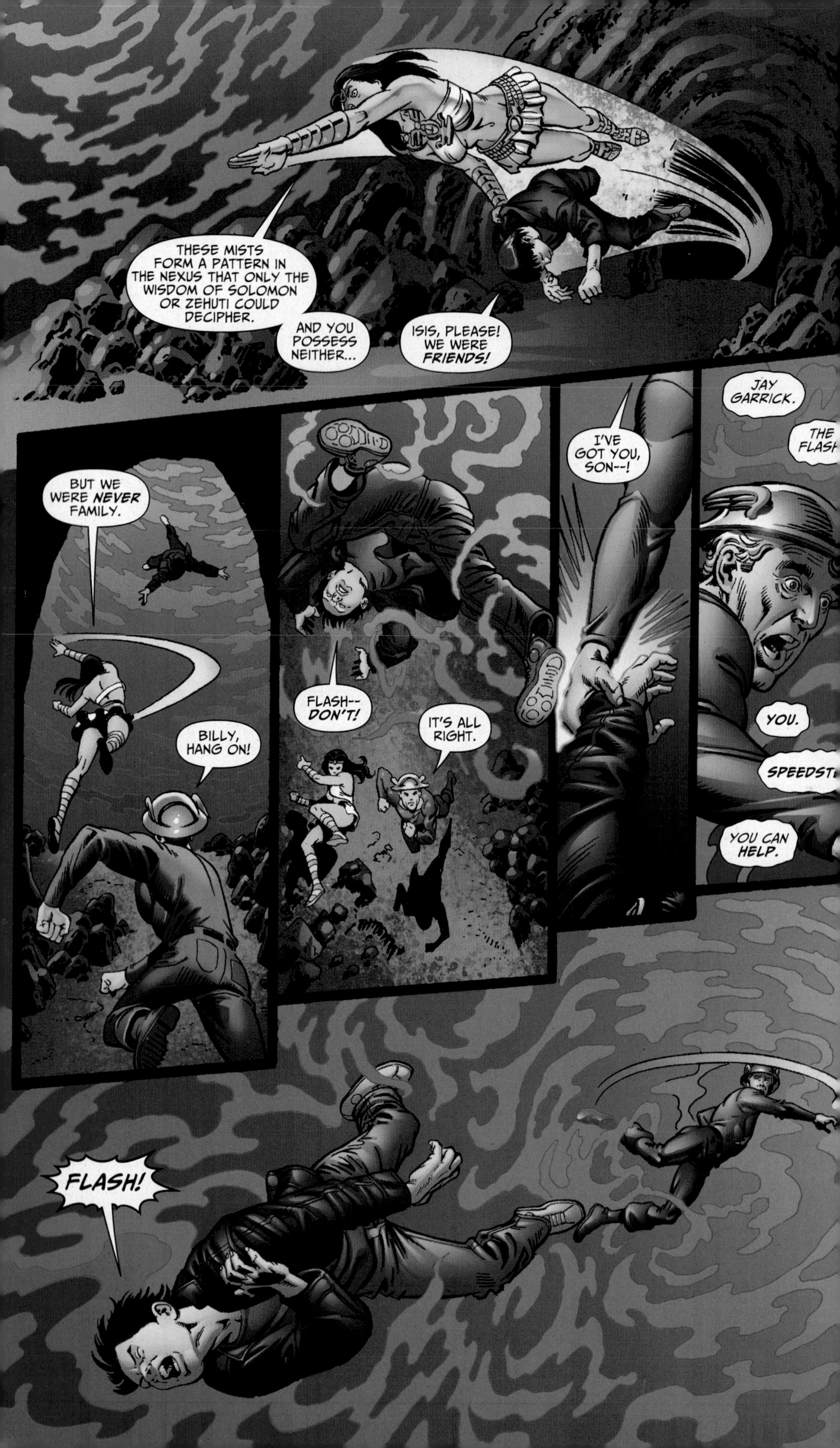
THESE MISTS FORM A PATTERN IN THE NEXUS THAT ONLY THE WISDOM OF SOLOMON OR ZEHUTI COULD DECIPHER.
AND YOU POSSESS NEITHER...
ISIS, PLEASE! WE WERE *FRIENDS!*
BUT WE WERE *NEVER* FAMILY.
BILLY, HANG ON!
FLASH-- *DON'T!*
IT'S ALL RIGHT.
I'VE GOT YOU, SON--!
JAY GARRICK.
YOU.
YOU CAN HELP.
FLASH!

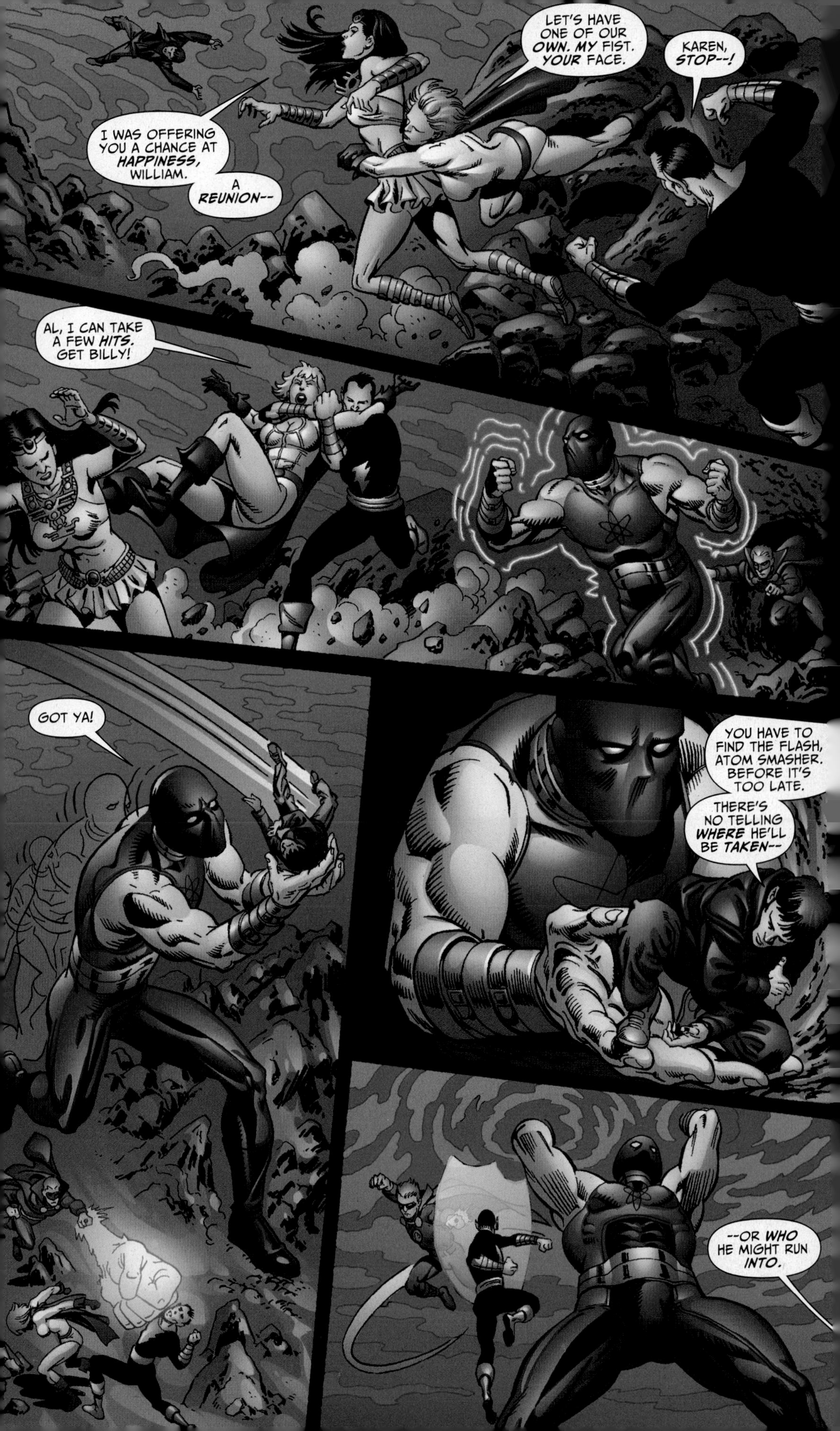

I WAS OFFERING YOU A CHANCE AT *HAPPINESS,* WILLIAM.
A *REUNION*--
LET'S HAVE ONE OF OUR *OWN. MY* FIST. *YOUR* FACE.
KAREN, *STOP*--!
AL, I CAN TAKE A FEW *HITS.* GET BILLY!
GOT YA!
YOU HAVE TO FIND THE FLASH, ATOM SMASHER. BEFORE IT'S TOO LATE.
THERE'S NO TELLING *WHERE* HE'LL BE *TAKEN*--
--OR *WHO* HE MIGHT RUN *INTO*.

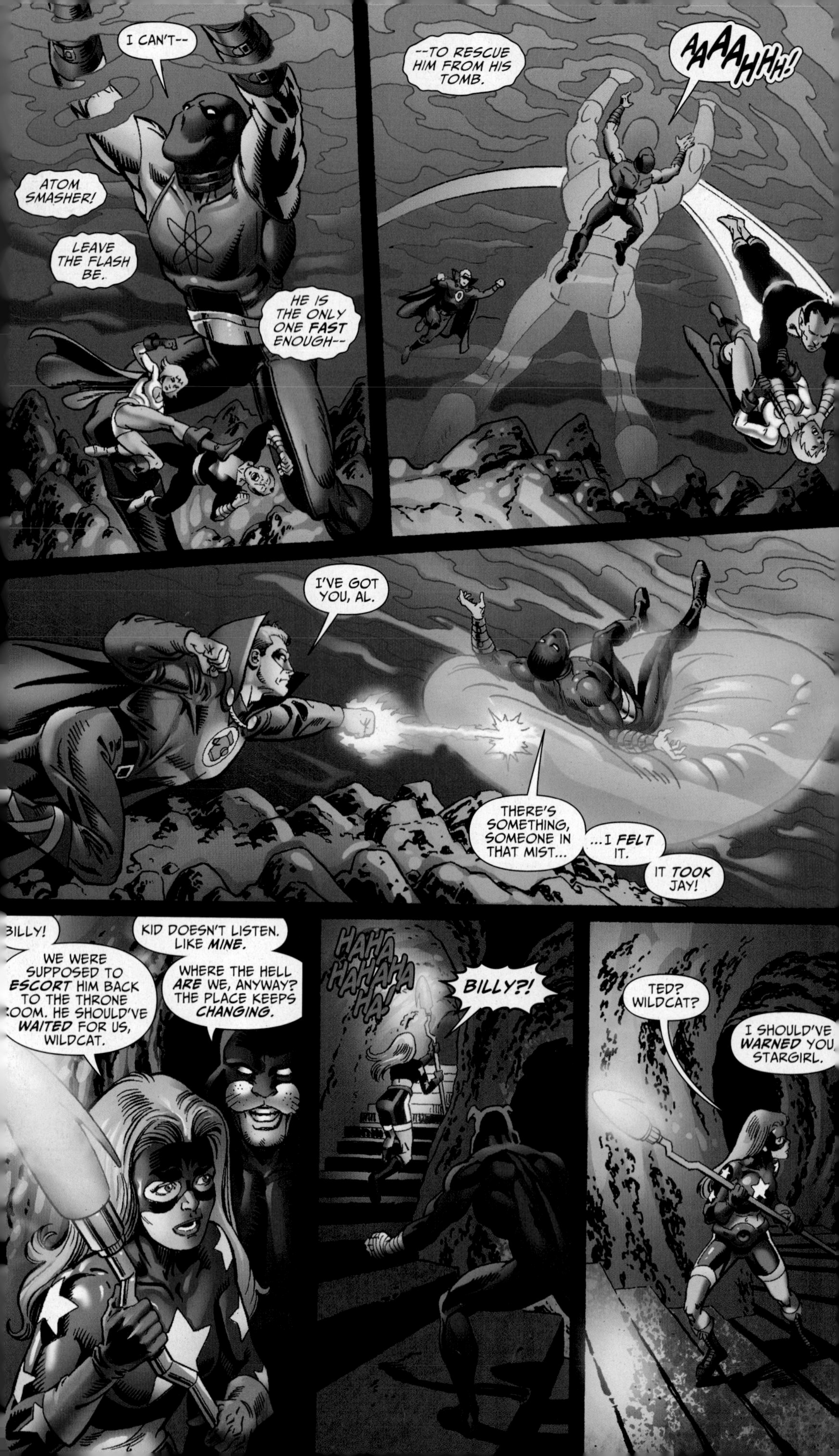
I CAN'T--
ATOM SMASHER!
LEAVE THE FLASH BE.
HE IS THE ONLY ONE FAST ENOUGH--
--TO RESCUE HIM FROM HIS TOMB.
AAAAHHH!
I'VE GOT YOU, AL.
THERE'S SOMETHING, SOMEONE IN THAT MIST...
...I FELT IT.
IT TOOK JAY!
BILLY!
WE WERE SUPPOSED TO ESCORT HIM BACK TO THE THRONE ROOM. HE SHOULD'VE WAITED FOR US, WILDCAT.
KID DOESN'T LISTEN. LIKE MINE.
WHERE THE HELL ARE WE, ANYWAY? THE PLACE KEEPS CHANGING.
HAHAHAHAHAHA!
BILLY?!
TED? WILDCAT?
I SHOULD'VE WARNED YOU, STARGIRL.

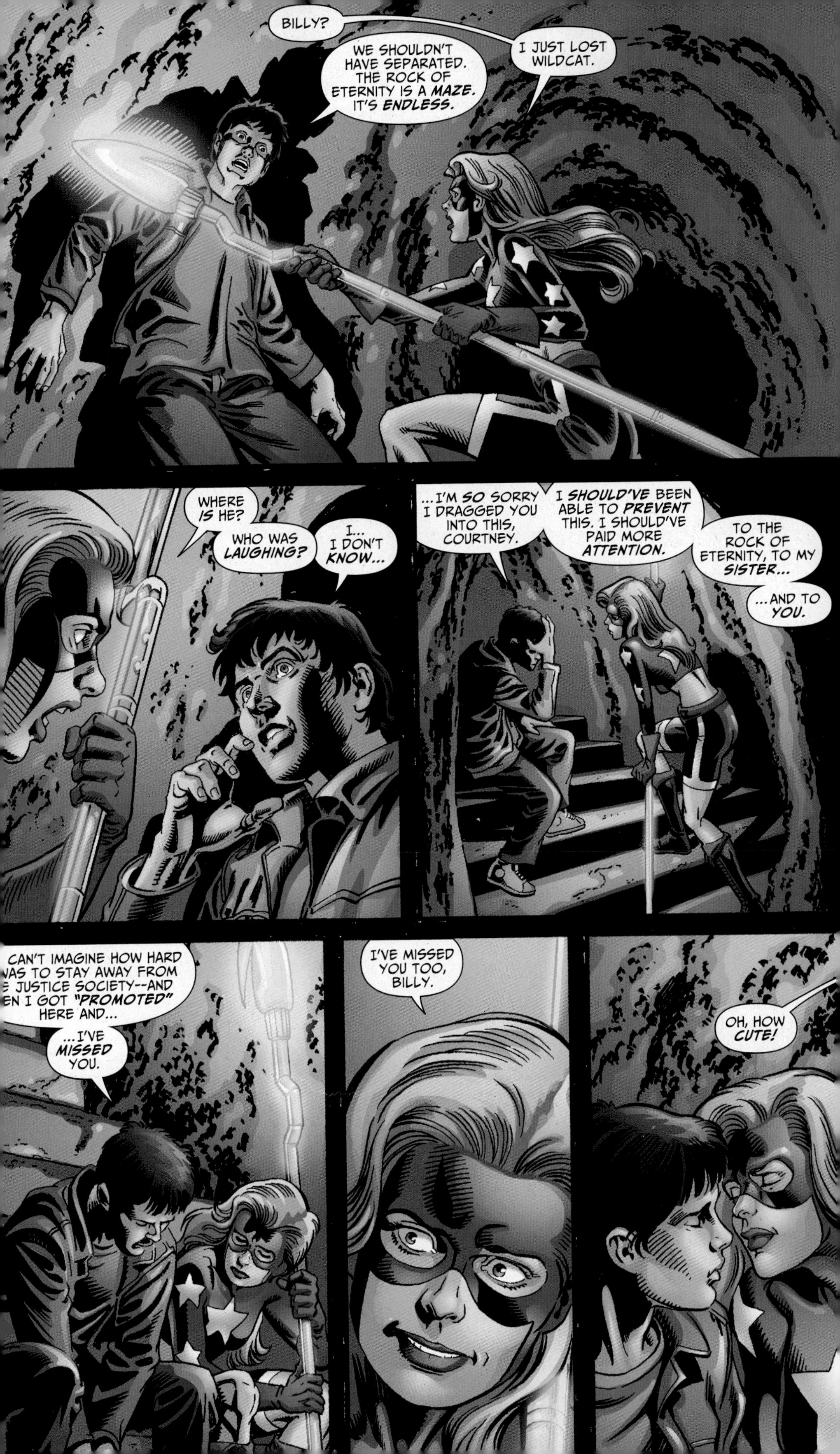
BILLY?
WE SHOULDN'T HAVE SEPARATED. THE ROCK OF ETERNITY IS A MAZE. IT'S ENDLESS.
I JUST LOST WILDCAT.
WHERE IS HE?
WHO WAS LAUGHING?
I... I DON'T KNOW...
...I'M SO SORRY I DRAGGED YOU INTO THIS, COURTNEY.
I SHOULD'VE BEEN ABLE TO PREVENT THIS. I SHOULD'VE PAID MORE ATTENTION.
TO THE ROCK OF ETERNITY, TO MY SISTER...
...AND TO YOU.
CAN'T IMAGINE HOW HARD WAS TO STAY AWAY FROM JUSTICE SOCIETY--AND EN I GOT "PROMOTED" HERE AND...
...I'VE MISSED YOU.
I'VE MISSED YOU TOO, BILLY.
OH, HOW CUTE!

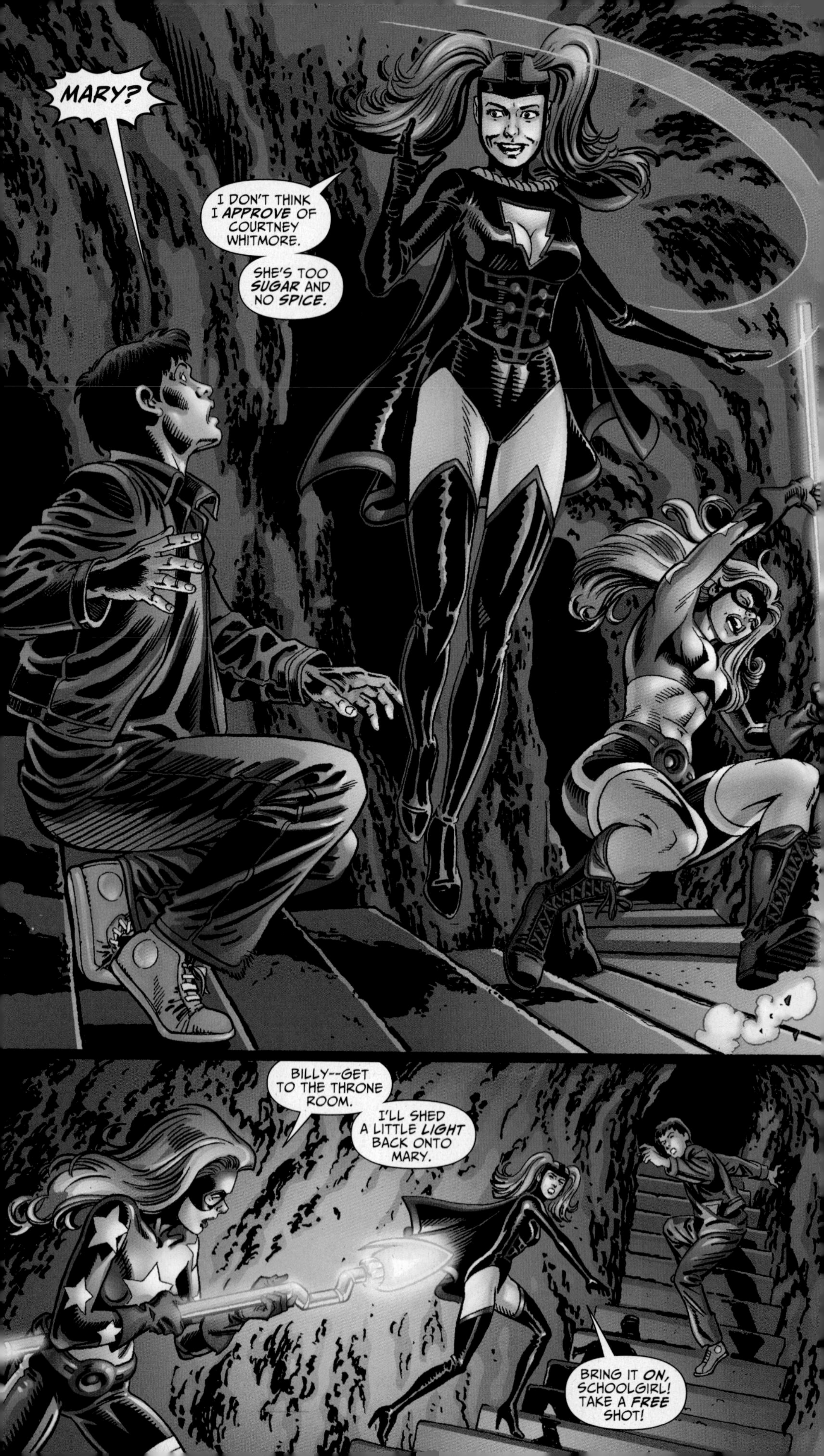
MARY?
I DON'T THINK I APPROVE OF COURTNEY WHITMORE.
SHE'S TOO SUGAR AND NO SPICE.
BILLY--GET TO THE THRONE ROOM.
I'LL SHED A LITTLE LIGHT BACK ONTO MARY.
BRING IT ON, SCHOOLGIRL! TAKE A FREE SHOT!

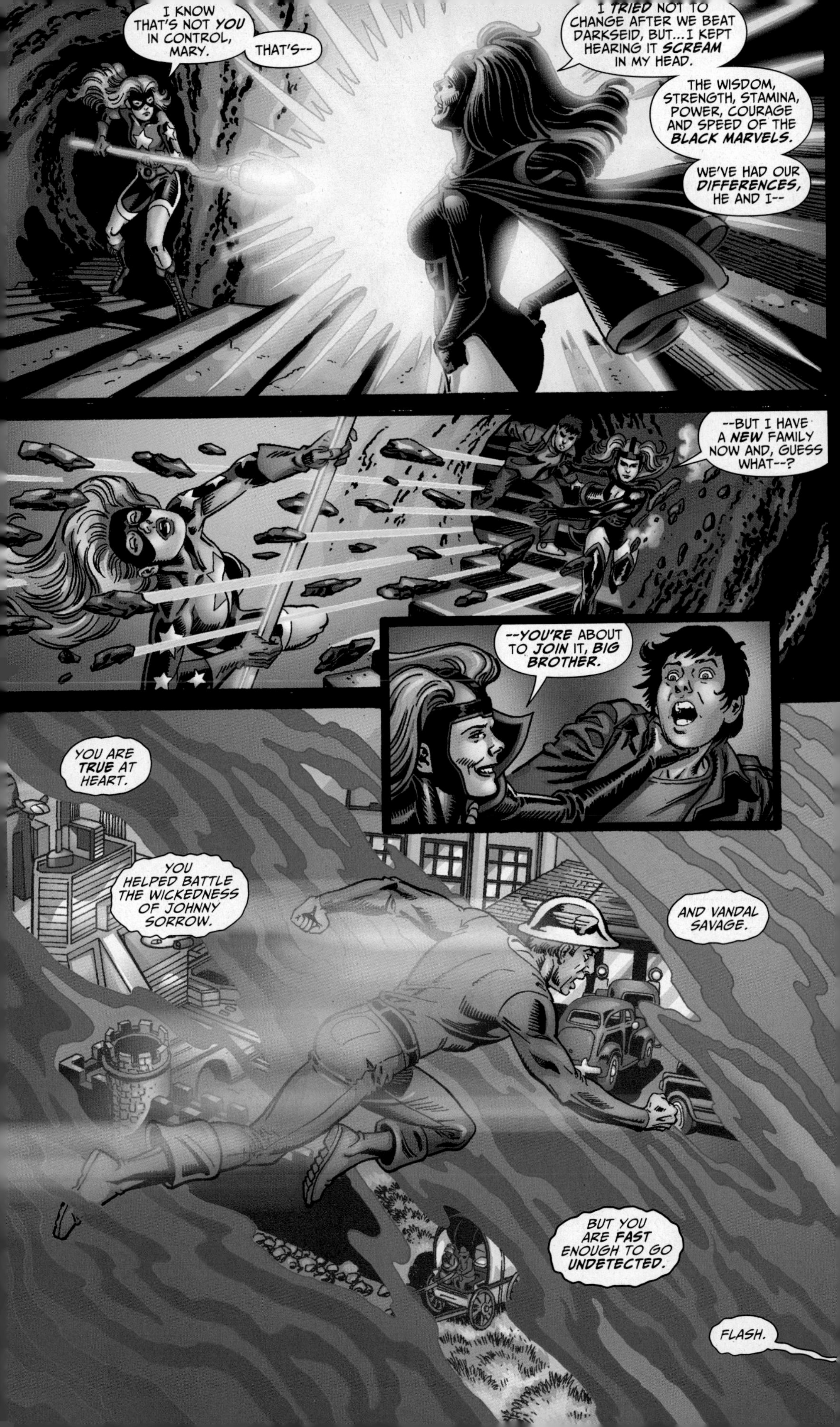
I KNOW THAT'S NOT *YOU* IN CONTROL, MARY.
THAT'S--
I *TRIED* NOT TO CHANGE AFTER WE BEAT DARKSEID, BUT... I KEPT HEARING IT *SCREAM* IN MY HEAD.
THE WISDOM, STRENGTH, STAMINA, POWER, COURAGE AND SPEED OF THE *BLACK MARVELS.*
WE'VE HAD OUR *DIFFERENCES,* HE AND I--
--BUT I HAVE A *NEW* FAMILY NOW AND, GUESS WHAT--?
--*YOU'RE* ABOUT TO *JOIN* IT, *BIG BROTHER.*
YOU ARE *TRUE* AT HEART.
YOU HELPED BATTLE THE WICKEDNESS OF JOHNNY SORROW.
AND VANDAL SAVAGE.
BUT YOU ARE *FAST* ENOUGH TO GO *UNDETECTED.*
FLASH.

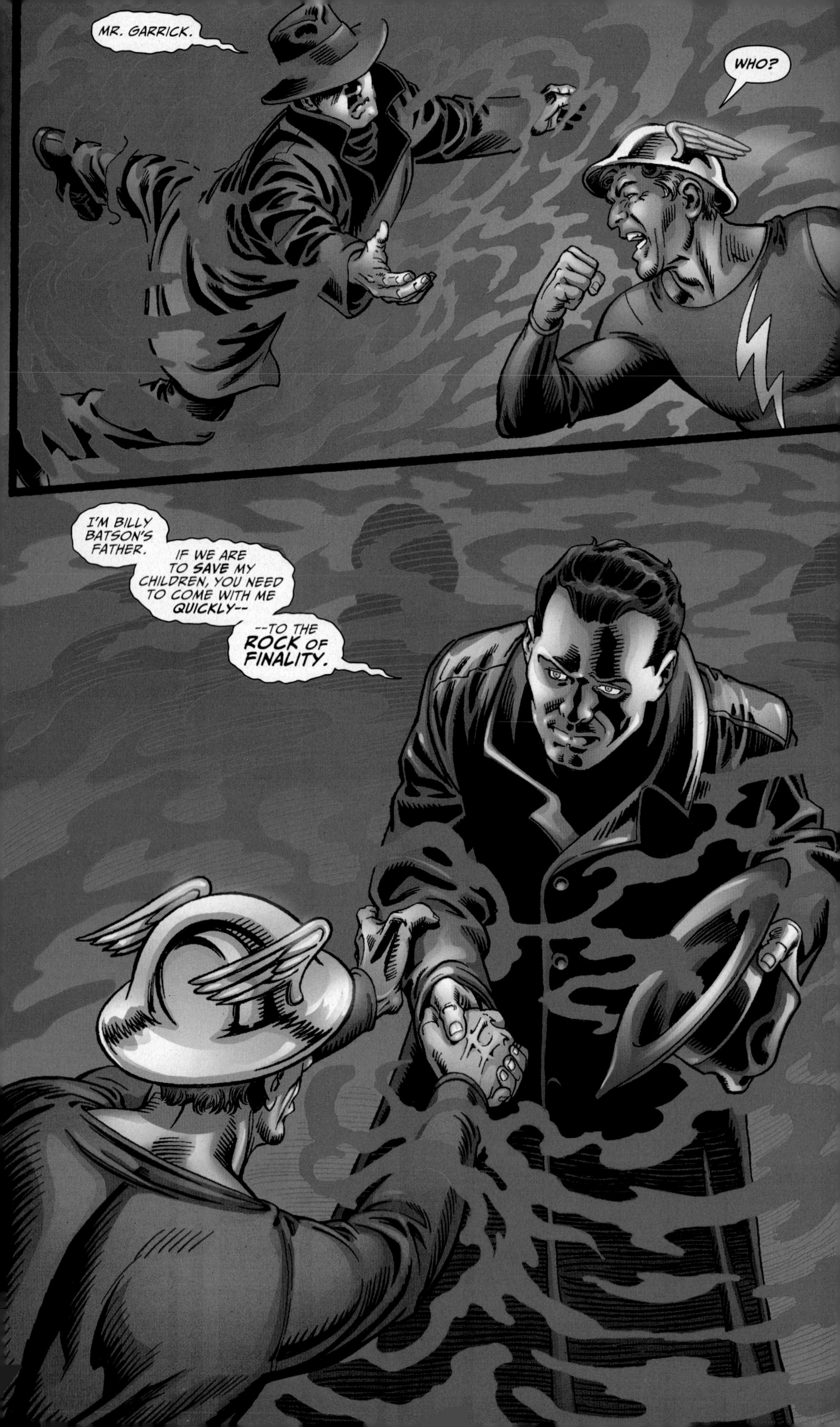
MR. GARRICK.
WHO?
I'M BILLY BATSON'S FATHER.
IF WE ARE TO SAVE MY CHILDREN, YOU NEED TO COME WITH ME QUICKLY--
--TO THE ROCK OF FINALITY.

USTICE SOCIETY OF AMERICA #25 cover A by Alex Ross
nterior pencils by Jerry Ordway and inks by Bob Wiacek and Ordway

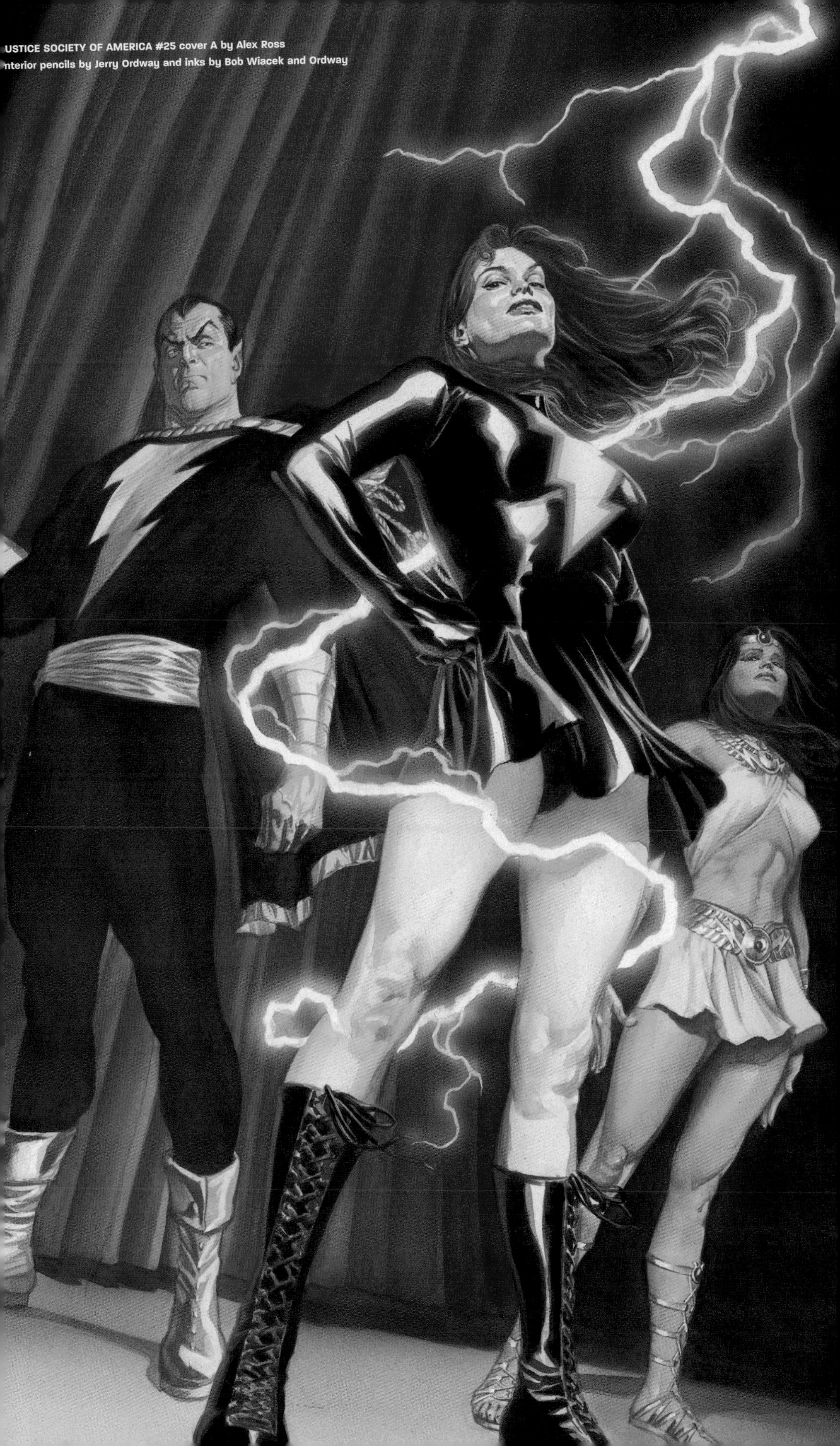

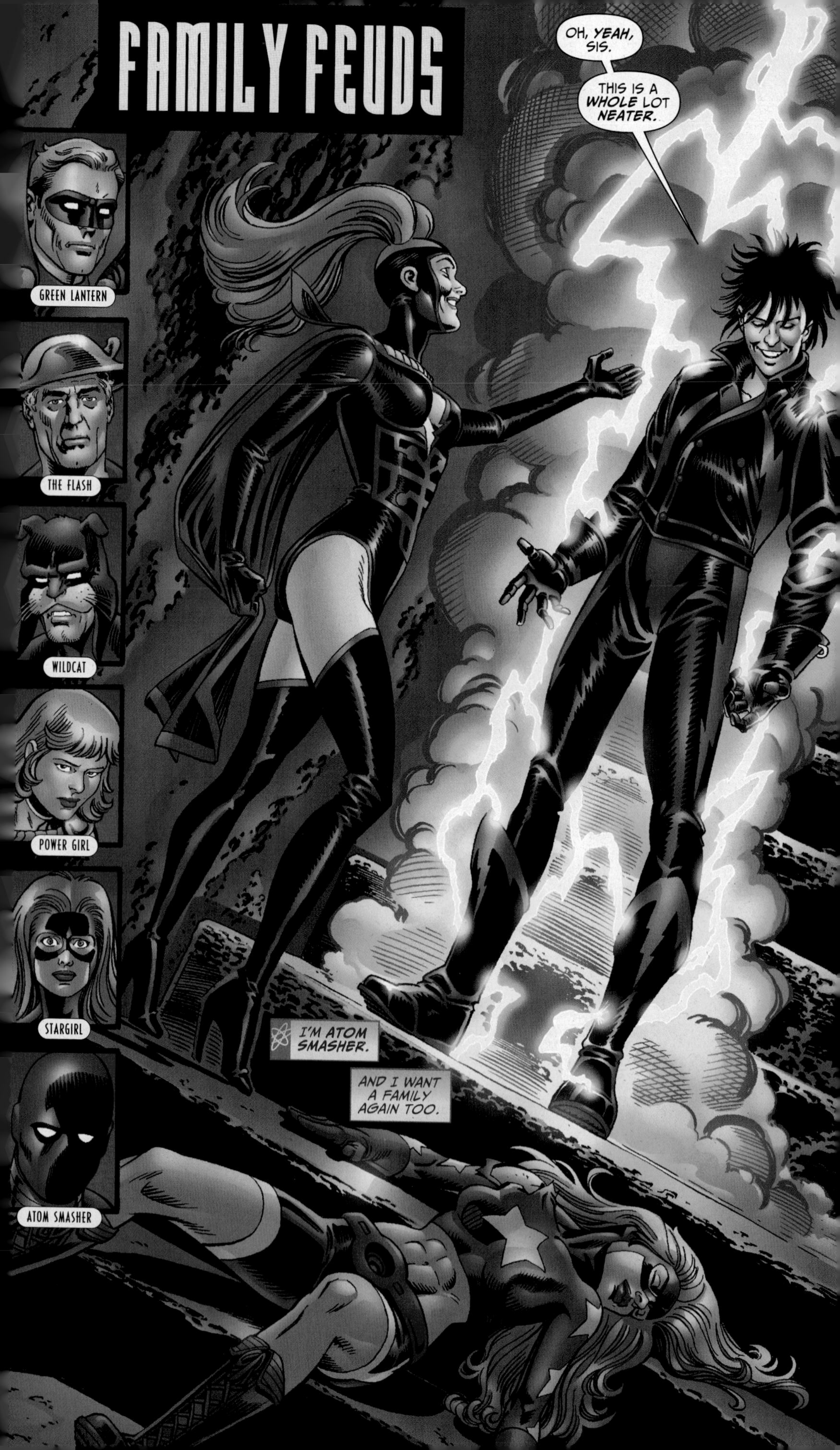
FAMILY FEUDS
GREEN LANTERN
THE FLASH
WILDCAT
POWER GIRL
STARGIRL
ATOM SMASHER
OH, YEAH, SIS.
THIS IS A WHOLE LOT NEATER.
I'M ATOM SMASHER.
AND I WANT A FAMILY AGAIN TOO.

THE PEOPLE OF 'AHNDAQ SURVIVED BLACK ADAM'S LIBERATION, THE SPECTRE'S INVASION AND THE TERROR CAUSED BY THE FOUR HORSEMEN.

THEY DESERVE CENTURIES OF PEACE.

BUT IT DIDN'T START TODAY.

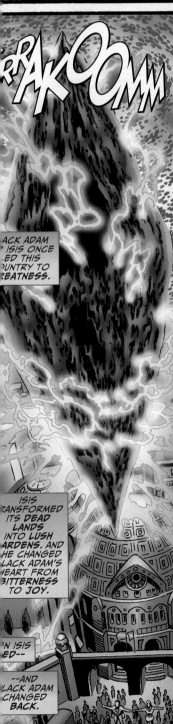

RRAKOOMM

BLACK ADAM AND ISIS ONCE LED THIS COUNTRY TO GREATNESS.

ISIS TRANSFORMED ITS DEAD LANDS INTO LUSH GARDENS. AND SHE CHANGED BLACK ADAM'S HEART FROM BITTERNESS TO JOY.

WHEN ISIS DIED--

--AND BLACK ADAM CHANGED BACK.

WHEN ISIS RETURNED--

--SHE CHANGED TOO.

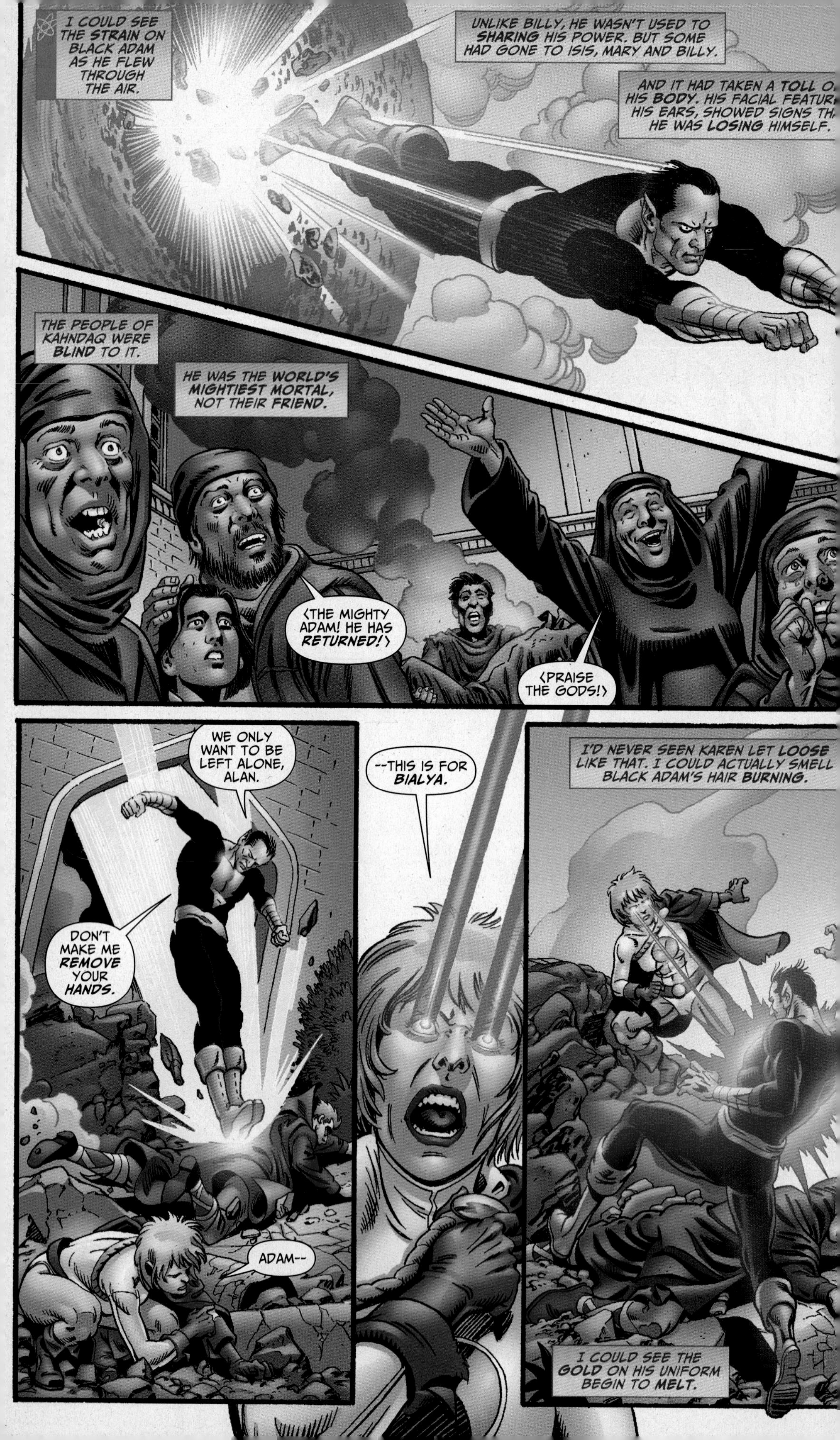

I COULD SEE THE STRAIN ON BLACK ADAM AS HE FLEW THROUGH THE AIR.
UNLIKE BILLY, HE WASN'T USED TO SHARING HIS POWER. BUT SOME HAD GONE TO ISIS, MARY AND BILLY.
AND IT HAD TAKEN A TOLL O HIS BODY. HIS FACIAL FEATUR HIS EARS, SHOWED SIGNS TH HE WAS LOSING HIMSELF.
THE PEOPLE OF KAHNDAQ WERE BLIND TO IT.
HE WAS THE WORLD'S MIGHTIEST MORTAL, NOT THEIR FRIEND.
‹THE MIGHTY ADAM! HE HAS RETURNED!›
‹PRAISE THE GODS!›
WE ONLY WANT TO BE LEFT ALONE, ALAN.
DON'T MAKE ME REMOVE YOUR HANDS.
ADAM--
--THIS IS FOR BIALYA.
I'D NEVER SEEN KAREN LET LOOSE LIKE THAT. I COULD ACTUALLY SMELL BLACK ADAM'S HAIR BURNING.
I COULD SEE THE GOLD ON HIS UNIFORM BEGIN TO MELT.

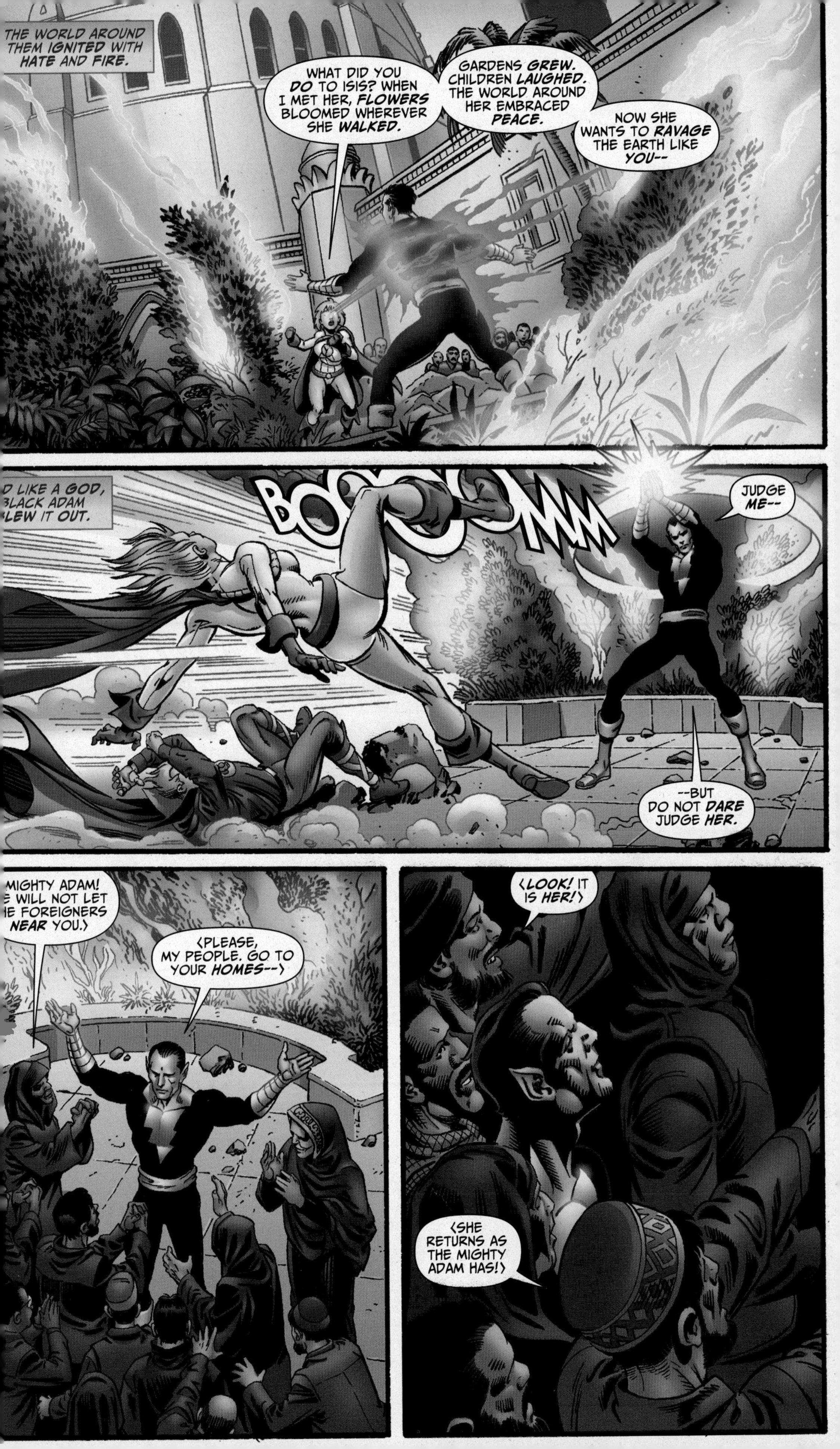
THE WORLD AROUND THEM IGNITED WITH HATE AND FIRE.
WHAT DID YOU DO TO ISIS? WHEN I MET HER, FLOWERS BLOOMED WHEREVER SHE WALKED.
GARDENS GREW. CHILDREN LAUGHED. THE WORLD AROUND HER EMBRACED PEACE.
NOW SHE WANTS TO RAVAGE THE EARTH LIKE YOU--
D LIKE A GOD, BLACK ADAM BLEW IT OUT.
BOOOOOMM
JUDGE ME--
--BUT DO NOT DARE JUDGE HER.
MIGHTY ADAM! E WILL NOT LET HE FOREIGNERS NEAR YOU.〉
〈PLEASE, MY PEOPLE. GO TO YOUR HOMES--〉
〈LOOK! IT IS HER!〉
〈SHE RETURNS AS THE MIGHTY ADAM HAS!〉

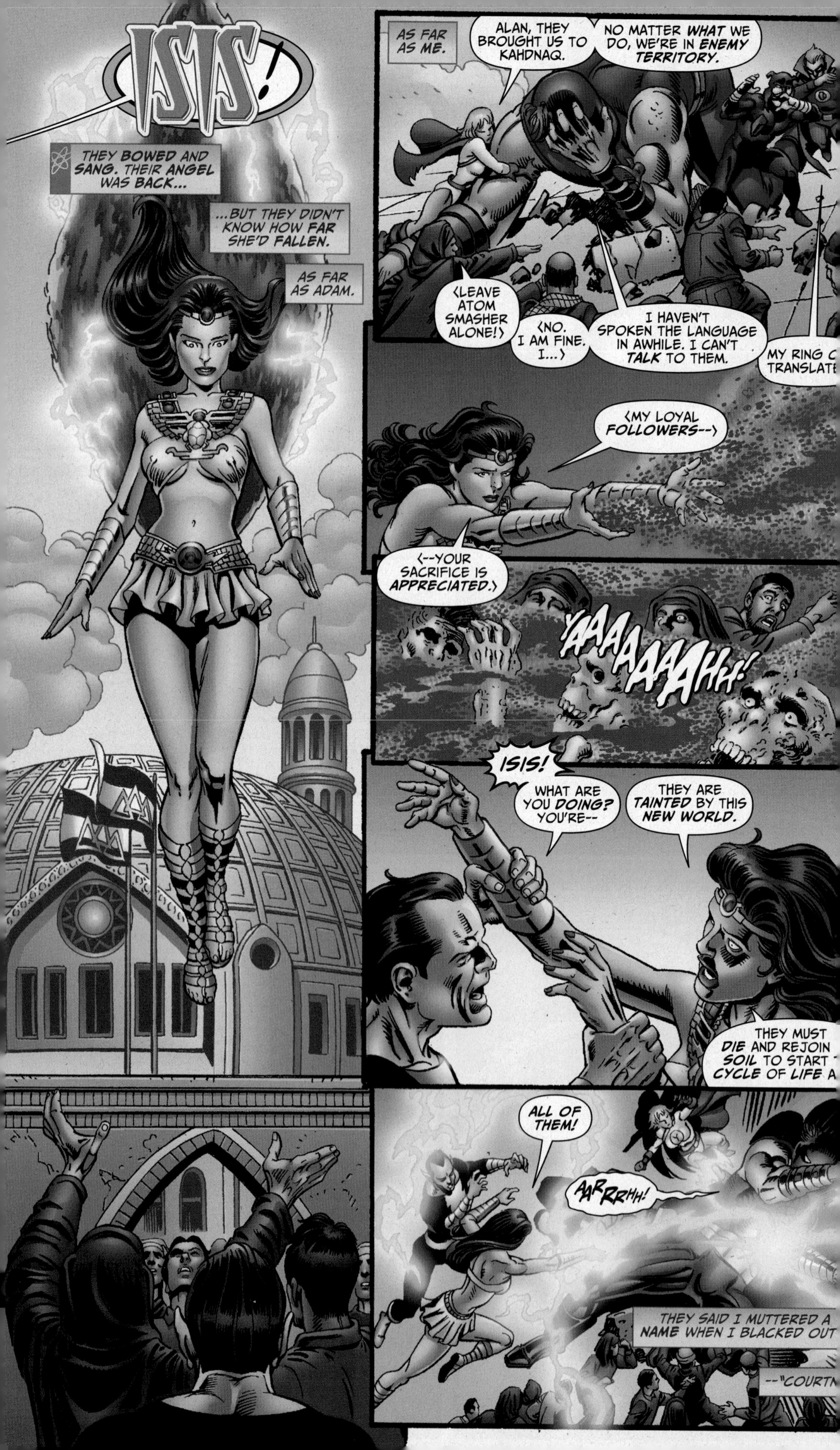
ISIS!
THEY BOWED AND SANG. THEIR ANGEL WAS BACK...
...BUT THEY DIDN'T KNOW HOW FAR SHE'D FALLEN.
AS FAR AS ADAM.
AS FAR AS ME.
ALAN, THEY BROUGHT US TO KAHDNAQ.
NO MATTER WHAT WE DO, WE'RE IN ENEMY TERRITORY.
‹LEAVE ATOM SMASHER ALONE!›
‹NO. I AM FINE. I...›
I HAVEN'T SPOKEN THE LANGUAGE IN AWHILE. I CAN'T TALK TO THEM.
MY RING C TRANSLATE
‹MY LOYAL FOLLOWERS--›
‹--YOUR SACRIFICE IS APPRECIATED.›
YAAAAAAAAHH!
ISIS!
WHAT ARE YOU DOING? YOU'RE--
THEY ARE TAINTED BY THIS NEW WORLD.
THEY MUST DIE AND REJOIN SOIL TO START CYCLE OF LIFE A
ALL OF THEM!
AARRRHH!
THEY SAID I MUTTERED A NAME WHEN I BLACKED OUT
--"COURTN

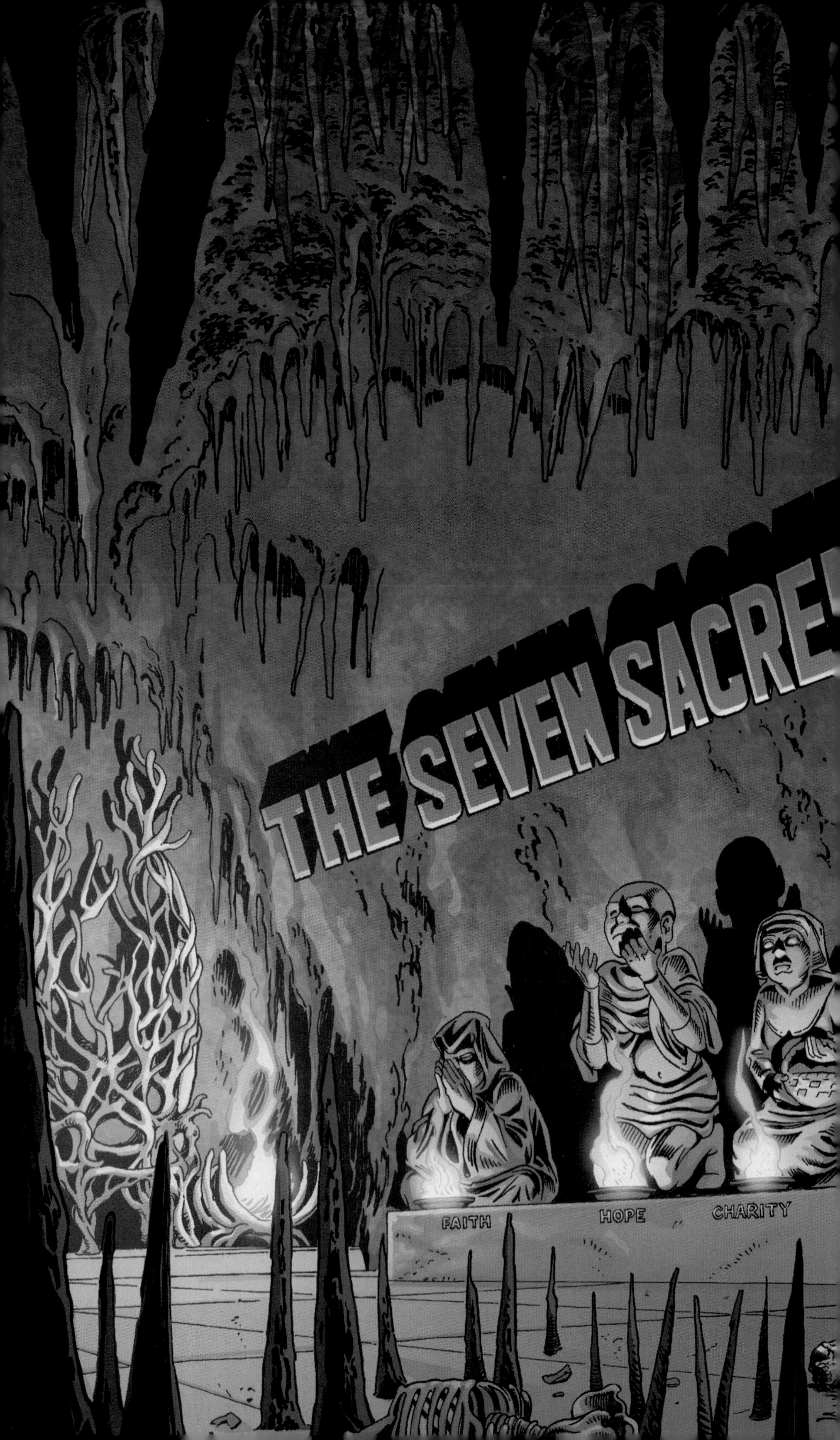
THE SEVEN SACRE
FAITH
HOPE
CHARITY

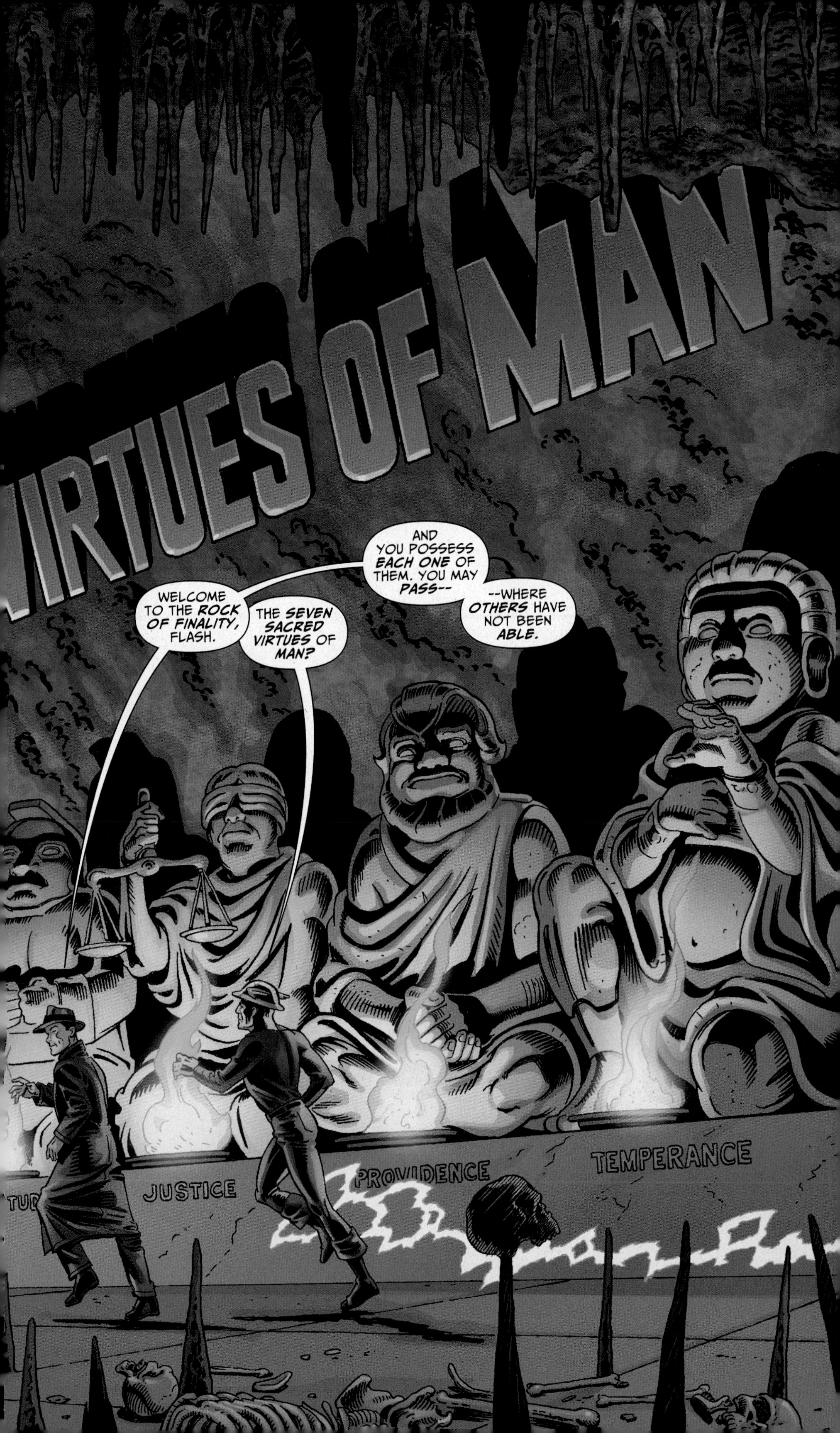
VIRTUES OF MAN
WELCOME TO THE ROCK OF FINALITY, FLASH.
THE SEVEN SACRED VIRTUES OF MAN?
AND YOU POSSESS EACH ONE OF THEM. YOU MAY PASS--
--WHERE OTHERS HAVE NOT BEEN ABLE.
JUSTICE
PROVIDENCE
TEMPERANCE

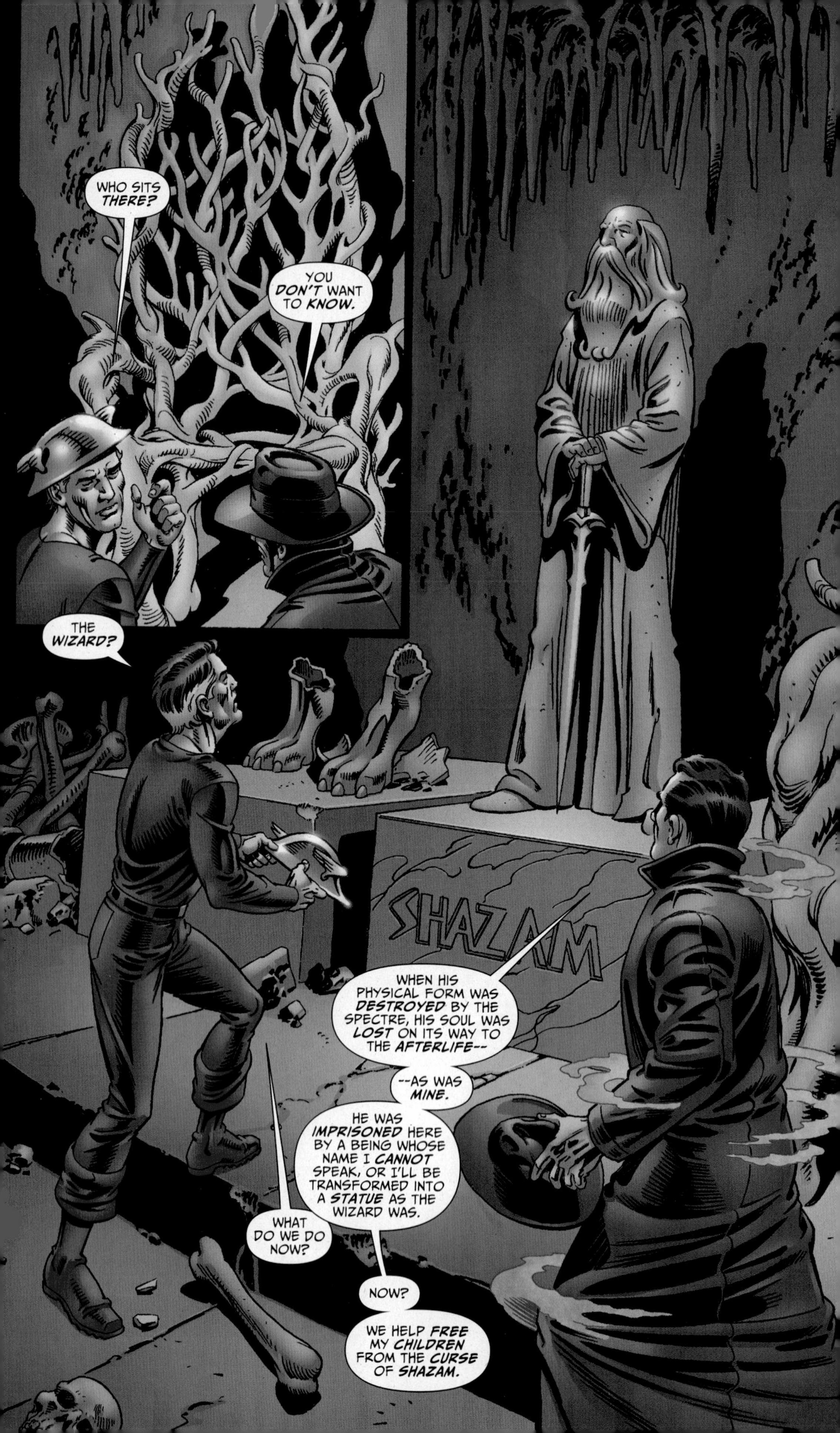
WHO SITS THERE?
YOU DON'T WANT TO KNOW.
THE WIZARD?
SHAZAM
WHEN HIS PHYSICAL FORM WAS DESTROYED BY THE SPECTRE, HIS SOUL WAS LOST ON ITS WAY TO THE AFTERLIFE--
--AS WAS MINE.
HE WAS IMPRISONED HERE BY A BEING WHOSE NAME I CANNOT SPEAK, OR I'LL BE TRANSFORMED INTO A STATUE AS THE WIZARD WAS.
WHAT DO WE DO NOW?
NOW?
WE HELP FREE MY CHILDREN FROM THE CURSE OF SHAZAM.

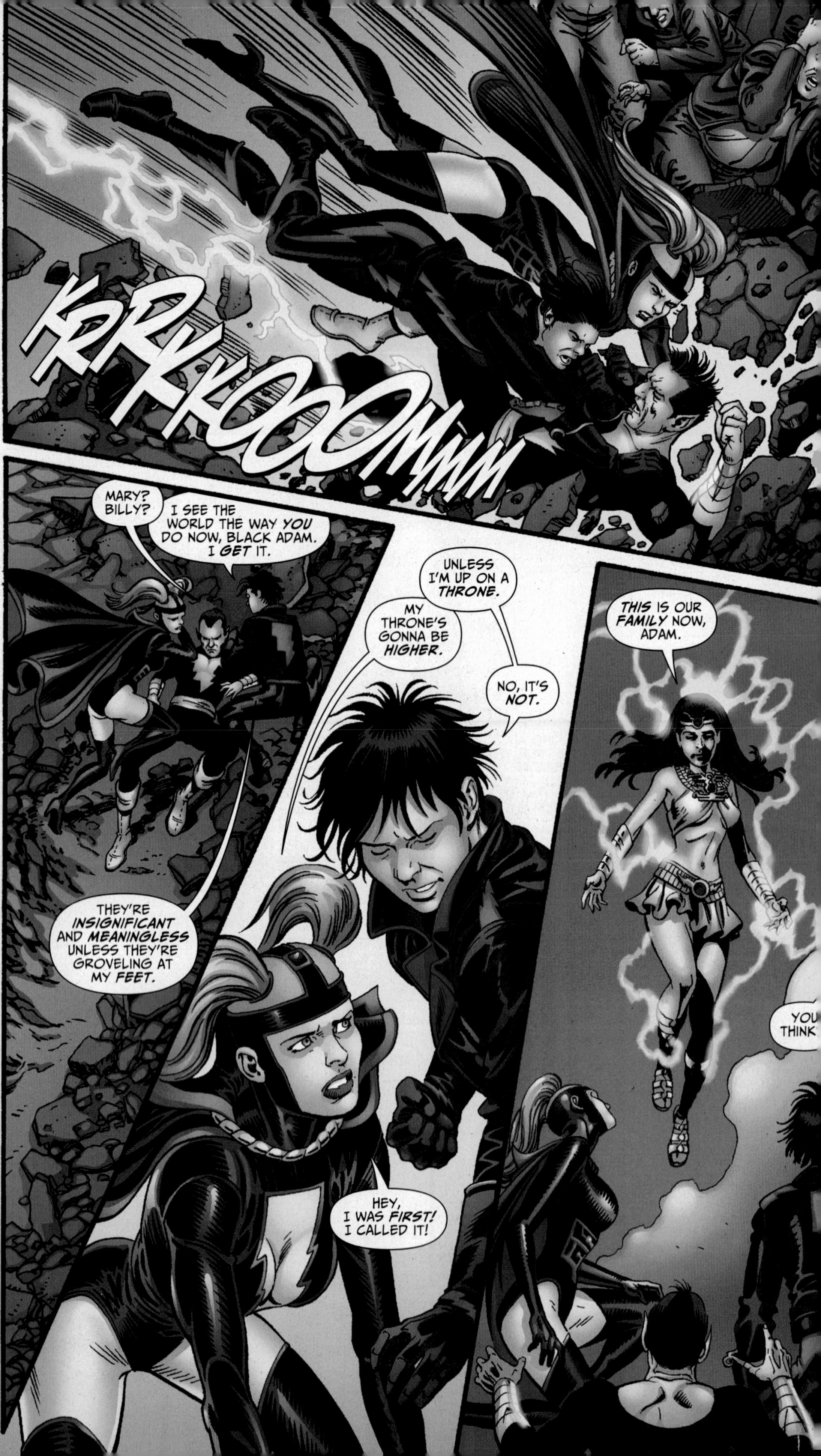
KRRKKOOOMMM
MARY? BILLY?
I SEE THE WORLD THE WAY YOU DO NOW, BLACK ADAM. I GET IT.
THEY'RE INSIGNIFICANT AND MEANINGLESS UNLESS THEY'RE GROVELING AT MY FEET.
UNLESS I'M UP ON A THRONE.
MY THRONE'S GONNA BE HIGHER.
NO, IT'S NOT.
HEY, I WAS FIRST! I CALLED IT!
THIS IS OUR FAMILY NOW, ADAM.
YOU THINK

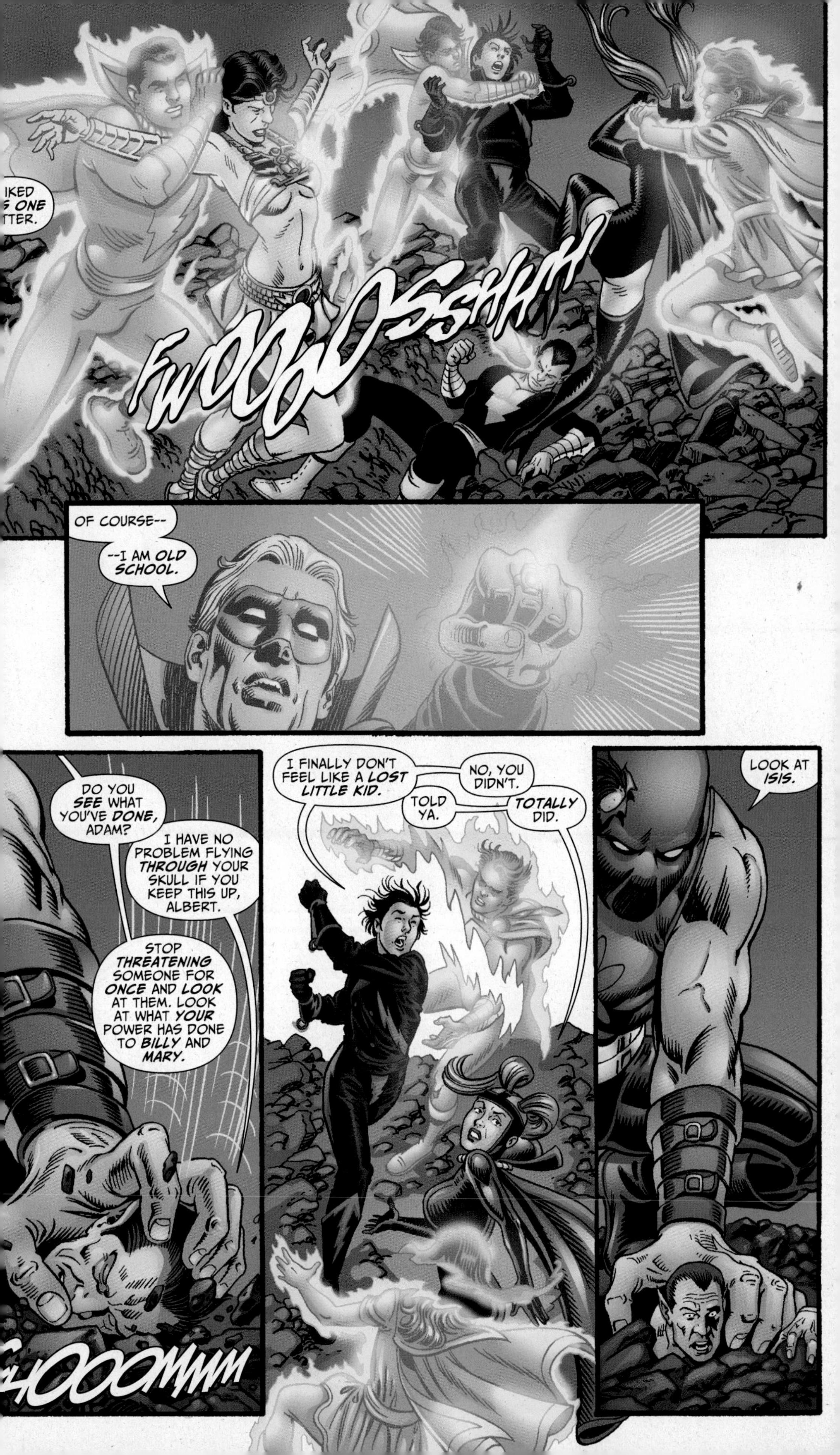
IKED
S ONE
TTER.
FWOOOOSSHHH
OF COURSE--
--I AM OLD SCHOOL.
DO YOU SEE WHAT YOU'VE DONE, ADAM?
I HAVE NO PROBLEM FLYING THROUGH YOUR SKULL IF YOU KEEP THIS UP, ALBERT.
STOP THREATENING SOMEONE FOR ONCE AND LOOK AT THEM. LOOK AT WHAT YOUR POWER HAS DONE TO BILLY AND MARY.
HOOOMMM
I FINALLY DON'T FEEL LIKE A LOST LITTLE KID.
NO, YOU DIDN'T.
TOLD YA.
TOTALLY DID.
LOOK AT ISIS.

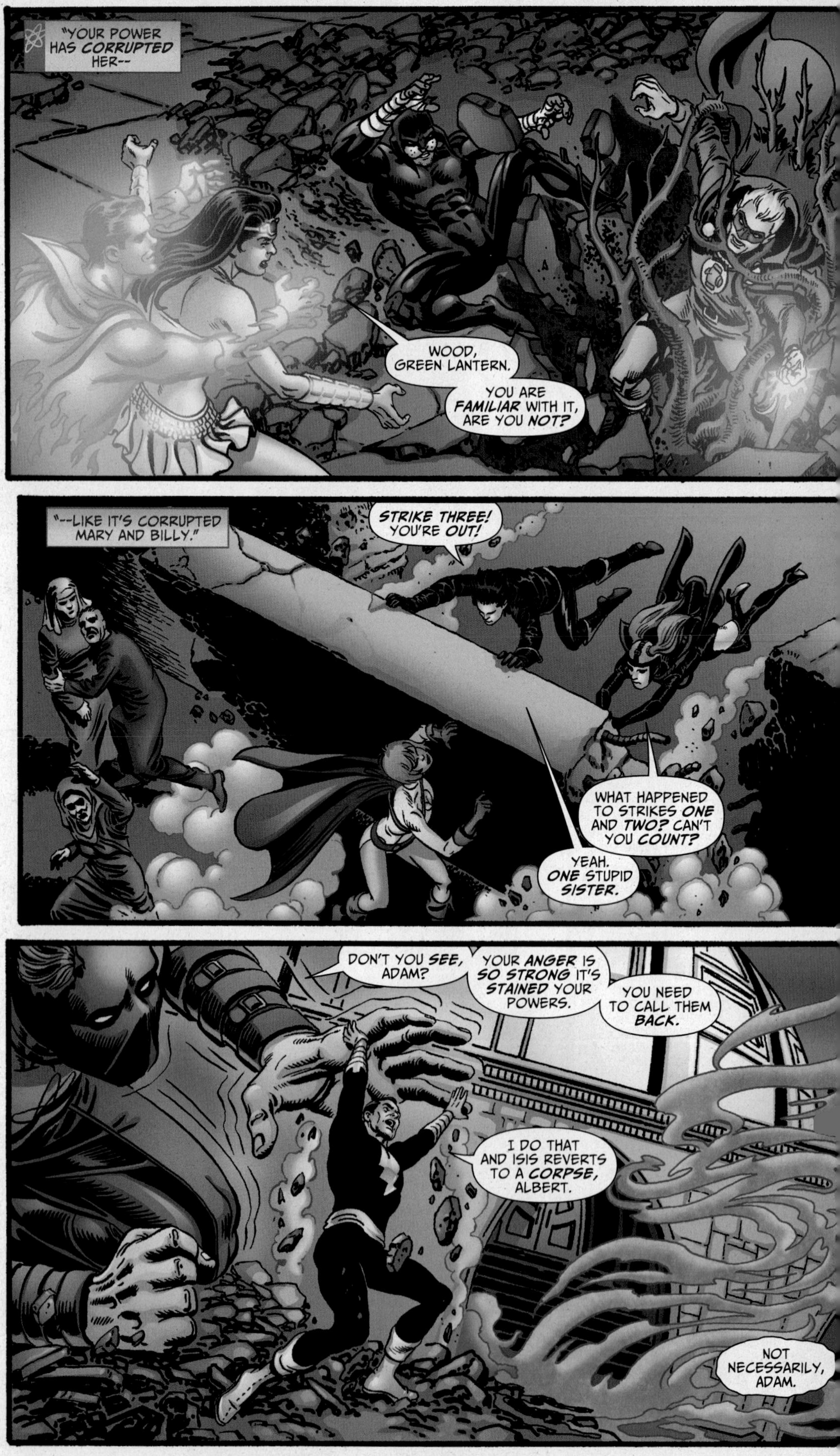
"YOUR POWER HAS CORRUPTED HER--
WOOD, GREEN LANTERN.
YOU ARE FAMILIAR WITH IT, ARE YOU NOT?
"--LIKE IT'S CORRUPTED MARY AND BILLY."
STRIKE THREE! YOU'RE OUT!
WHAT HAPPENED TO STRIKES ONE AND TWO? CAN'T YOU COUNT?
YEAH. ONE STUPID SISTER.
DON'T YOU SEE, ADAM?
YOUR ANGER IS SO STRONG IT'S STAINED YOUR POWERS.
YOU NEED TO CALL THEM BACK.
I DO THAT AND ISIS REVERTS TO A CORPSE, ALBERT.
NOT NECESSARILY, ADAM.

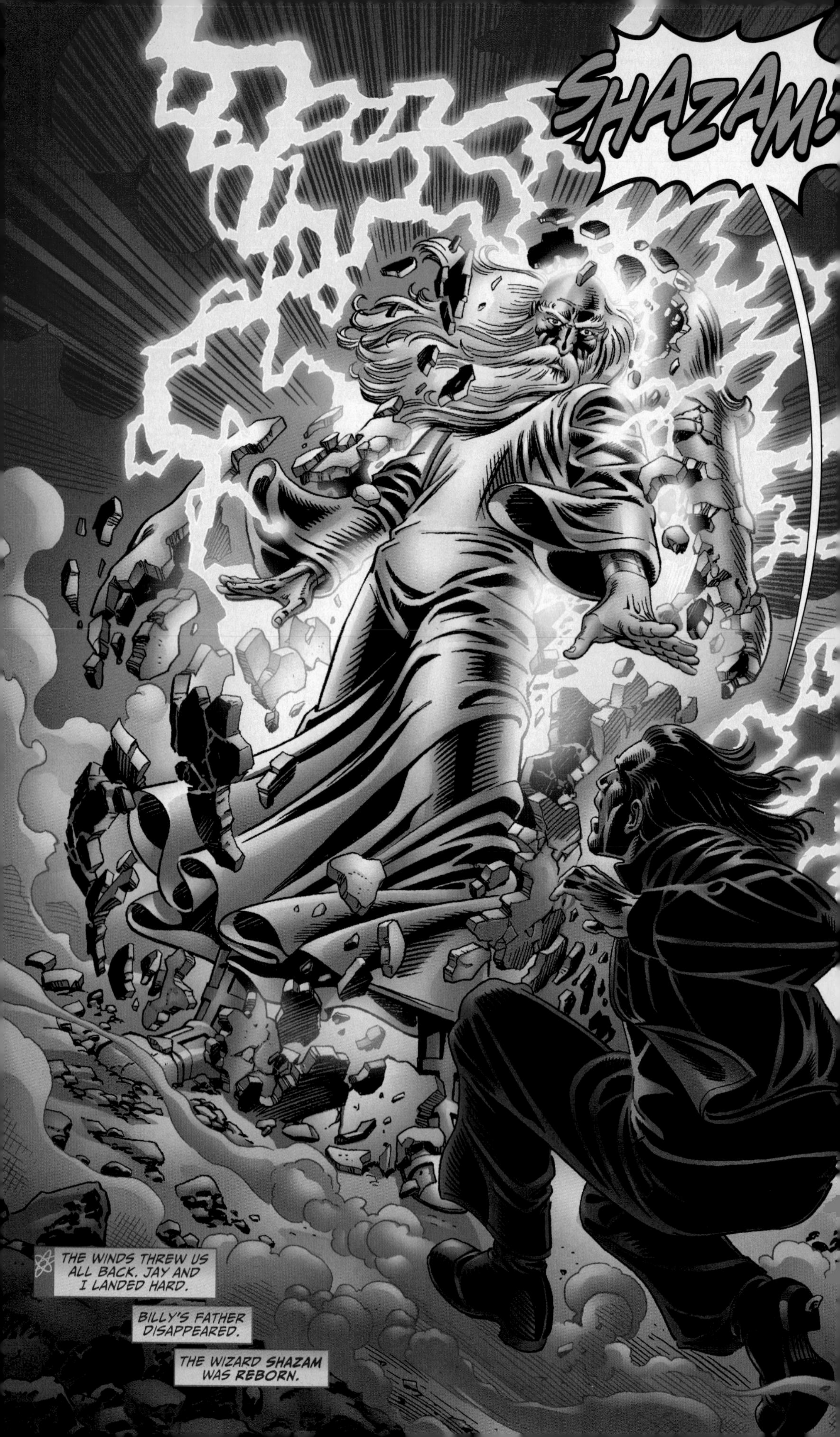
SHAZAM!
THE WINDS THREW US ALL BACK. JAY AND I LANDED HARD.
BILLY'S FATHER DISAPPEARED.
THE WIZARD SHAZAM WAS REBORN.

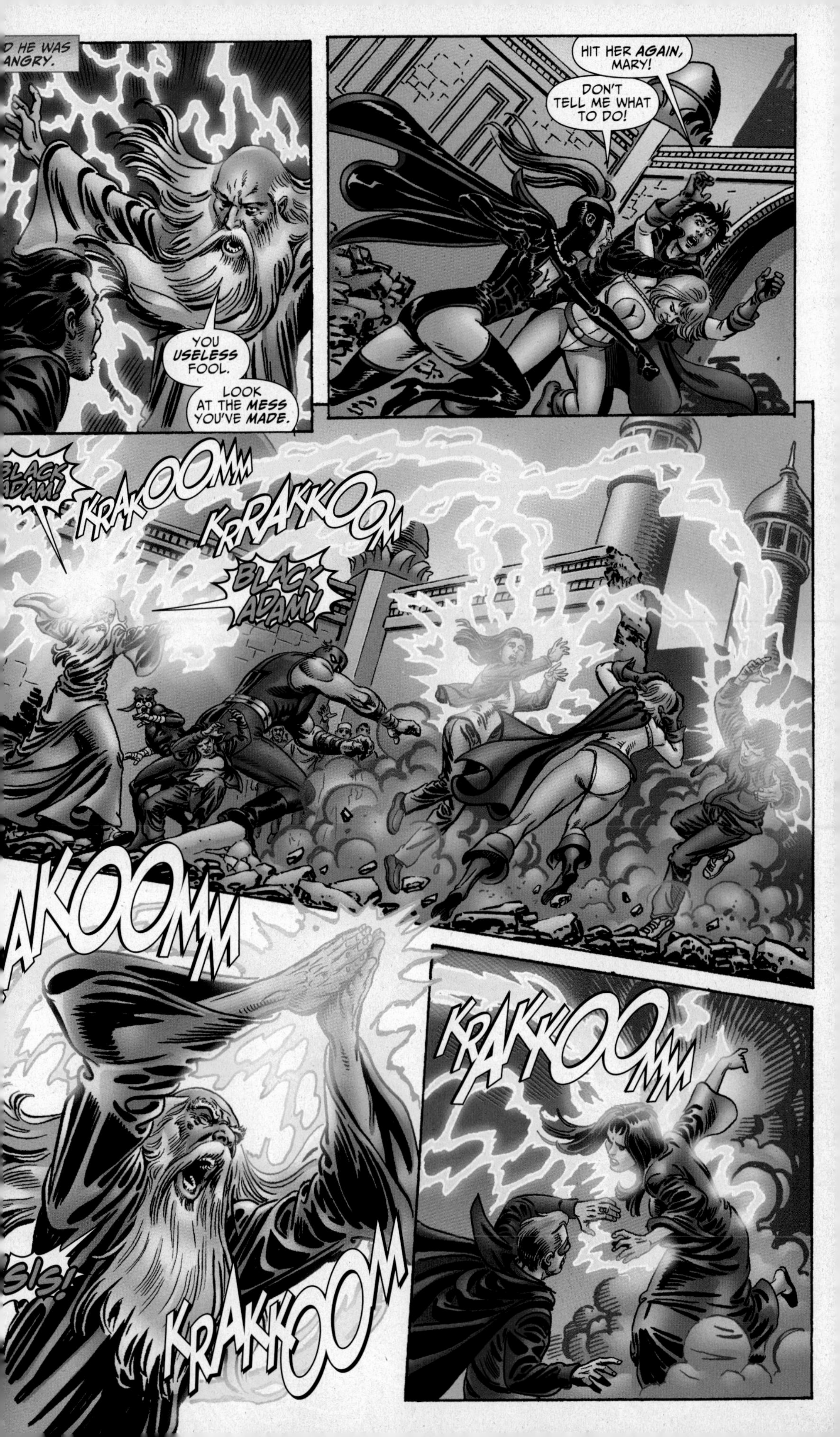

D HE WAS ANGRY.
YOU USELESS FOOL.
LOOK AT THE MESS YOU'VE MADE.
HIT HER AGAIN, MARY!
DON'T TELL ME WHAT TO DO!
BLACK ADAM!
KRAKOOMM
KRRAKKOOM
BLACK ADAM!
AKOOMM
KRAKKOOMM
SIS!
KRAKKOOM

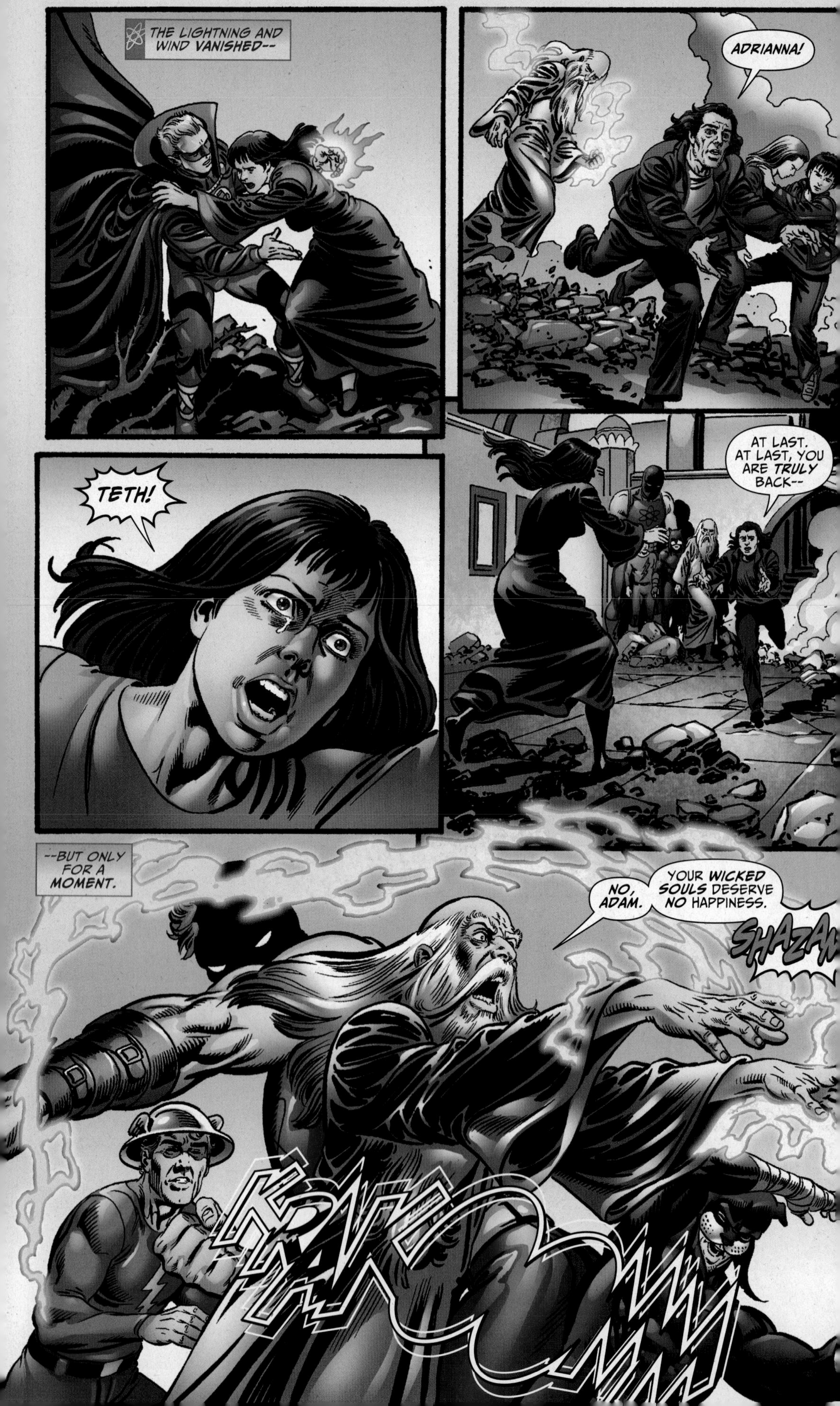
THE LIGHTNING AND WIND VANISHED--
ADRIANNA!
TETH!
AT LAST. AT LAST, YOU ARE TRULY BACK--
--BUT ONLY FOR A MOMENT.
NO, ADAM.
YOUR WICKED SOULS DESERVE NO HAPPINESS.
SHAZAM
KRAKOOM

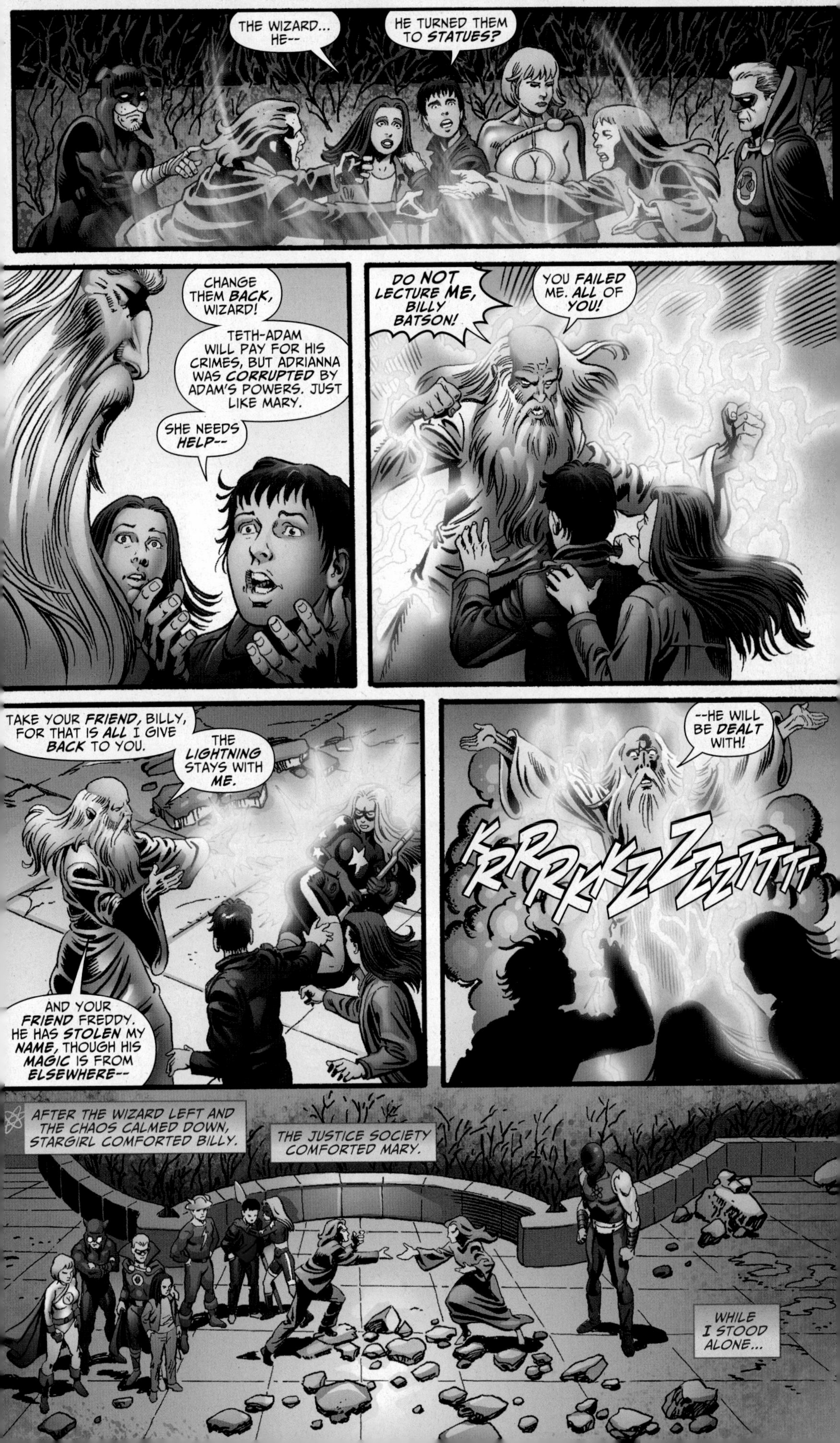
THE WIZARD... HE--
HE TURNED THEM TO STATUES?
CHANGE THEM BACK, WIZARD!
TETH-ADAM WILL PAY FOR HIS CRIMES, BUT ADRIANNA WAS CORRUPTED BY ADAM'S POWERS. JUST LIKE MARY.
SHE NEEDS HELP--
DO NOT LECTURE ME, BILLY BATSON!
YOU FAILED ME. ALL OF YOU!
TAKE YOUR FRIEND, BILLY, FOR THAT IS ALL I GIVE BACK TO YOU.
THE LIGHTNING STAYS WITH ME.
AND YOUR FRIEND FREDDY. HE HAS STOLEN MY NAME, THOUGH HIS MAGIC IS FROM ELSEWHERE--
--HE WILL BE DEALT WITH!
KRRRKKZZZZZTTTTT
AFTER THE WIZARD LEFT AND THE CHAOS CALMED DOWN, STARGIRL COMFORTED BILLY.
THE JUSTICE SOCIETY COMFORTED MARY.
WHILE I STOOD ALONE...

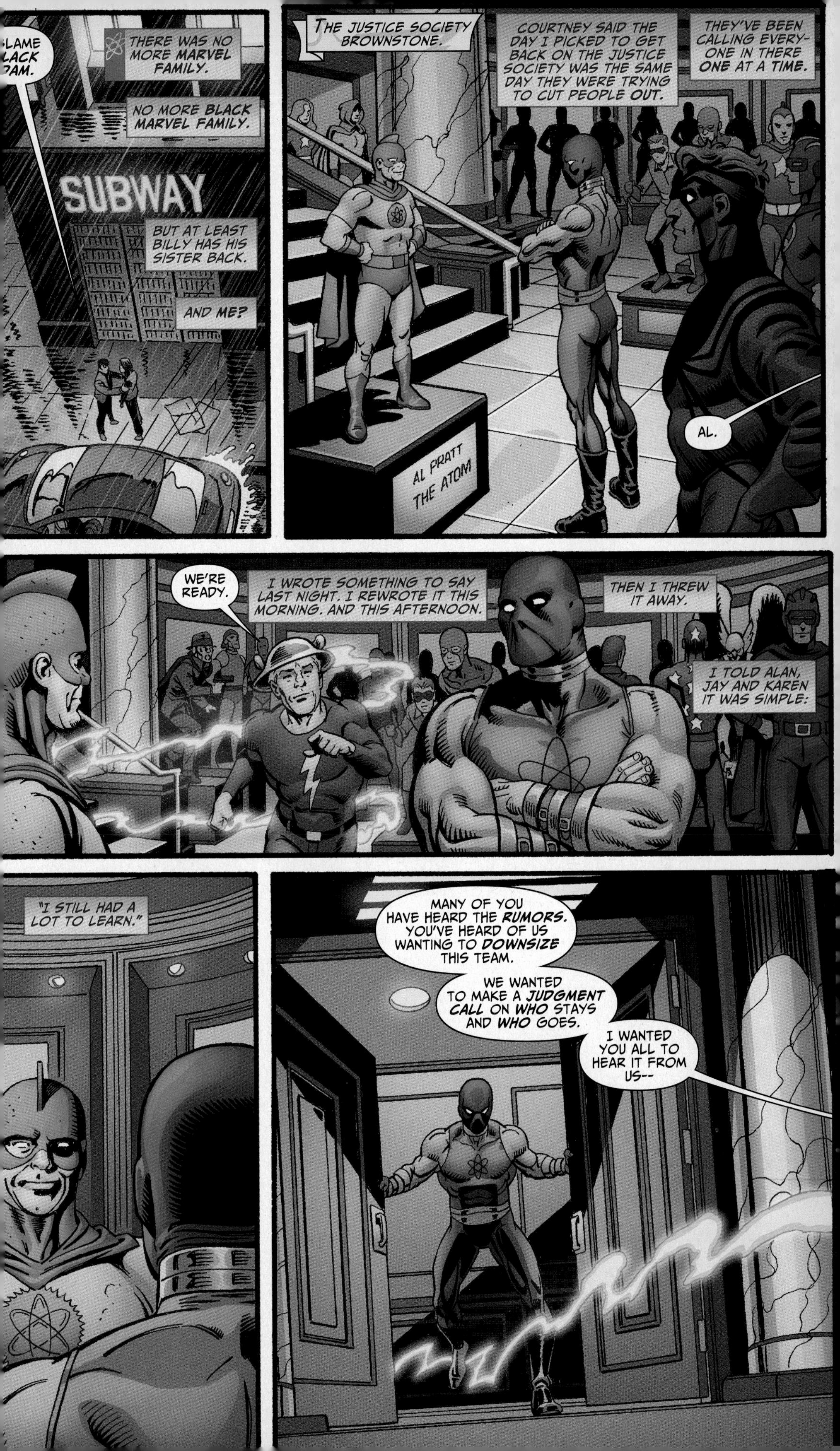

-LAME
BLACK
-DAM.
THERE WAS NO MORE MARVEL FAMILY.
NO MORE BLACK MARVEL FAMILY.
SUBWAY
BUT AT LEAST BILLY HAS HIS SISTER BACK.
AND ME?
THE JUSTICE SOCIETY BROWNSTONE.
COURTNEY SAID THE DAY I PICKED TO GET BACK ON THE JUSTICE SOCIETY WAS THE SAME DAY THEY WERE TRYING TO CUT PEOPLE OUT.
THEY'VE BEEN CALLING EVERY-ONE IN THERE ONE AT A TIME.
AL PRATT THE ATOM
AL.
WE'RE READY.
I WROTE SOMETHING TO SAY LAST NIGHT. I REWROTE IT THIS MORNING. AND THIS AFTERNOON.
THEN I THREW IT AWAY.
I TOLD ALAN, JAY AND KAREN IT WAS SIMPLE:
"I STILL HAD A LOT TO LEARN."
MANY OF YOU HAVE HEARD THE RUMORS. YOU'VE HEARD OF US WANTING TO DOWNSIZE THIS TEAM.
WE WANTED TO MAKE A JUDGMENT CALL ON WHO STAYS AND WHO GOES.
I WANTED YOU ALL TO HEAR IT FROM US--

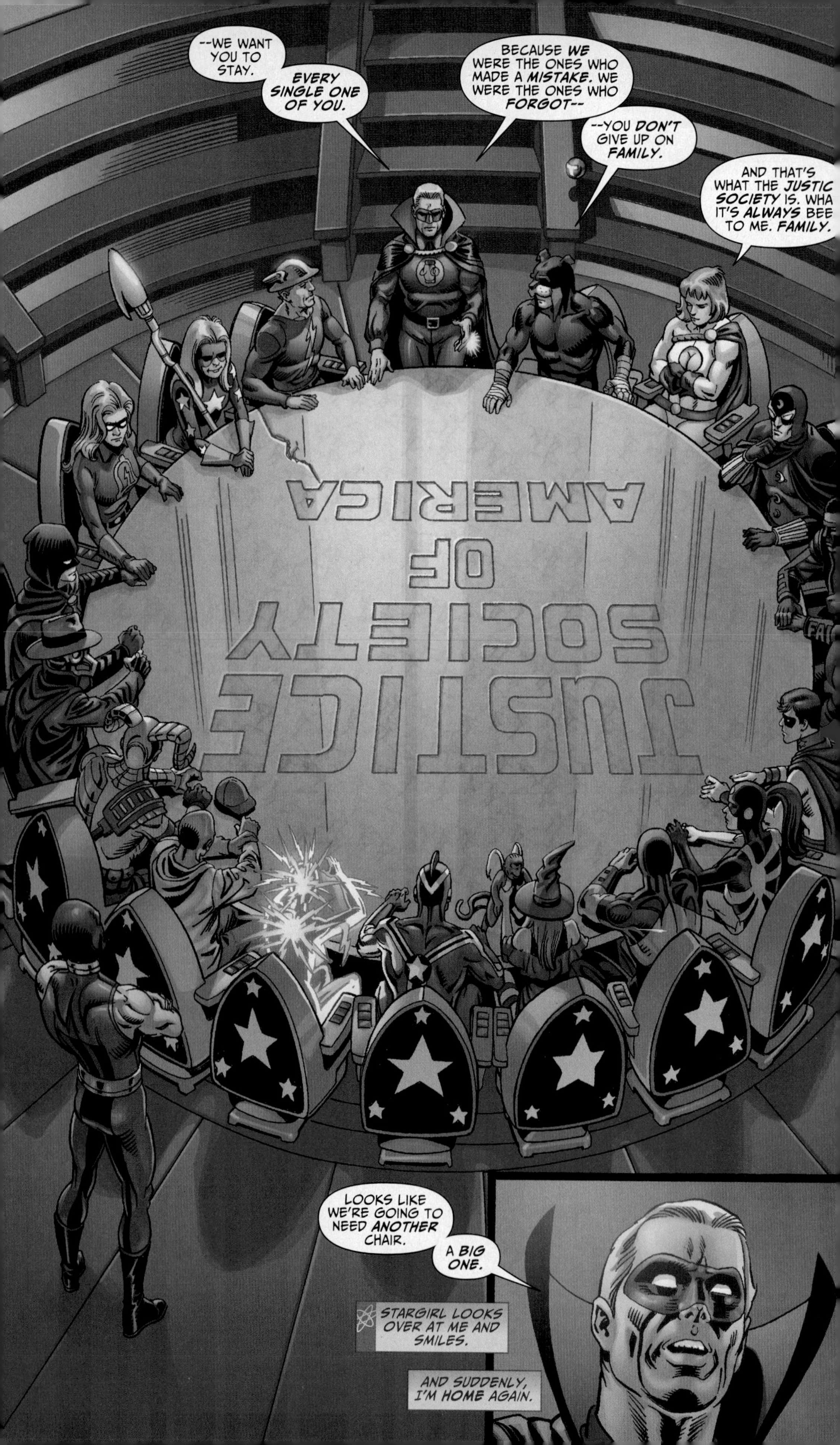
--WE WANT YOU TO STAY.
EVERY SINGLE ONE OF YOU.
BECAUSE WE WERE THE ONES WHO MADE A MISTAKE. WE WERE THE ONES WHO FORGOT--
--YOU DON'T GIVE UP ON FAMILY.
AND THAT'S WHAT THE JUSTIC SOCIETY IS. WHA IT'S ALWAYS BEE TO ME. FAMILY.
JUSTICE SOCIETY OF AMERICA
LOOKS LIKE WE'RE GOING TO NEED ANOTHER CHAIR.
A BIG ONE.
STARGIRL LOOKS OVER AT ME AND SMILES.
AND SUDDENLY, I'M HOME AGAIN.

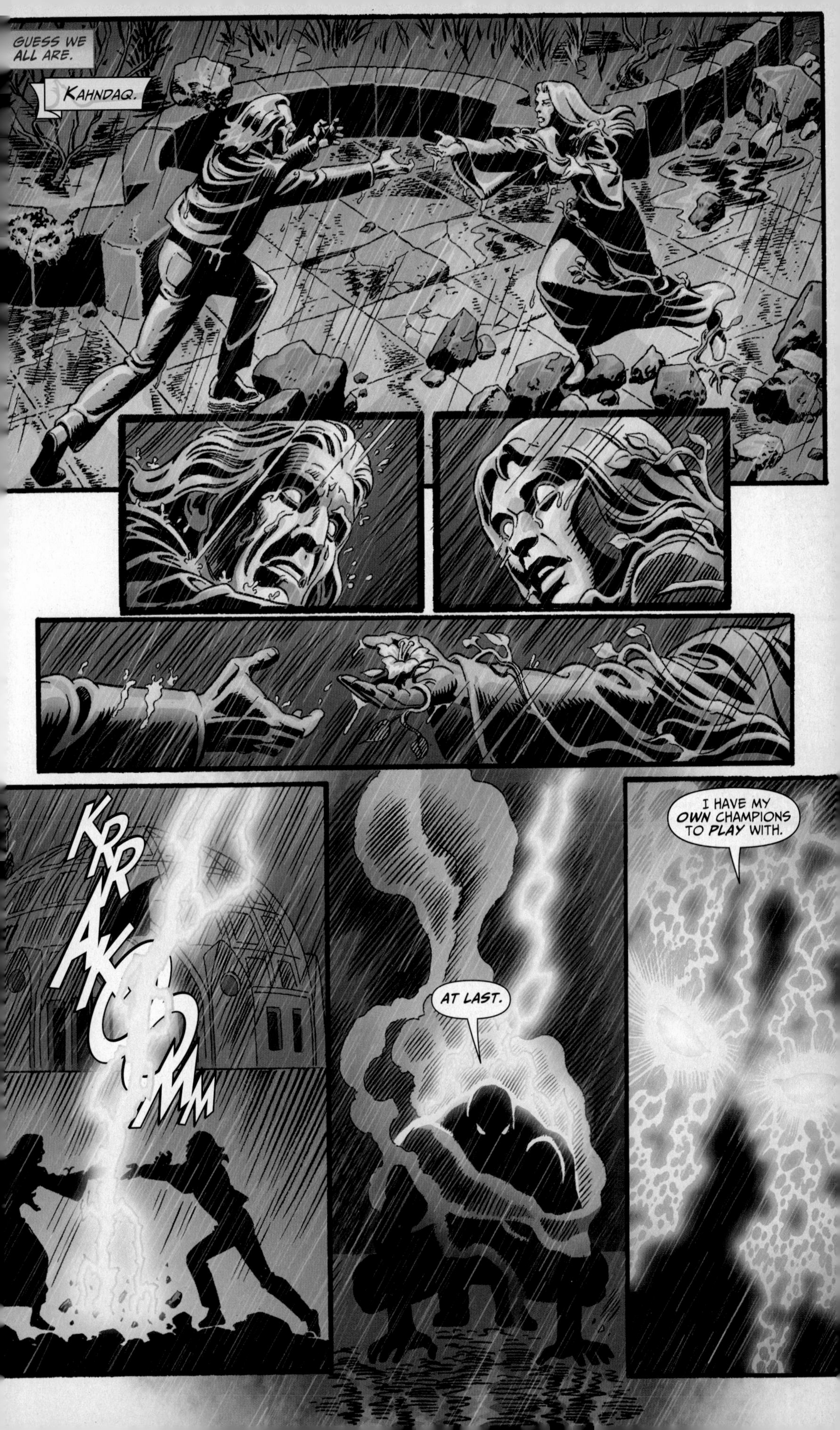
GUESS WE ALL ARE.
KAHNDAQ.
KRRAKOOM
AT LAST.
I HAVE MY OWN CHAMPIONS TO PLAY WITH.

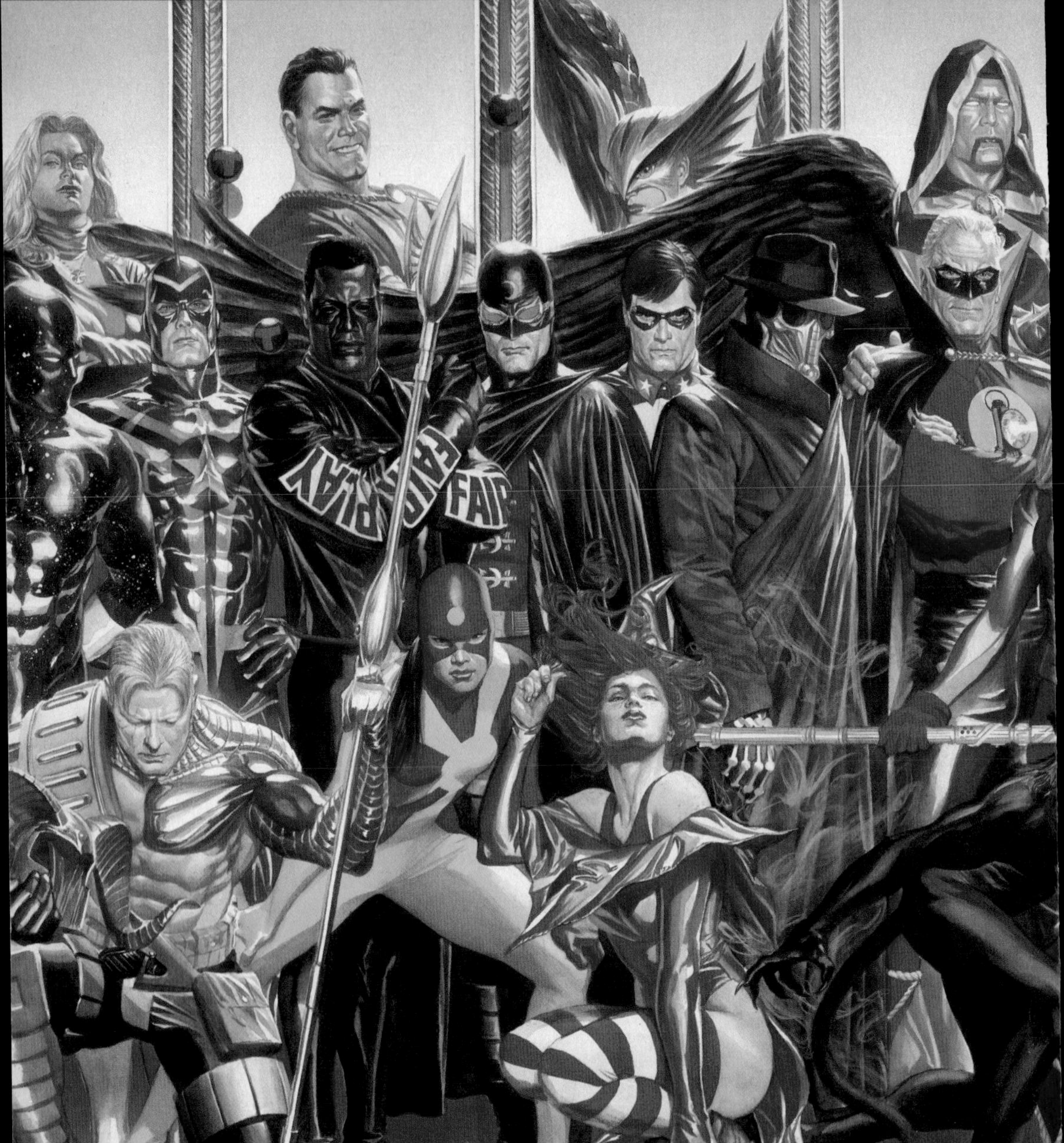
FAIR PLAY
FAIR

JUSTICE SOCIETY OF AMERICA #26 cover by Alex Ross
Interior art by Dale Eaglesham & Nathan Massengill

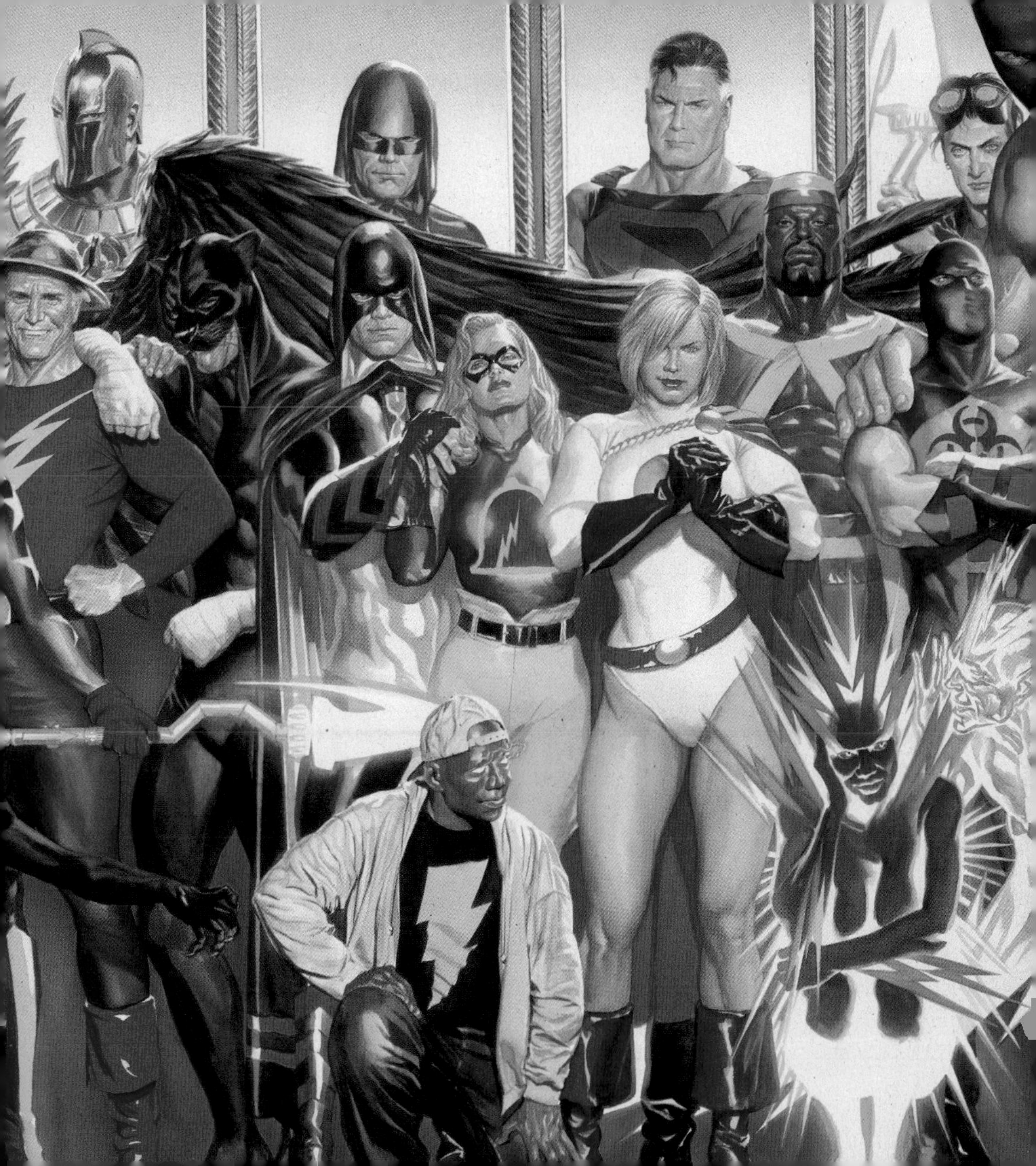

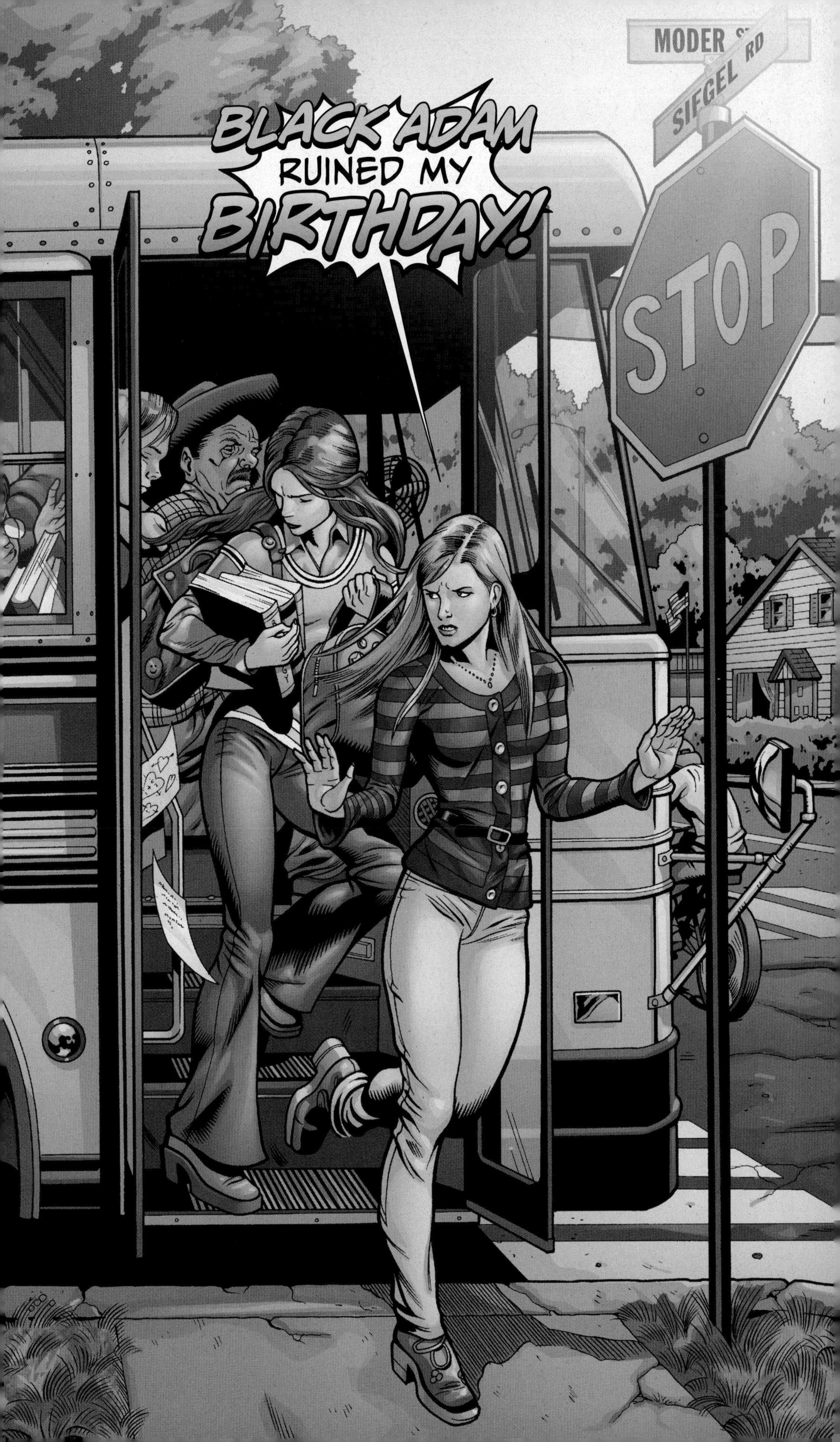
BLACK ADAM RUINED MY BIRTHDAY!
SIFGEL RD
STOP

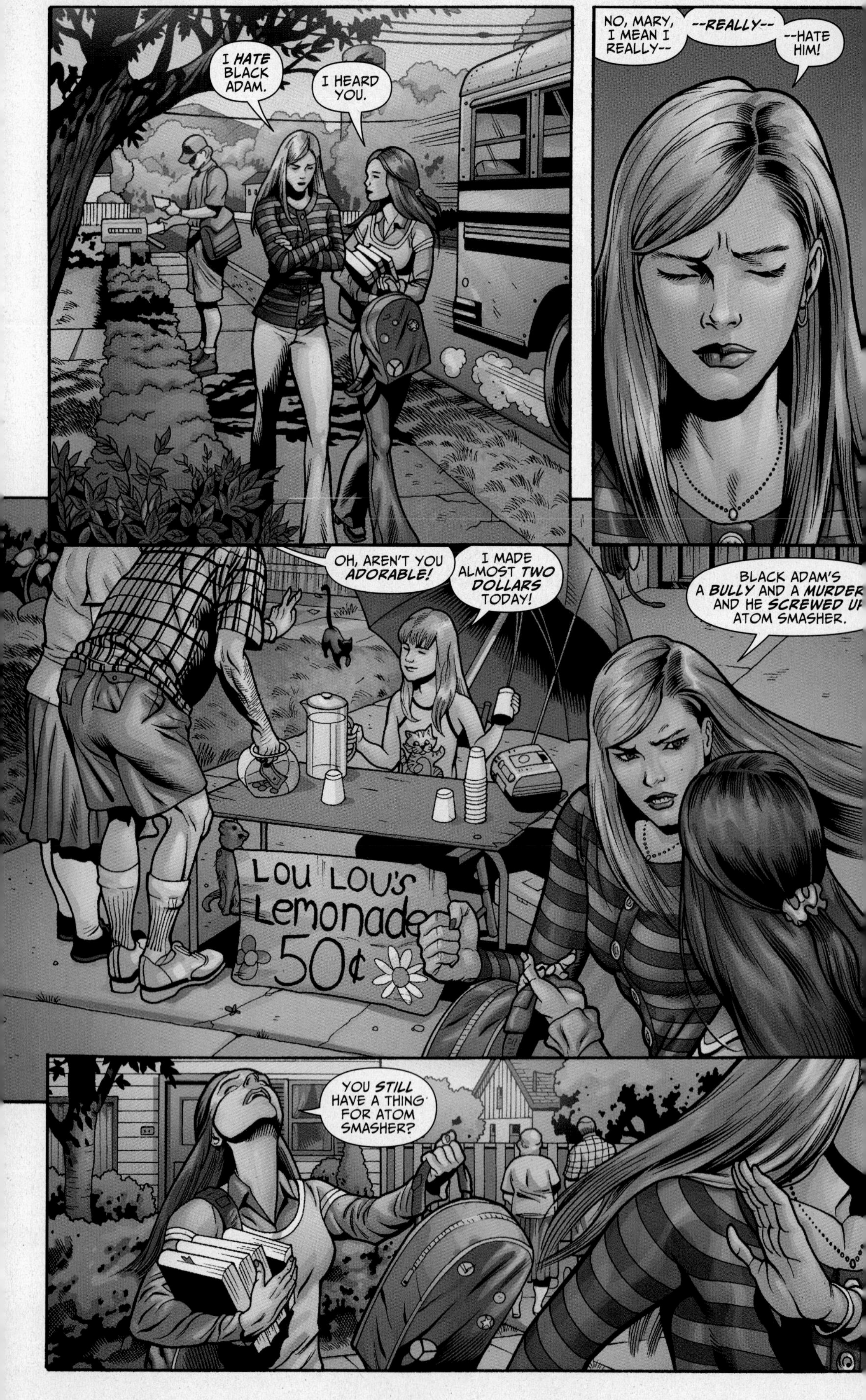
I HATE BLACK ADAM.
I HEARD YOU.
NO, MARY, I MEAN I REALLY--
--REALLY--
--HATE HIM!
OH, AREN'T YOU ADORABLE!
I MADE ALMOST TWO DOLLARS TODAY!
LOU LOU'S Lemonade 50¢
YOU STILL HAVE A THING FOR ATOM SMASHER?

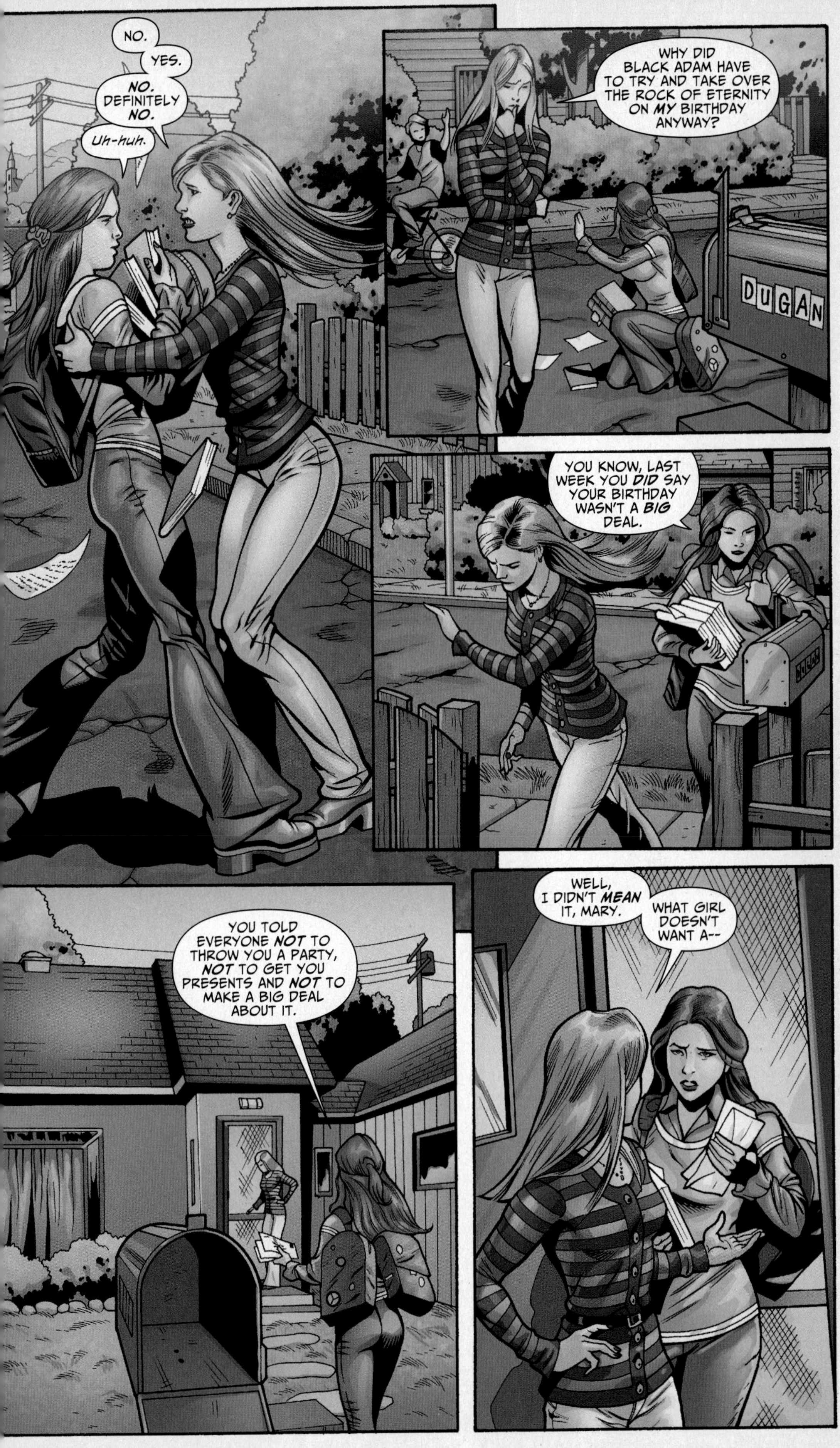
NO.
YES.
NO. DEFINITELY NO.
Uh-huh.
WHY DID BLACK ADAM HAVE TO TRY AND TAKE OVER THE ROCK OF ETERNITY ON MY BIRTHDAY ANYWAY?
DUGAN
YOU KNOW, LAST WEEK YOU DID SAY YOUR BIRTHDAY WASN'T A BIG DEAL.
YOU TOLD EVERYONE NOT TO THROW YOU A PARTY, NOT TO GET YOU PRESENTS AND NOT TO MAKE A BIG DEAL ABOUT IT.
WELL, I DIDN'T MEAN IT, MARY.
WHAT GIRL DOESN'T WANT A--

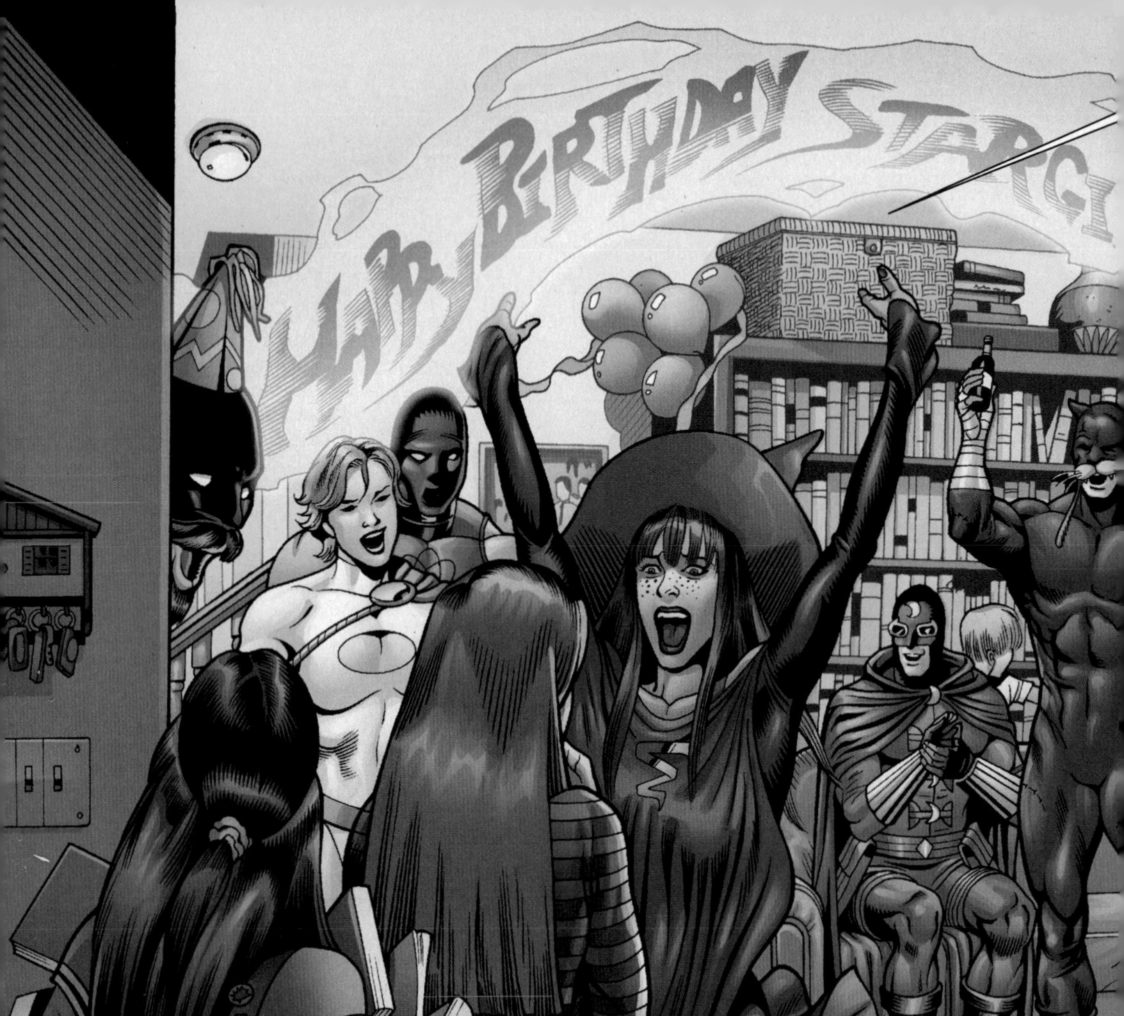

HAPPY BIRTHDAY STARGI

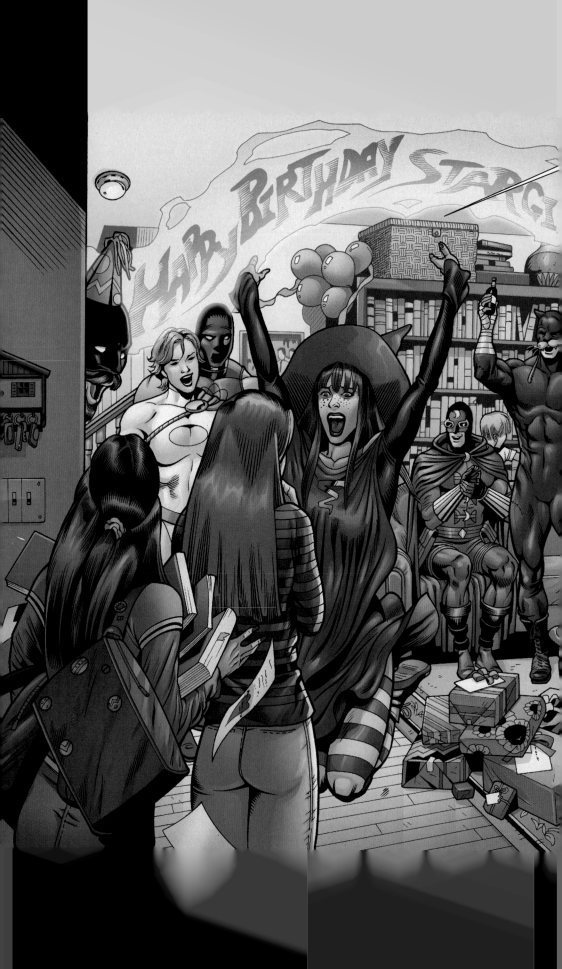

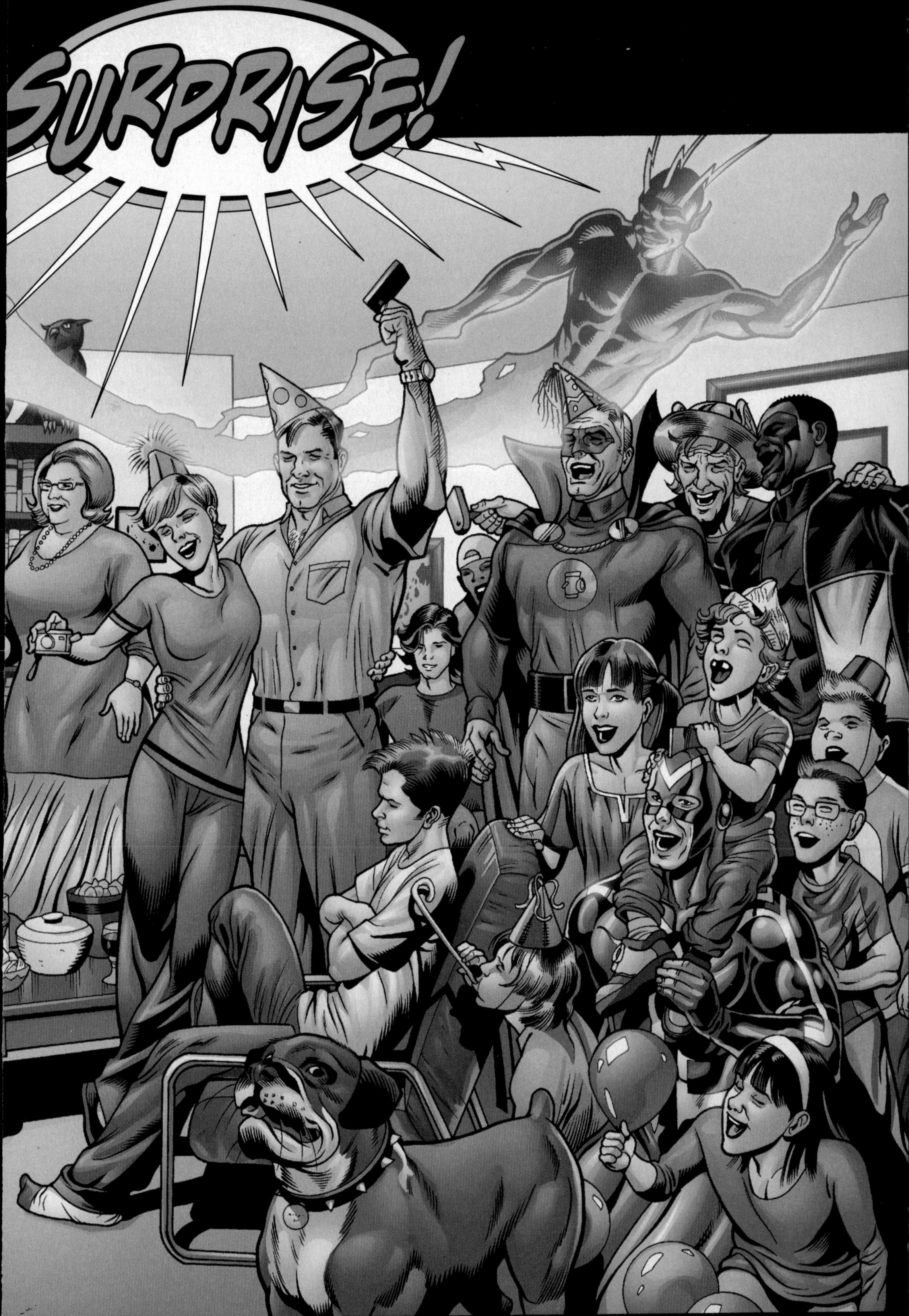
SURPRISE!

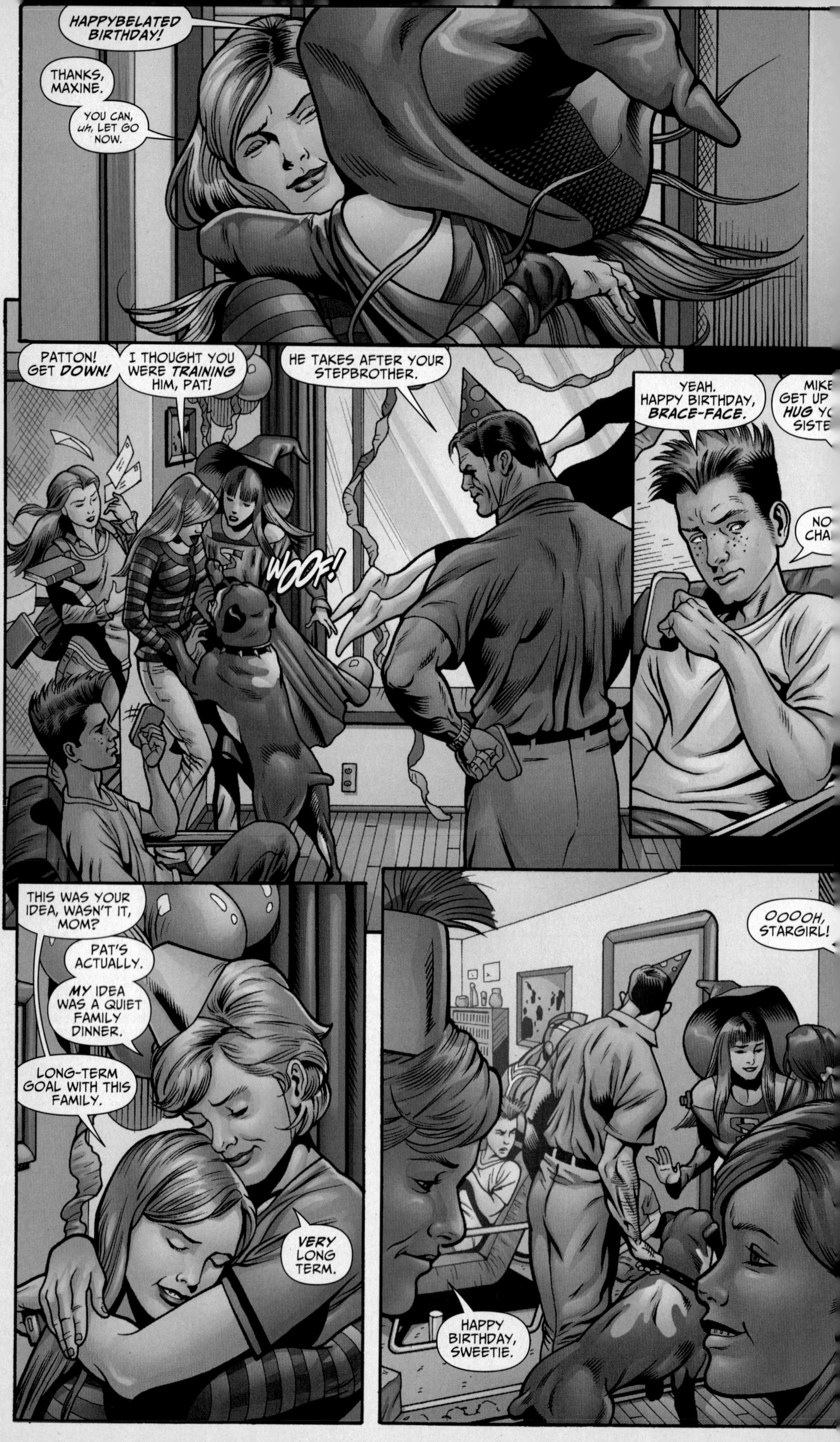
HAPPYBELATED BIRTHDAY!
THANKS, MAXINE.
YOU CAN, *uh,* LET GO NOW.
PATTON! GET *DOWN!*
I THOUGHT YOU WERE *TRAINING* HIM, PAT!
HE TAKES AFTER YOUR STEPBROTHER.
WOOF!
YEAH. HAPPY BIRTHDAY, *BRACE-FACE.*
MIKE GET UP *HUG* Y SISTE
NO CHA
THIS WAS YOUR IDEA, WASN'T IT, MOM?
PAT'S ACTUALLY.
MY IDEA WAS A QUIET FAMILY DINNER.
LONG-TERM GOAL WITH THIS FAMILY.
VERY LONG TERM.
OOOOH, STARGIRL!
HAPPY BIRTHDAY, SWEETIE.

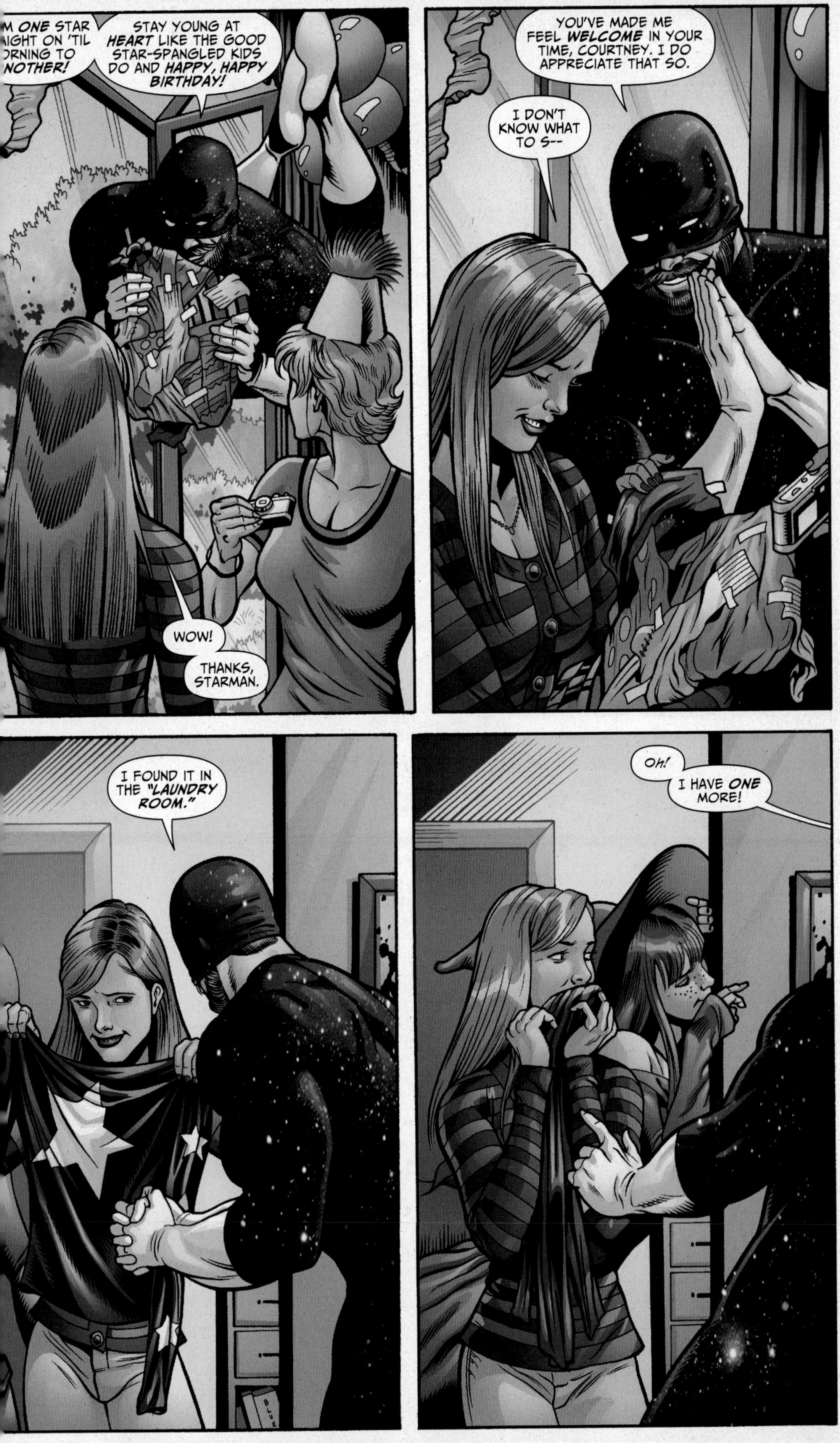

M ONE STAR
IGHT ON 'TIL
ORNING TO
NOTHER!
STAY YOUNG AT HEART LIKE THE GOOD STAR-SPANGLED KIDS DO AND HAPPY, HAPPY BIRTHDAY!
WOW!
THANKS, STARMAN.
YOU'VE MADE ME FEEL WELCOME IN YOUR TIME, COURTNEY. I DO APPRECIATE THAT SO.
I DON'T KNOW WHAT TO S--
I FOUND IT IN THE "LAUNDRY ROOM."
Oh!
I HAVE ONE MORE!

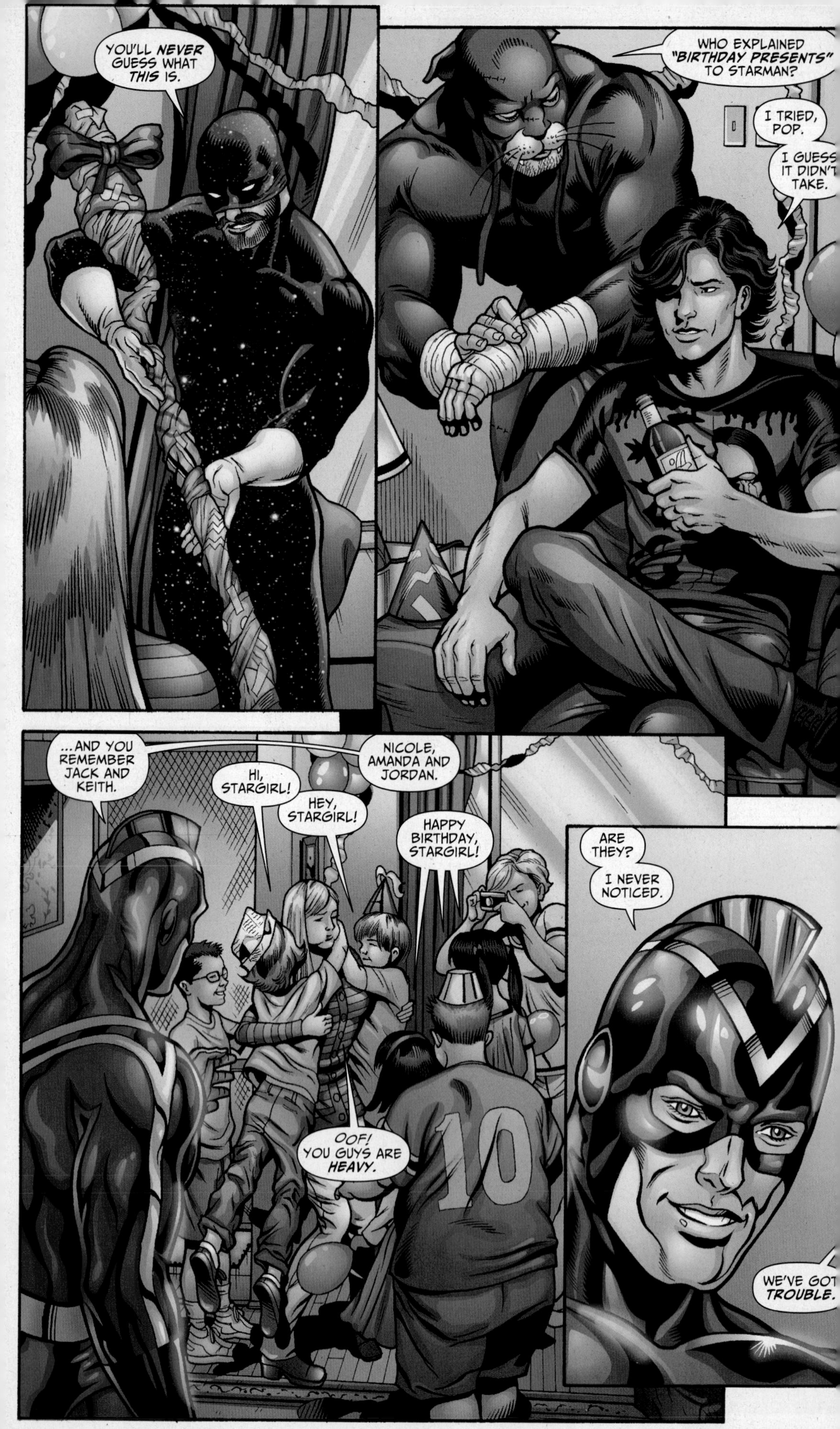
YOU'LL NEVER GUESS WHAT THIS IS.
WHO EXPLAINED "BIRTHDAY PRESENTS" TO STARMAN?
I TRIED, POP.
I GUESS IT DIDN'T TAKE.
...AND YOU REMEMBER JACK AND KEITH.
NICOLE, AMANDA AND JORDAN.
HI, STARGIRL!
HEY, STARGIRL!
HAPPY BIRTHDAY, STARGIRL!
OOF! YOU GUYS ARE HEAVY.
ARE THEY?
I NEVER NOTICED.
WE'VE GOT TROUBLE.

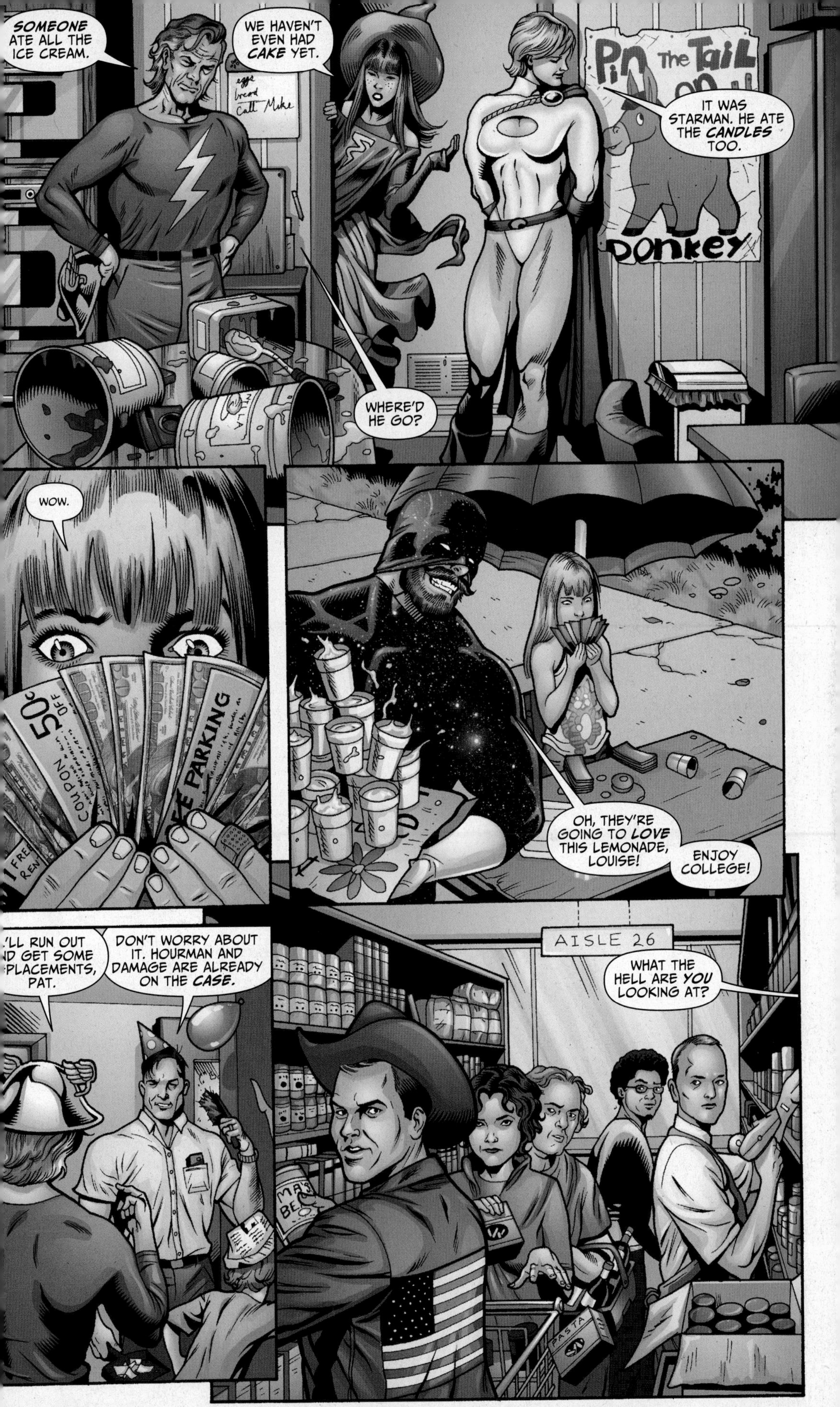
SOMEONE ATE ALL THE ICE CREAM.
eggs bread Call Mike
WE HAVEN'T EVEN HAD CAKE YET.
Pin The TaiL on
DONKEY
IT WAS STARMAN. HE ATE THE CANDLES TOO.
WHERE'D HE GO?
WOW.
50¢ OFF
COUPON
E PARKING
OH, THEY'RE GOING TO LOVE THIS LEMONADE, LOUISE!
ENJOY COLLEGE!
'LL RUN OUT ND GET SOME PLACEMENTS, PAT.
DON'T WORRY ABOUT IT. HOURMAN AND DAMAGE ARE ALREADY ON THE CASE.
AISLE 26
WHAT THE HELL ARE YOU LOOKING AT?
PASTA

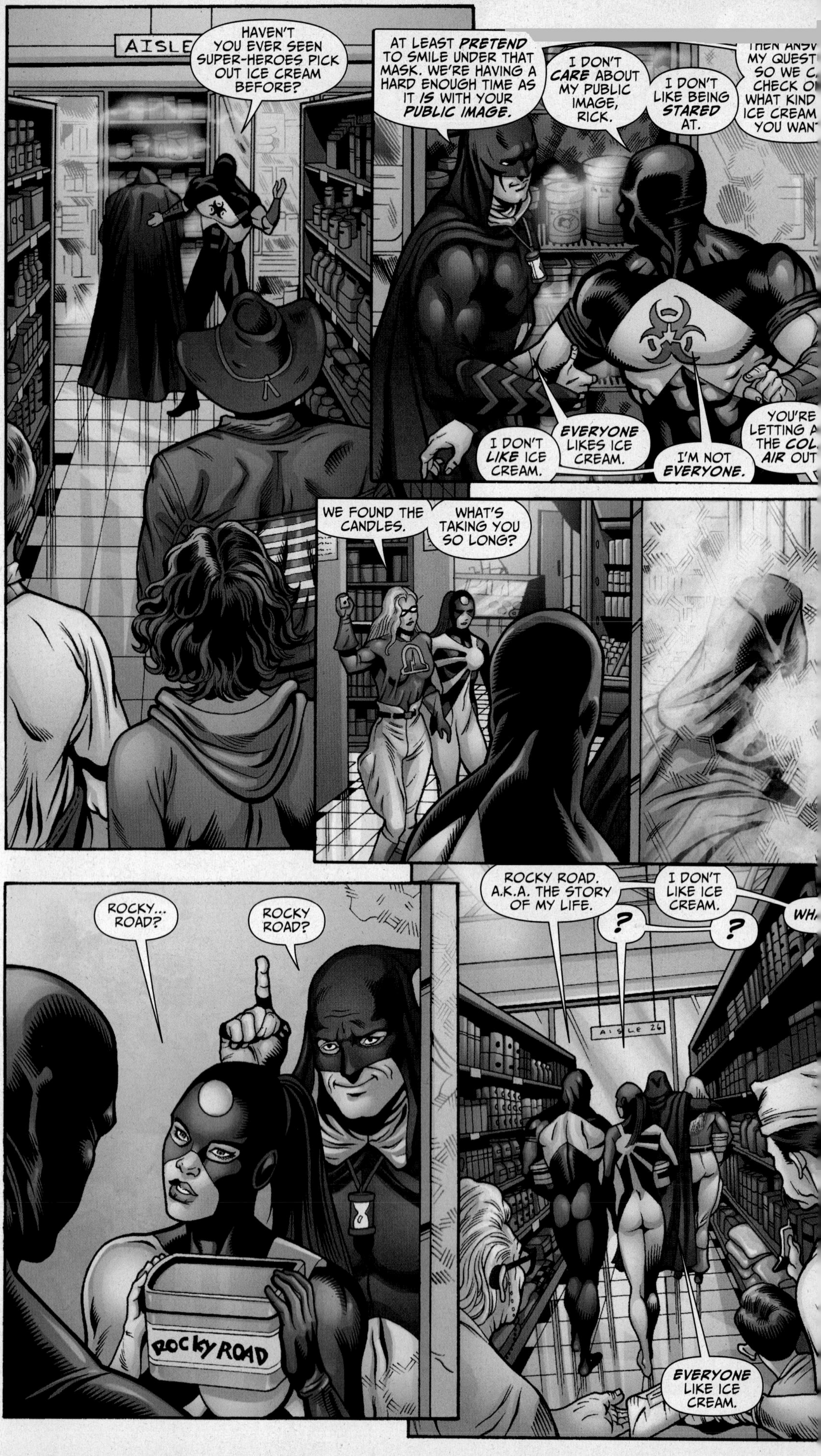
AISLE
HAVEN'T YOU EVER SEEN SUPER-HEROES PICK OUT ICE CREAM BEFORE?
AT LEAST PRETEND TO SMILE UNDER THAT MASK. WE'RE HAVING A HARD ENOUGH TIME AS IT IS WITH YOUR PUBLIC IMAGE.
I DON'T CARE ABOUT MY PUBLIC IMAGE, RICK.
I DON'T LIKE BEING STARED AT.
I DON'T LIKE ICE CREAM.
EVERYONE LIKES ICE CREAM.
I'M NOT EVERYONE.
WE FOUND THE CANDLES.
WHAT'S TAKING YOU SO LONG?
ROCKY... ROAD?
ROCKY ROAD?
ROCKY ROAD
ROCKY ROAD. A.K.A. THE STORY OF MY LIFE.
?
I DON'T LIKE ICE CREAM.
?
AISLE 26
EVERYONE LIKE ICE CREAM.

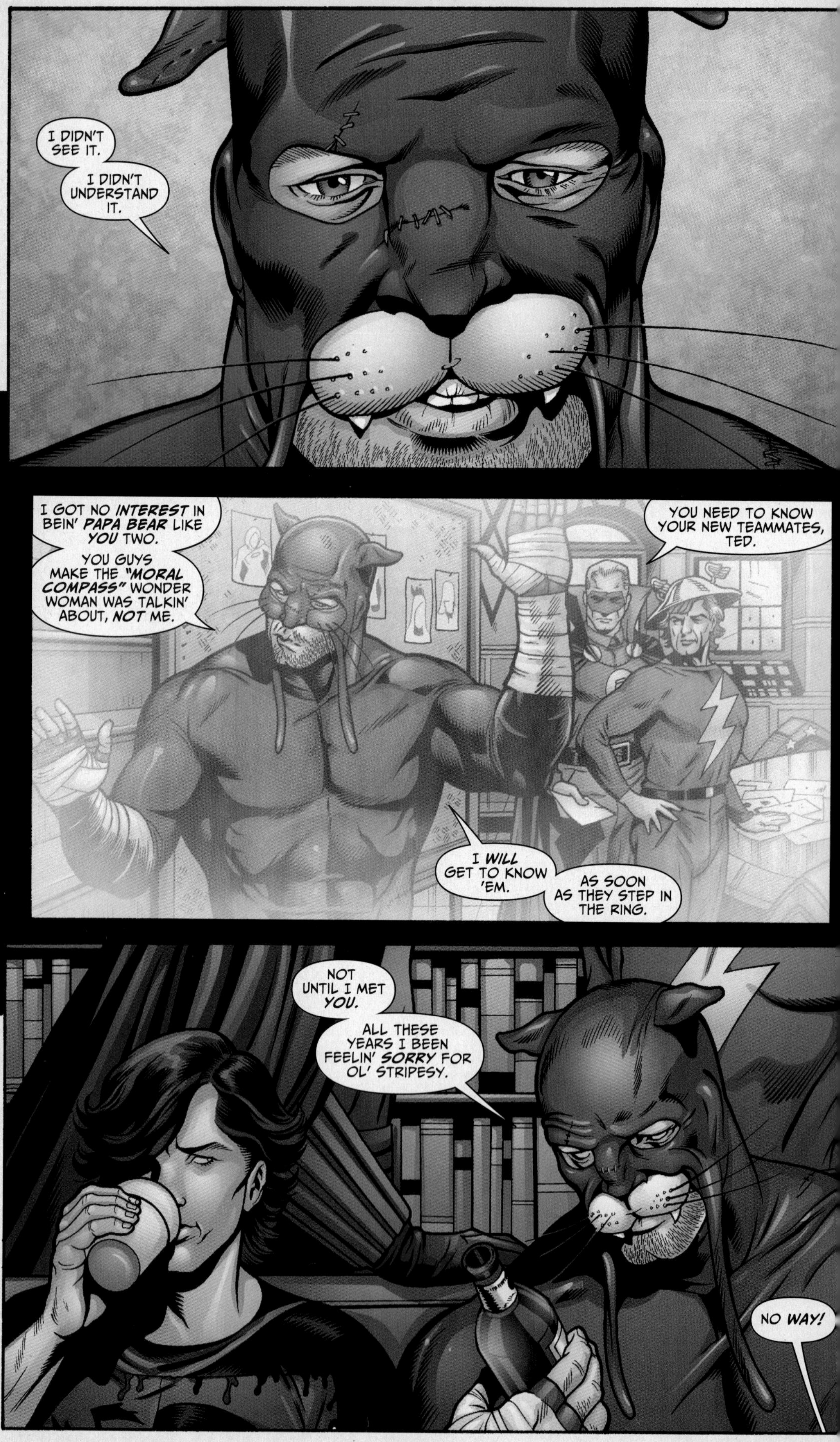

I DIDN'T SEE IT.
I DIDN'T UNDERSTAND IT.
I GOT NO INTEREST IN BEIN' PAPA BEAR LIKE YOU TWO.
YOU GUYS MAKE THE "MORAL COMPASS" WONDER WOMAN WAS TALKIN' ABOUT, NOT ME.
YOU NEED TO KNOW YOUR NEW TEAMMATES, TED.
I WILL GET TO KNOW 'EM.
AS SOON AS THEY STEP IN THE RING.
NOT UNTIL I MET YOU.
ALL THESE YEARS I BEEN FEELIN' SORRY FOR OL' STRIPESY.
NO WAY!

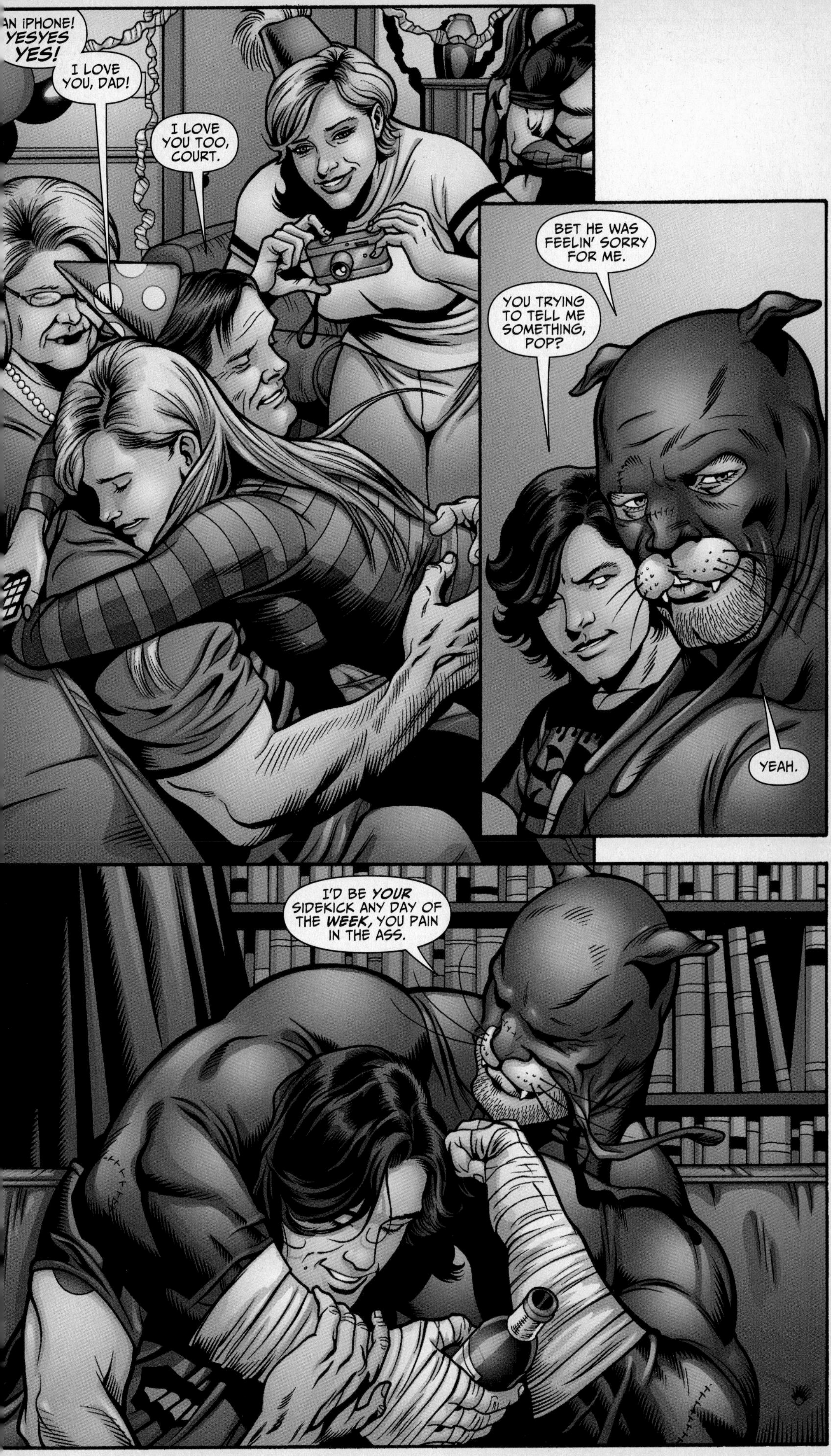
AN iPHONE! YESYES YES!
I LOVE YOU, DAD!
I LOVE YOU TOO, COURT.
BET HE WAS FEELIN' SORRY FOR ME.
YOU TRYING TO TELL ME SOMETHING, POP?
YEAH.
I'D BE YOUR SIDEKICK ANY DAY OF THE WEEK, YOU PAIN IN THE ASS.

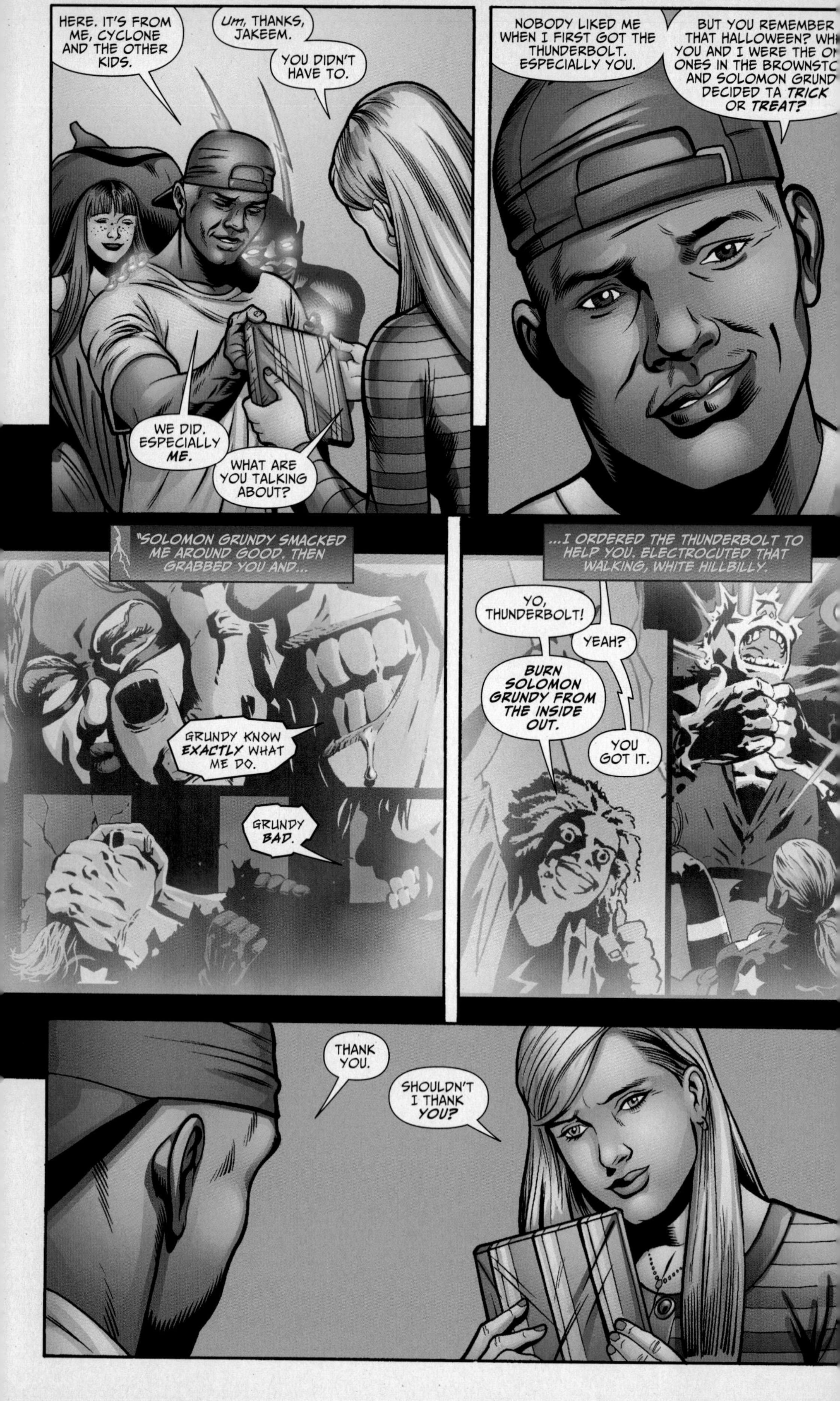
HERE. IT'S FROM ME, CYCLONE AND THE OTHER KIDS.
Um, THANKS, JAKEEM.
YOU DIDN'T HAVE TO.
WE DID. ESPECIALLY *ME.*
WHAT ARE YOU TALKING ABOUT?
NOBODY LIKED ME WHEN I FIRST GOT THE THUNDERBOLT. ESPECIALLY YOU.
BUT YOU REMEMBER THAT HALLOWEEN? WH YOU AND I WERE THE ON ONES IN THE BROWNSTO AND SOLOMON GRUND DECIDED TA *TRICK* OR *TREAT?*
"SOLOMON GRUNDY SMACKED ME AROUND GOOD. THEN GRABBED YOU AND...
GRUNDY KNOW *EXACTLY* WHAT ME DO.
GRUNDY *BAD.*
...I ORDERED THE THUNDERBOLT TO HELP YOU. ELECTROCUTED THAT WALKING, WHITE HILLBILLY.
YO, THUNDERBOLT!
YEAH?
BURN SOLOMON GRUNDY FROM THE INSIDE OUT.
YOU GOT IT.
THANK YOU.
SHOULDN'T I THANK *YOU?*

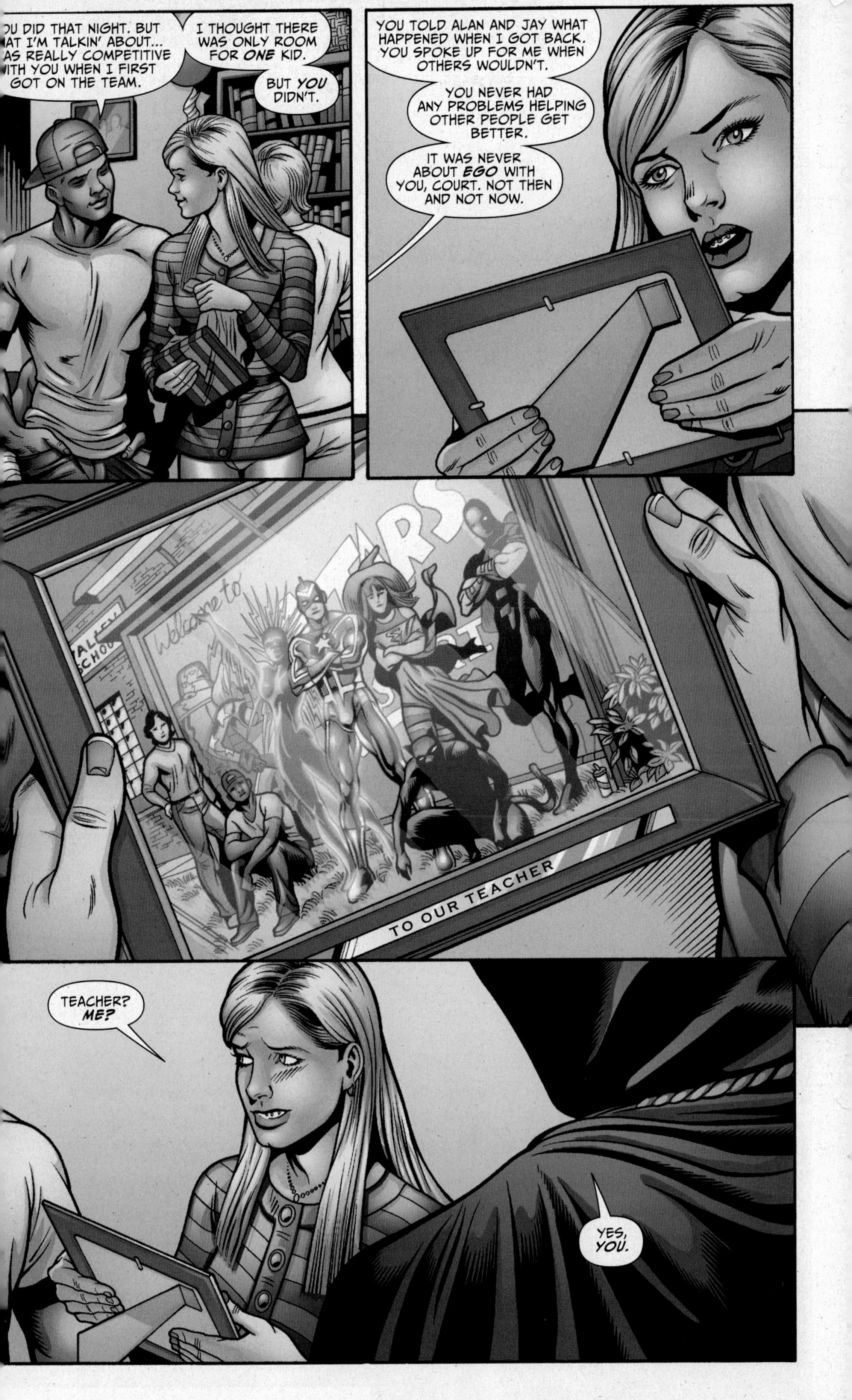

OU DID THAT NIGHT. BUT
AT I'M TALKIN' ABOUT...
AS REALLY COMPETITIVE
ITH YOU WHEN I FIRST
GOT ON THE TEAM.
I THOUGHT THERE WAS ONLY ROOM FOR ONE KID.
BUT YOU DIDN'T.
YOU TOLD ALAN AND JAY WHAT HAPPENED WHEN I GOT BACK. YOU SPOKE UP FOR ME WHEN OTHERS WOULDN'T.
YOU NEVER HAD ANY PROBLEMS HELPING OTHER PEOPLE GET BETTER.
IT WAS NEVER ABOUT EGO WITH YOU, COURT. NOT THEN AND NOT NOW.
Welcome to
TO OUR TEACHER
TEACHER? ME?
YES, YOU.

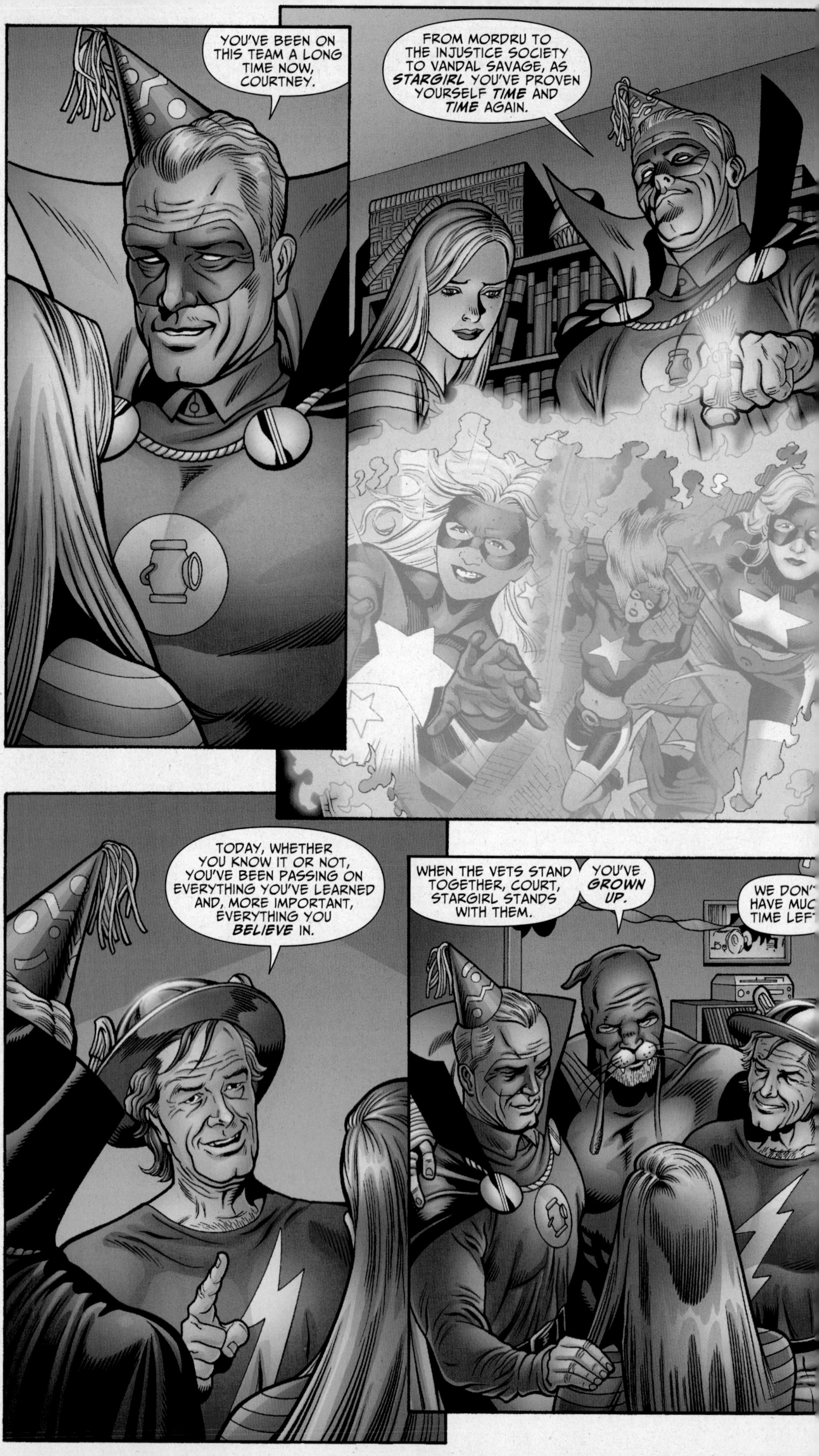
YOU'VE BEEN ON THIS TEAM A LONG TIME NOW, COURTNEY.
FROM MORDRU TO THE INJUSTICE SOCIETY TO VANDAL SAVAGE, AS STARGIRL YOU'VE PROVEN YOURSELF TIME AND TIME AGAIN.
TODAY, WHETHER YOU KNOW IT OR NOT, YOU'VE BEEN PASSING ON EVERYTHING YOU'VE LEARNED AND, MORE IMPORTANT, EVERYTHING YOU BELIEVE IN.
WHEN THE VETS STAND TOGETHER, COURT, STARGIRL STANDS WITH THEM.
YOU'VE GROWN UP.

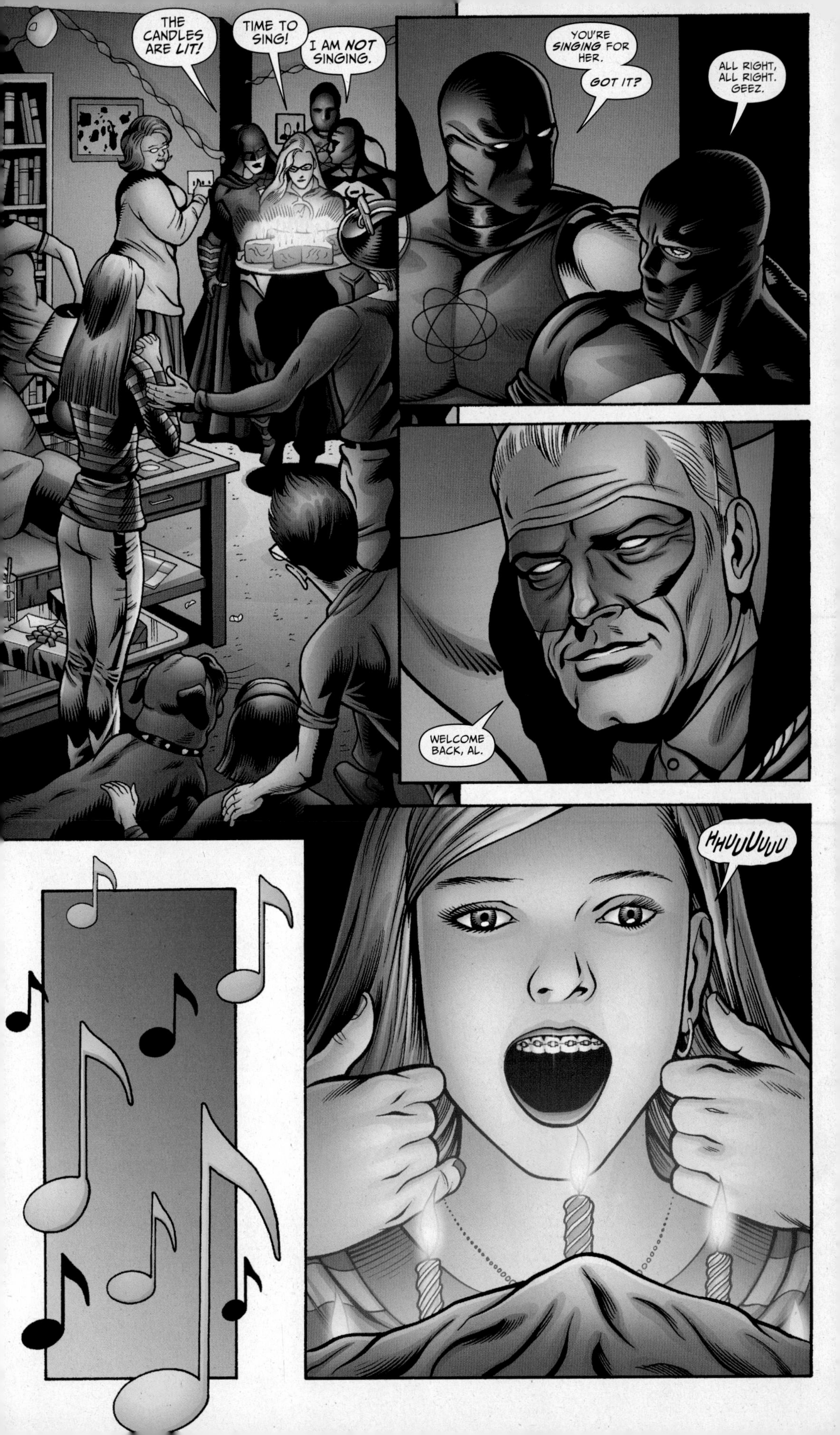
THE CANDLES ARE LIT!
TIME TO SING!
I AM NOT SINGING.
YOU'RE SINGING FOR HER.
GOT IT?
ALL RIGHT, ALL RIGHT. GEEZ.
WELCOME BACK, AL.
HHUUUUUU

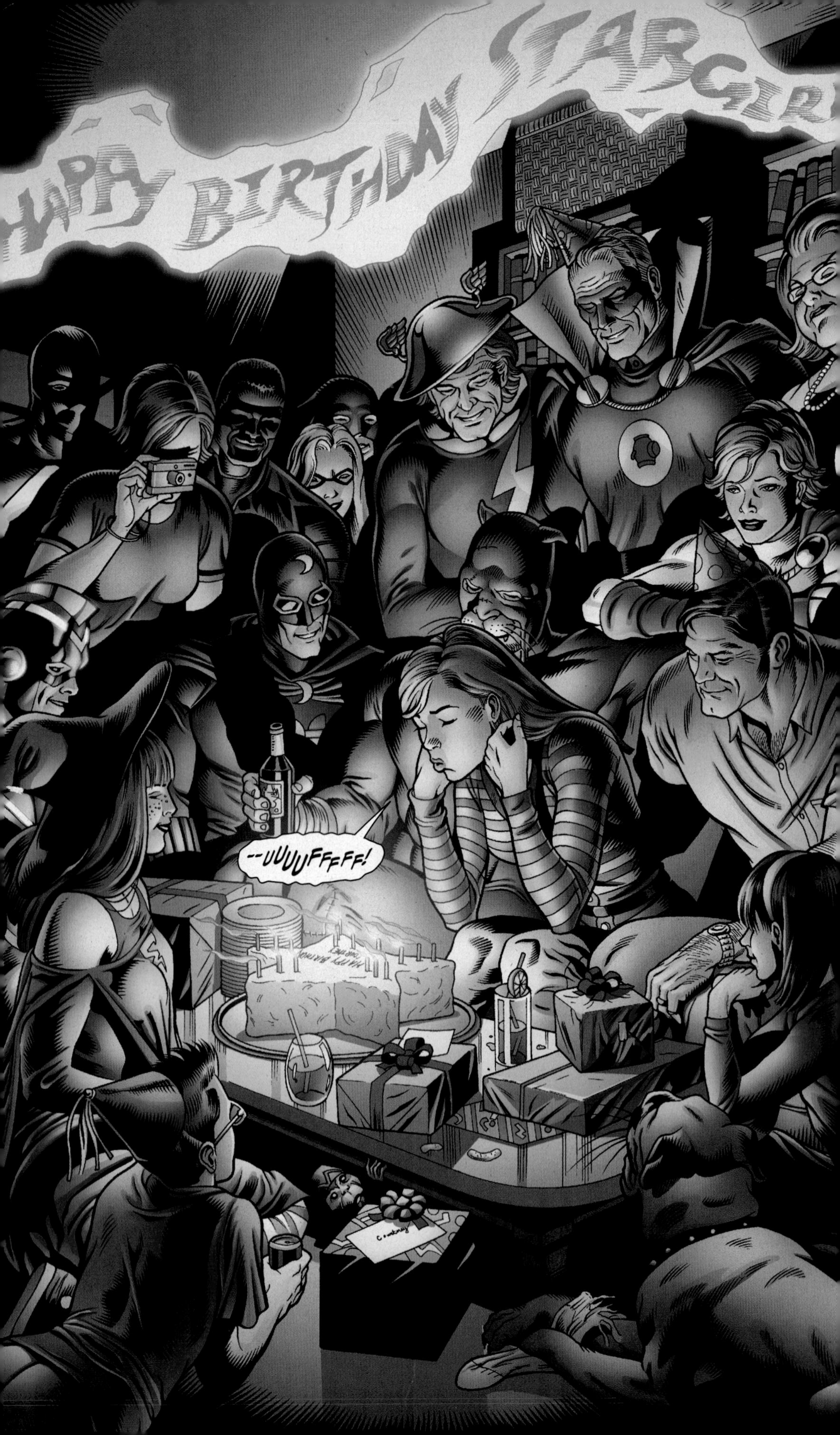

HAPPY BIRTHDAY STARGIRL
--UUUUFFFFF!
HAPPY BIRTHDAY COURTNEY
Courtney

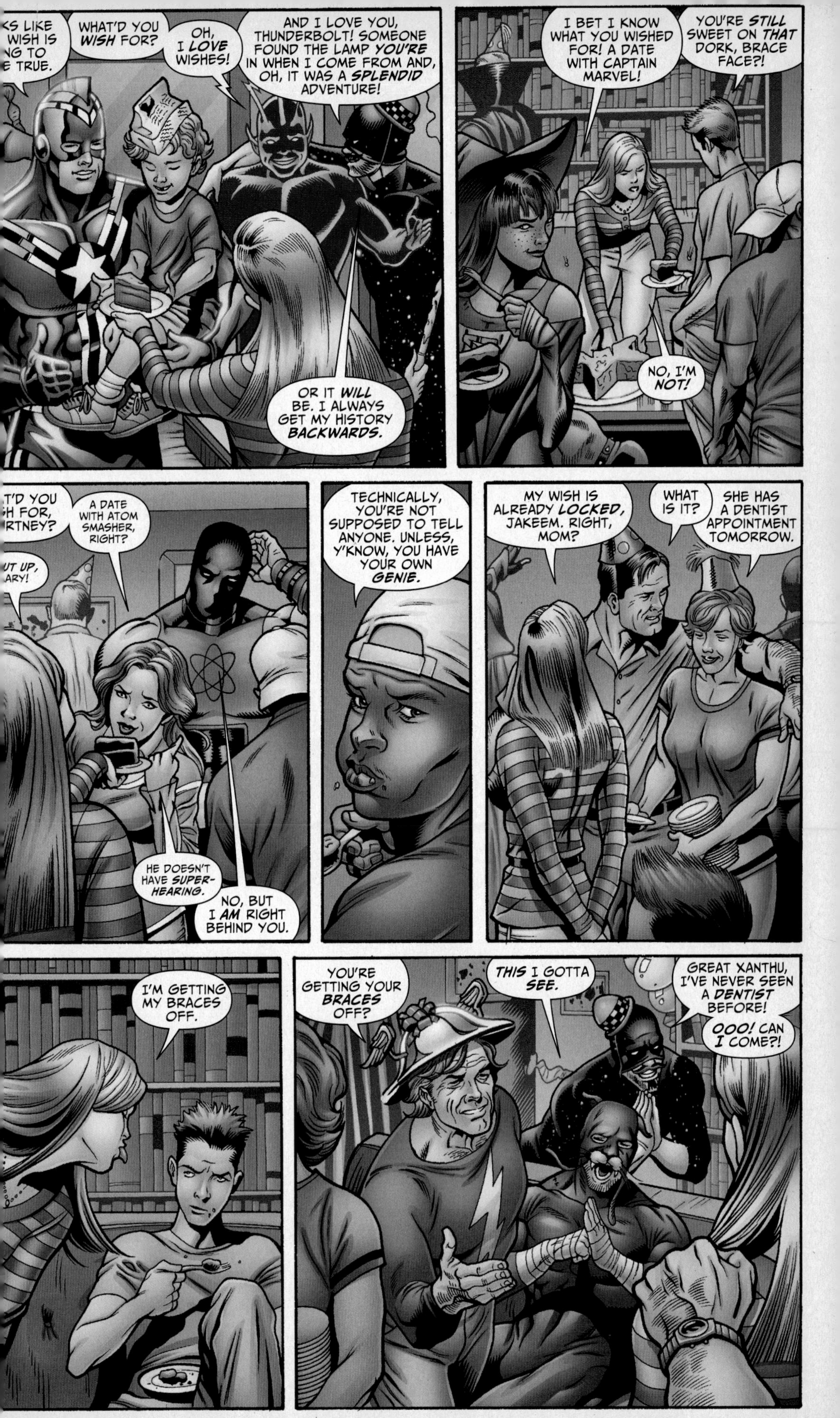

KS LIKE
WISH IS
NG TO
E TRUE.
WHAT'D YOU WISH FOR?
OH, I LOVE WISHES!
AND I LOVE YOU, THUNDERBOLT! SOMEONE FOUND THE LAMP YOU'RE IN WHEN I COME FROM AND, OH, IT WAS A SPLENDID ADVENTURE!
OR IT WILL BE. I ALWAYS GET MY HISTORY BACKWARDS.
I BET I KNOW WHAT YOU WISHED FOR! A DATE WITH CAPTAIN MARVEL!
YOU'RE STILL SWEET ON THAT DORK, BRACE FACE?!
NO, I'M NOT!
T'D YOU
H FOR,
RTNEY?
A DATE WITH ATOM SMASHER, RIGHT?
UT UP,
ARY!
HE DOESN'T HAVE SUPER-HEARING.
NO, BUT I AM RIGHT BEHIND YOU.
TECHNICALLY, YOU'RE NOT SUPPOSED TO TELL ANYONE. UNLESS, Y'KNOW, YOU HAVE YOUR OWN GENIE.
MY WISH IS ALREADY LOCKED, JAKEEM. RIGHT, MOM?
WHAT IS IT?
SHE HAS A DENTIST APPOINTMENT TOMORROW.
I'M GETTING MY BRACES OFF.
YOU'RE GETTING YOUR BRACES OFF?
THIS I GOTTA SEE.
GREAT XANTHU, I'VE NEVER SEEN A DENTIST BEFORE!
OOO! CAN I COME?!

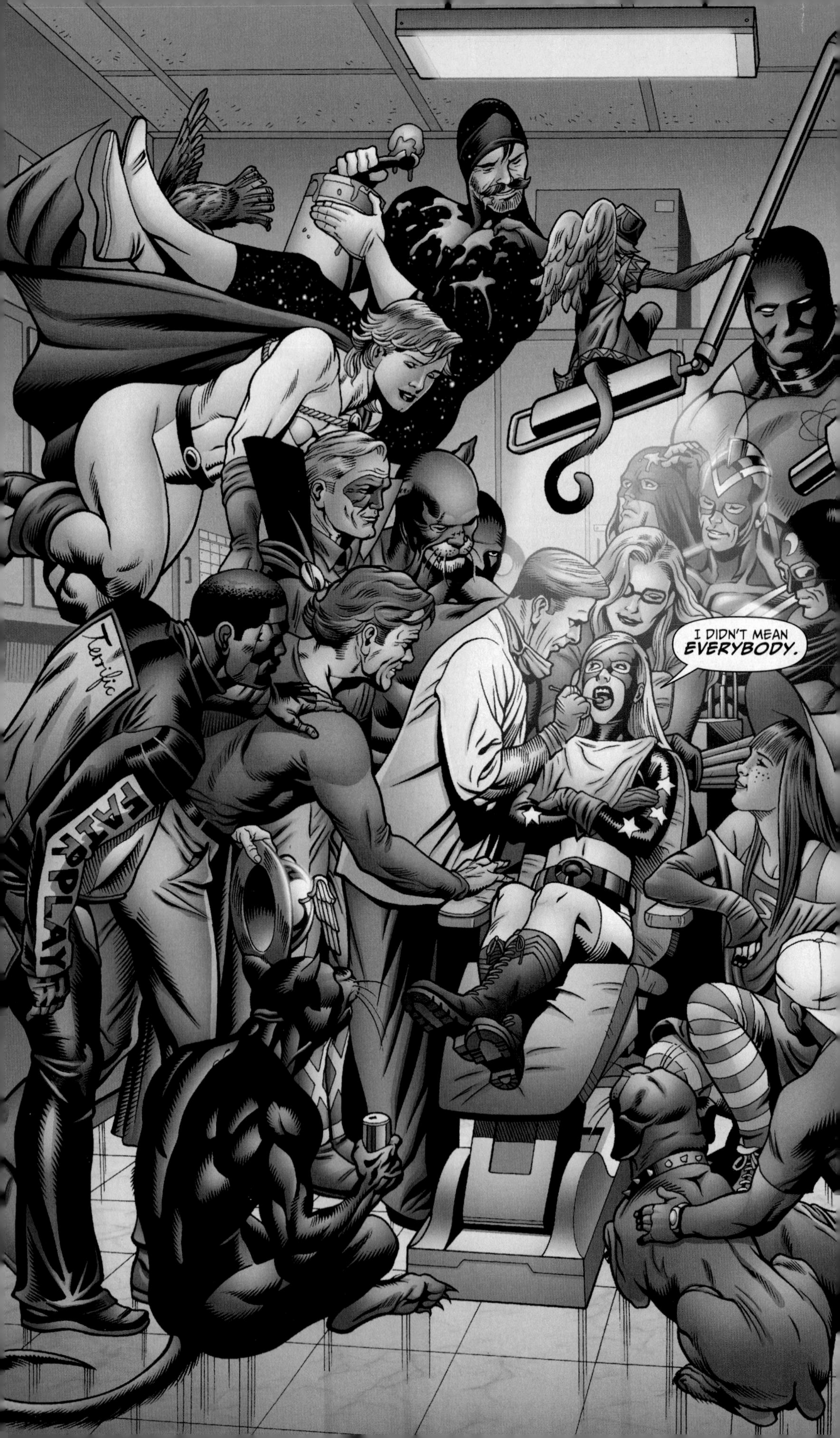
Terrific
I DIDN'T MEAN EVERYBODY.

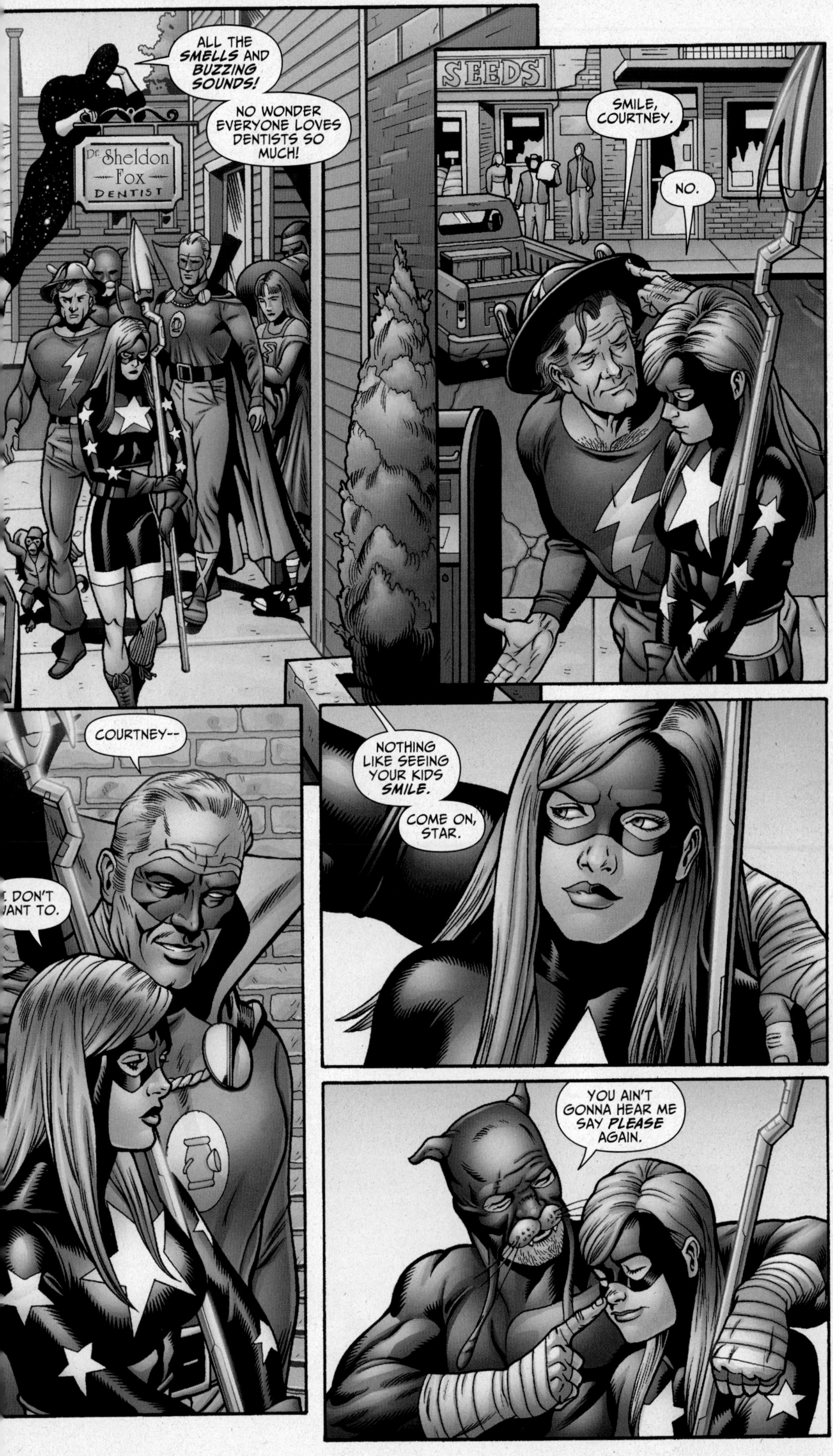
ALL THE SMELLS AND BUZZING SOUNDS!
NO WONDER EVERYONE LOVES DENTISTS SO MUCH!
Dr. Sheldon Fox DENTIST
SEEDS
SMILE, COURTNEY.
NO.
COURTNEY--
I DON'T WANT TO.
NOTHING LIKE SEEING YOUR KIDS SMILE.
COME ON, STAR.
YOU AIN'T GONNA HEAR ME SAY PLEASE AGAIN.

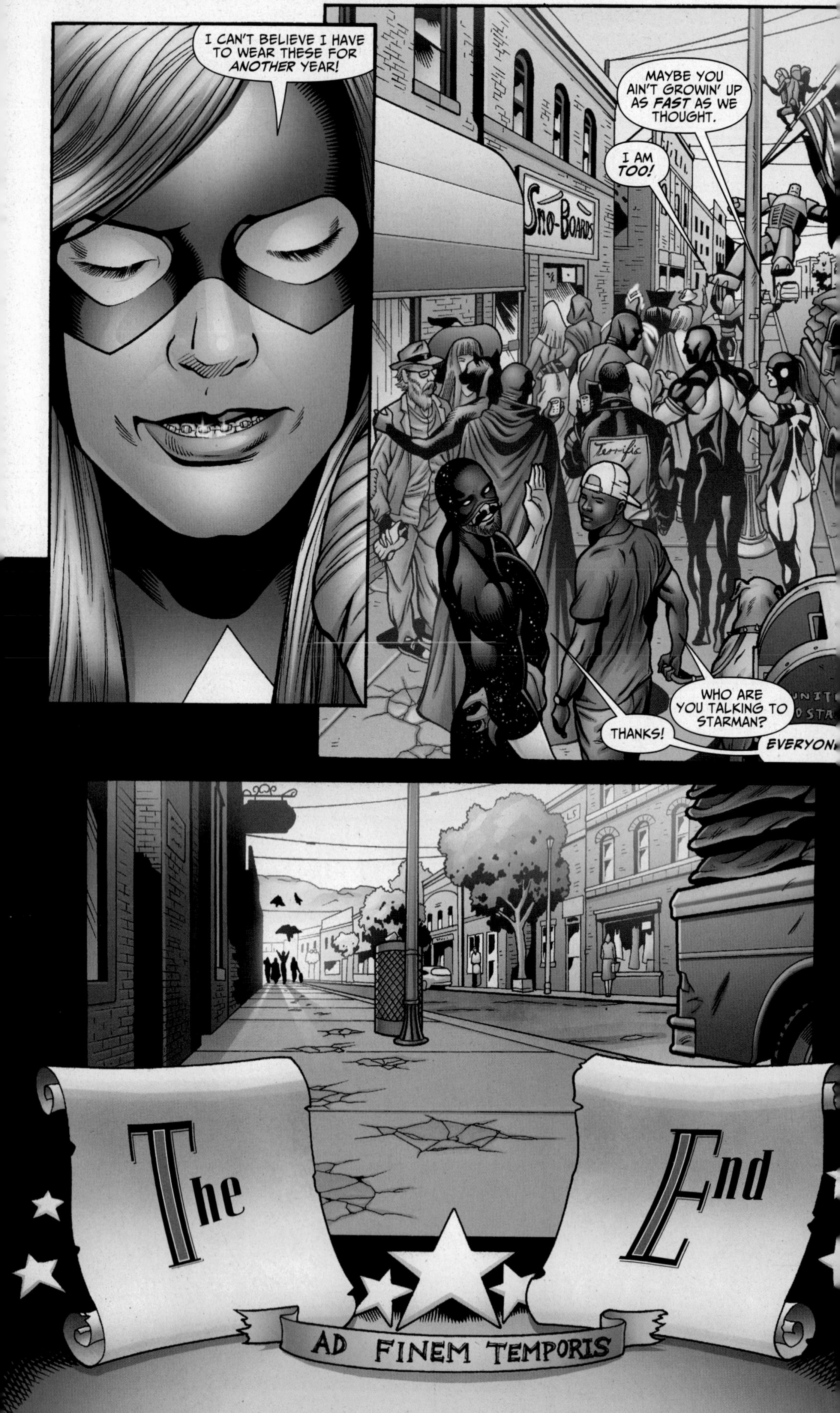
I CAN'T BELIEVE I HAVE TO WEAR THESE FOR ANOTHER YEAR!
MAYBE YOU AIN'T GROWIN' UP AS FAST AS WE THOUGHT.
I AM TOO!
Sno-Boards
Terrific
WHO ARE YOU TALKING TO STARMAN?
THANKS!
EVERYON
The End
AD FINEM TEMPORIS

USTICE SOCIETY OF AMERICA #27 cover by Jerry Ordway
terior art by Ordway & Bob Wiacek

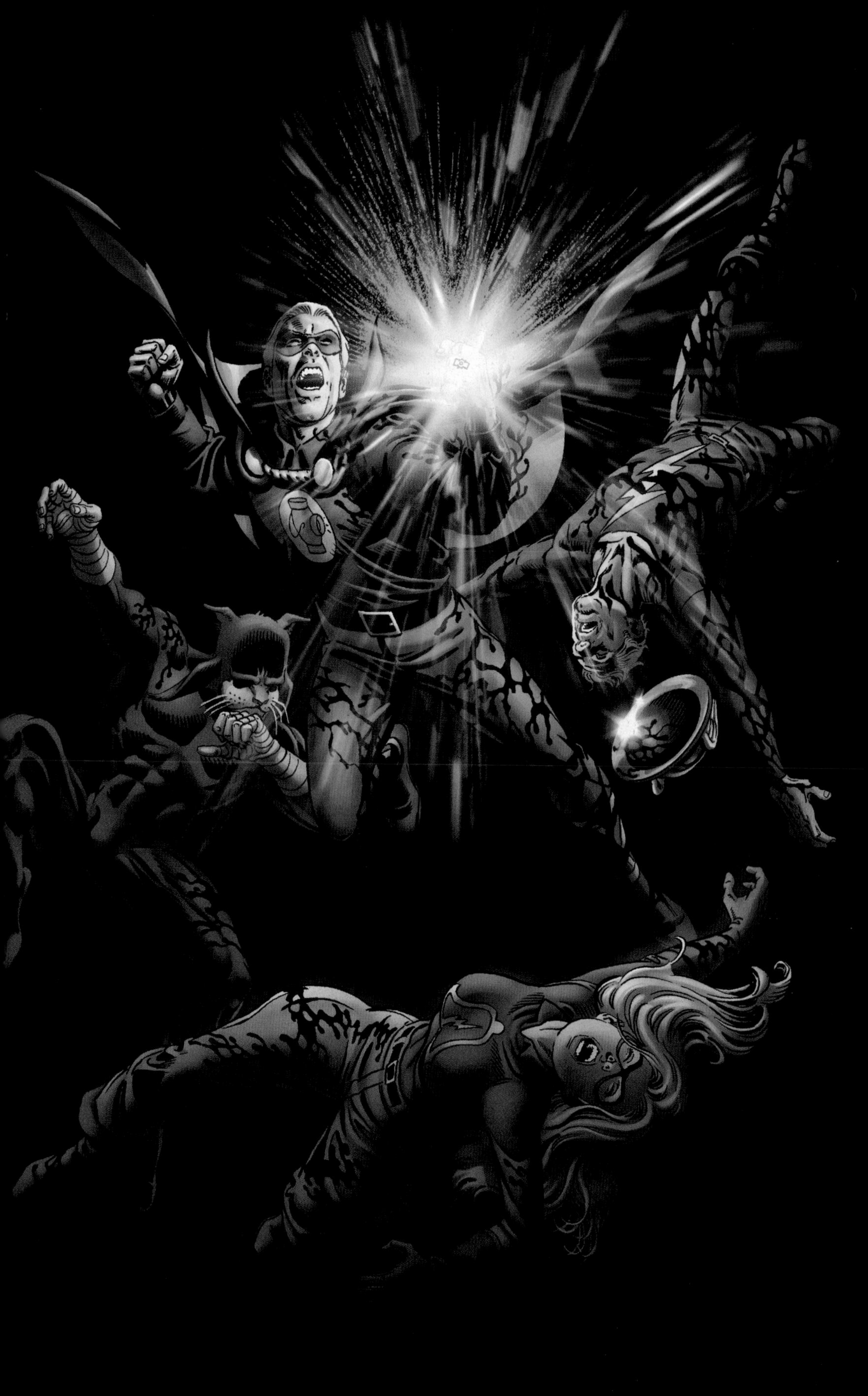

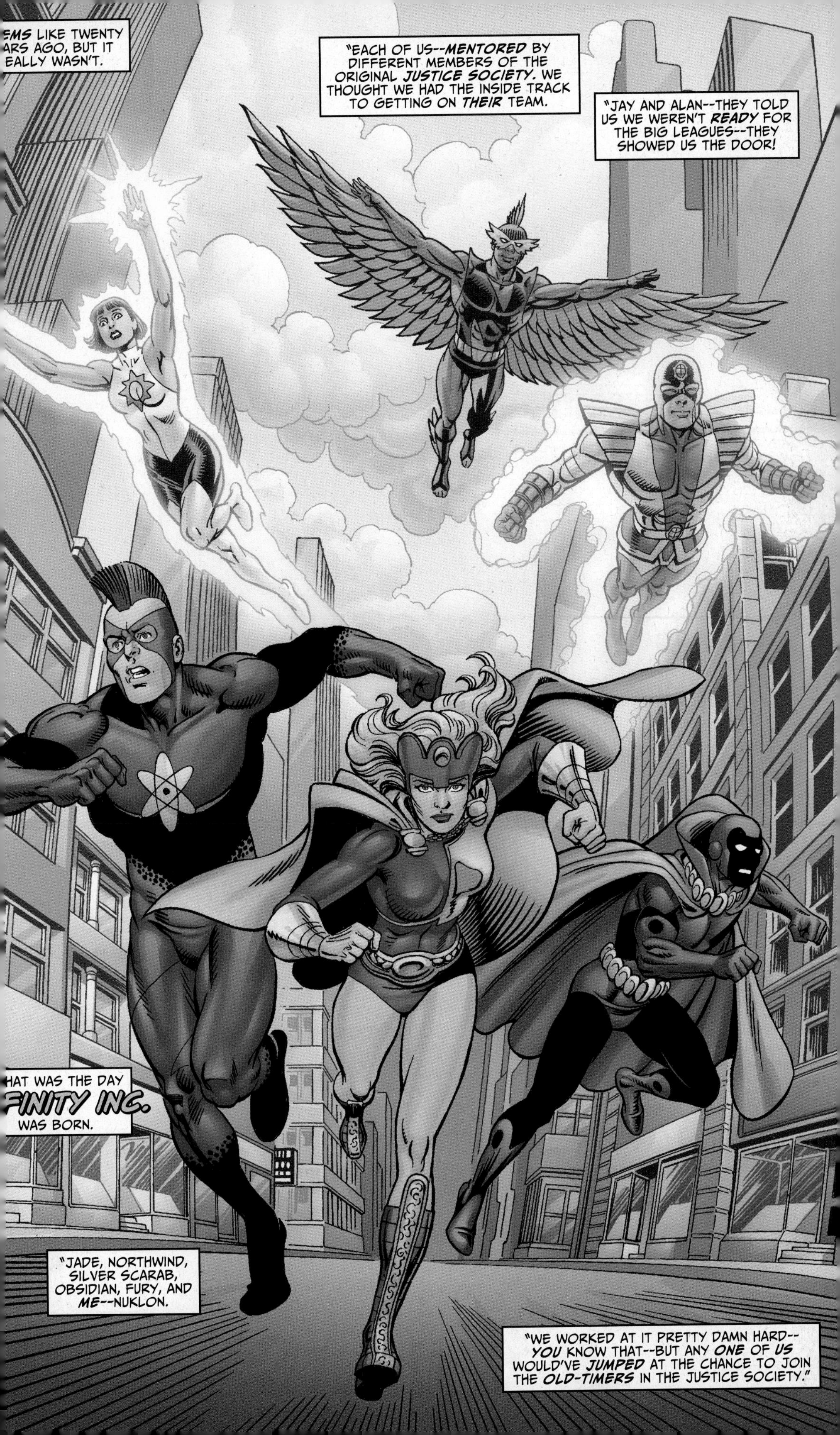
EMS LIKE TWENTY
ARS AGO, BUT IT
EALLY WASN'T.
"EACH OF US--MENTORED BY DIFFERENT MEMBERS OF THE ORIGINAL JUSTICE SOCIETY. WE THOUGHT WE HAD THE INSIDE TRACK TO GETTING ON THEIR TEAM.
"JAY AND ALAN--THEY TOLD US WE WEREN'T READY FOR THE BIG LEAGUES--THEY SHOWED US THE DOOR!
HAT WAS THE DAY
FINITY INC.
WAS BORN.
"JADE, NORTHWIND, SILVER SCARAB, OBSIDIAN, FURY, AND ME--NUKLON.
"WE WORKED AT IT PRETTY DAMN HARD--YOU KNOW THAT--BUT ANY ONE OF US WOULD'VE JUMPED AT THE CHANCE TO JOIN THE OLD-TIMERS IN THE JUSTICE SOCIETY."

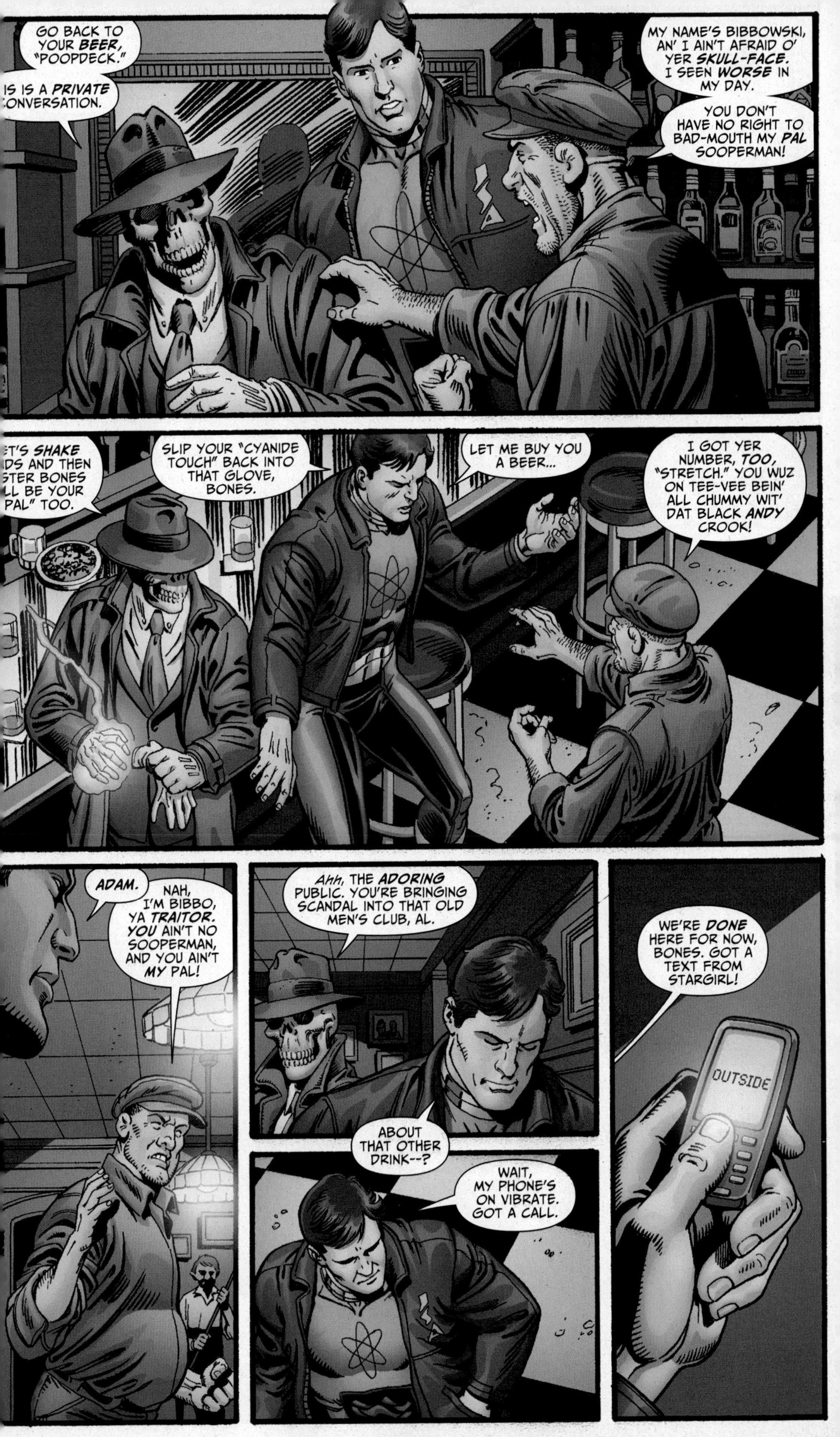
GO BACK TO YOUR BEER, "POOPDECK."
IS IS A PRIVATE CONVERSATION.
MY NAME'S BIBBOWSKI, AN' I AIN'T AFRAID O' YER SKULL-FACE. I SEEN WORSE IN MY DAY.
YOU DON'T HAVE NO RIGHT TO BAD-MOUTH MY PAL SOOPERMAN!
ET'S SHAKE DS AND THEN STER BONES LL BE YOUR PAL" TOO.
SLIP YOUR "CYANIDE TOUCH" BACK INTO THAT GLOVE, BONES.
LET ME BUY YOU A BEER...
I GOT YER NUMBER, TOO, "STRETCH." YOU WUZ ON TEE-VEE BEIN' ALL CHUMMY WIT' DAT BLACK ANDY CROOK!
ADAM.
NAH, I'M BIBBO, YA TRAITOR. YOU AIN'T NO SOOPERMAN, AND YOU AIN'T MY PAL!
Ahh, THE ADORING PUBLIC. YOU'RE BRINGING SCANDAL INTO THAT OLD MEN'S CLUB, AL.
ABOUT THAT OTHER DRINK--?
WAIT, MY PHONE'S ON VIBRATE. GOT A CALL.
WE'RE DONE HERE FOR NOW, BONES. GOT A TEXT FROM STARGIRL!
OUTSIDE

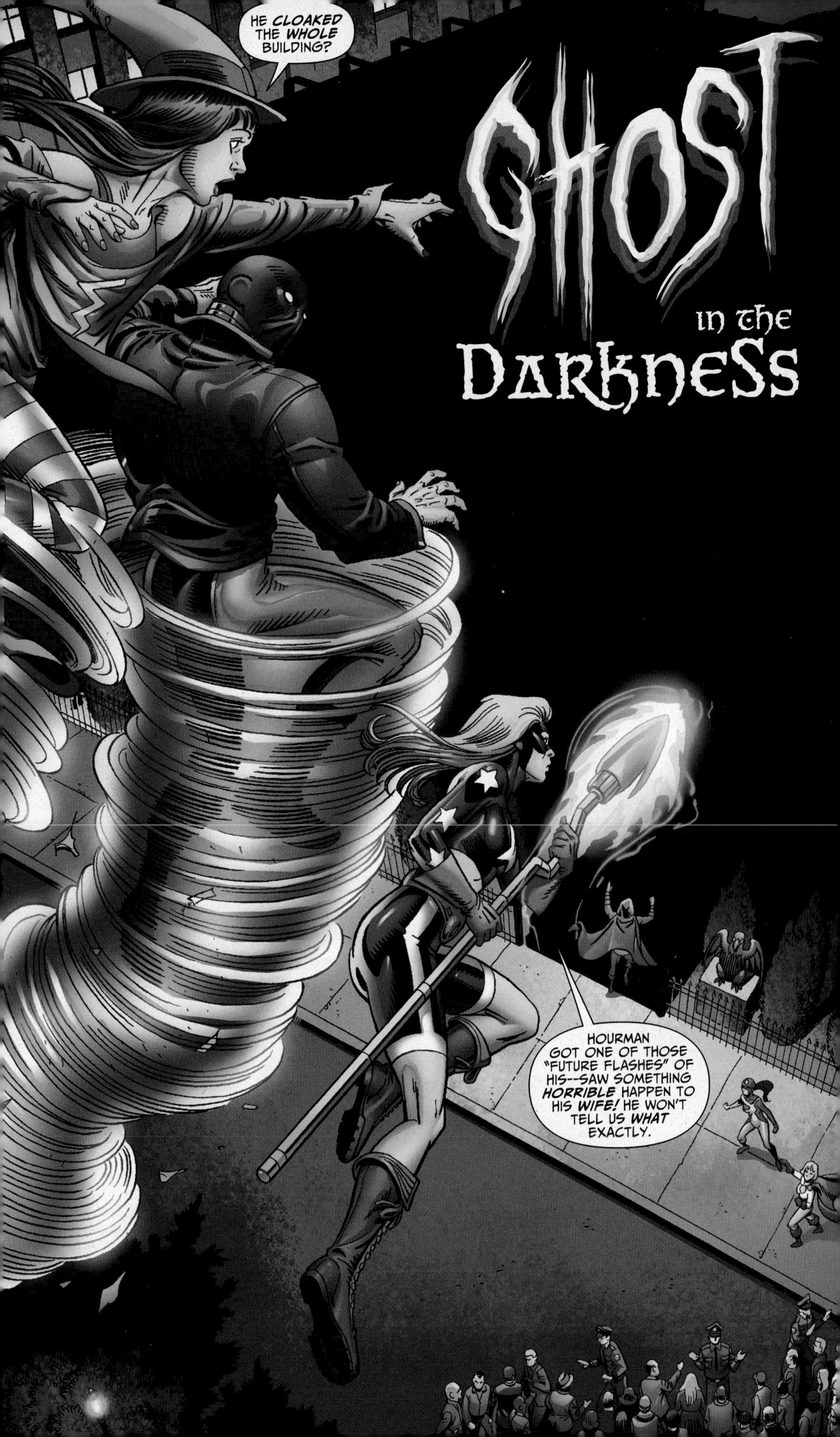
HE CLOAKED THE WHOLE BUILDING?
GHOST in the DARKNESS
HOURMAN GOT ONE OF THOSE "FUTURE FLASHES" OF HIS--SAW SOMETHING HORRIBLE HAPPEN TO HIS WIFE! HE WON'T TELL US WHAT EXACTLY.

OBSIDIAN, SOMETHING REALLY *BAD* IS GOING TO HAPPEN IN ABOUT SEVENTEEN MINUTES!

LET MY *WIFE* GO! LET THEM *ALL* GO! WHAT THE HELL ARE YOU TRYING TO ACCOMPLISH?

THERE IS A DANGEROUS *PRESENCE* OUTSIDE THE BUILDING. I AM ONLY DOING MY JOB, HOURMAN, AS *SECURITY* FOR THE J.S.A..

GEEZ, REMIND ME *NEVER* TO COME BETWEEN *HIM* AND HIS *WIFE!*

POWER GIRL DEPLOYED THE OTHERS TO GUARD THE PERIMETER, BUT NO *THREAT'S* BEEN FOUND.

MAYBE HOURMAN'S "PEEK" INTO THE FUTURE WAS ALREADY *AVERTED?*

IF HE'S HARMED HER, I'LL--!

REST YOUR KNUCKLES, TYLER.

OBSIDIAN--BUDDY-- WHAT'S UP? HOURMAN IS CONVINCED *DOOMSDAY* IS COMING.

NO ONE HAS BEEN HARMED. THE HEADQUARTERS IS IN LOCKDOWN MODE, ALBERT.

IF THE THREAT'S OUT *HERE,* WHY HE KICK THE RES OF US TO THE CURB?

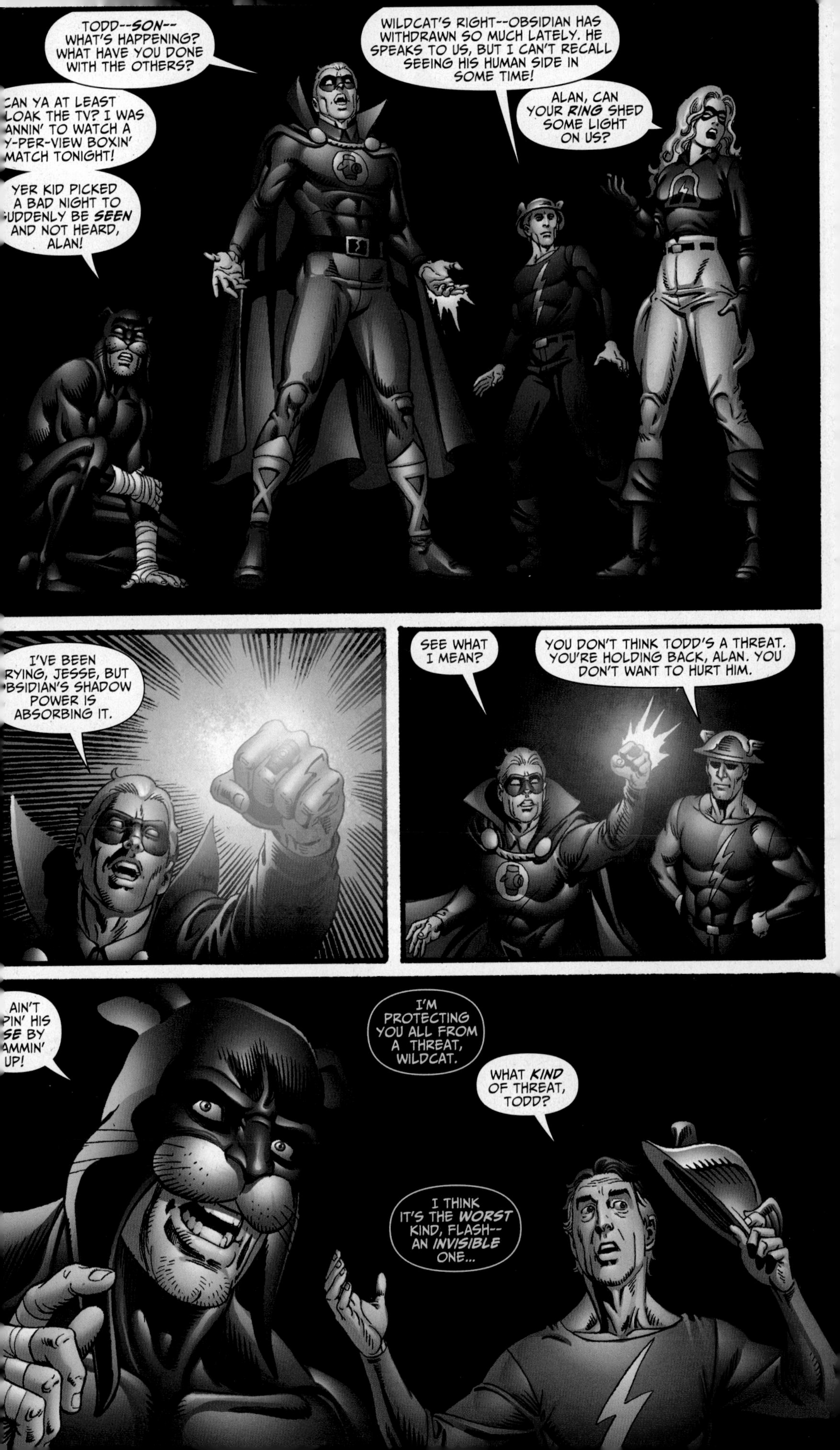

TODD--SON-- WHAT'S HAPPENING? WHAT HAVE YOU DONE WITH THE OTHERS?
CAN YA AT LEAST LOAK THE TV? I WAS ANNIN' TO WATCH A Y-PER-VIEW BOXIN' MATCH TONIGHT!
YER KID PICKED A BAD NIGHT TO UDDENLY BE SEEN AND NOT HEARD, ALAN!
WILDCAT'S RIGHT--OBSIDIAN HAS WITHDRAWN SO MUCH LATELY. HE SPEAKS TO US, BUT I CAN'T RECALL SEEING HIS HUMAN SIDE IN SOME TIME!
ALAN, CAN YOUR RING SHED SOME LIGHT ON US?
I'VE BEEN RYING, JESSE, BUT BSIDIAN'S SHADOW POWER IS ABSORBING IT.
SEE WHAT I MEAN?
YOU DON'T THINK TODD'S A THREAT. YOU'RE HOLDING BACK, ALAN. YOU DON'T WANT TO HURT HIM.
AIN'T PIN' HIS SE BY AMMIN' UP!
I'M PROTECTING YOU ALL FROM A THREAT, WILDCAT.
WHAT KIND OF THREAT, TODD?
I THINK IT'S THE WORST KIND, FLASH-- AN INVISIBLE ONE...

"...A GHOST."

HEADS UP-- WE'VE GOT A BYSTANDER DOWN!

POWER GIRL--GET THE CROWD BACK! I'LL TE TO HIM! MY T-SPHERES AR CONTACTING EMERGENCY SERVICES NOW!

HEY, I RECOGNIZE HIM! HE'S BEEN HERE SINCE THIS ALL STARTED!

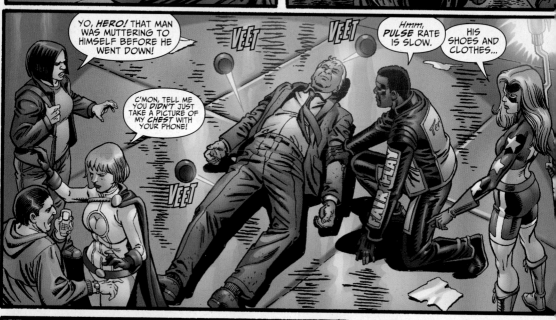

YO, *HERO!* THAT MAN WAS MUTTERING TO HIMSELF BEFORE HE WENT DOWN!

C'MON, TELL ME YOU *DIDN'T* JUST TAKE A PICTURE OF MY *CHEST* WITH YOUR PHONE!

VEET

VEET

VEET

Hmm, PULSE RATE IS SLOW.

HIS SHOES AND CLOTHES...

YES, THEY'RE *WORN* THROUGH. STARGIRL, CAN YOU *WARM* HIM WITH YOUR COSMIC ROD? HE'S GOING INTO *SHOCK.*

SIR--DON'T TRY TO SPEAK. MY NAME IS MR. TERRIFIC, AND I'VE CALLED FOR AN AMBULANCE.

MY NAME-- IS BILL. *WALKED* HERE--FROM *FAWCETT CITY.* *MAKE* THEM LET ME GO...

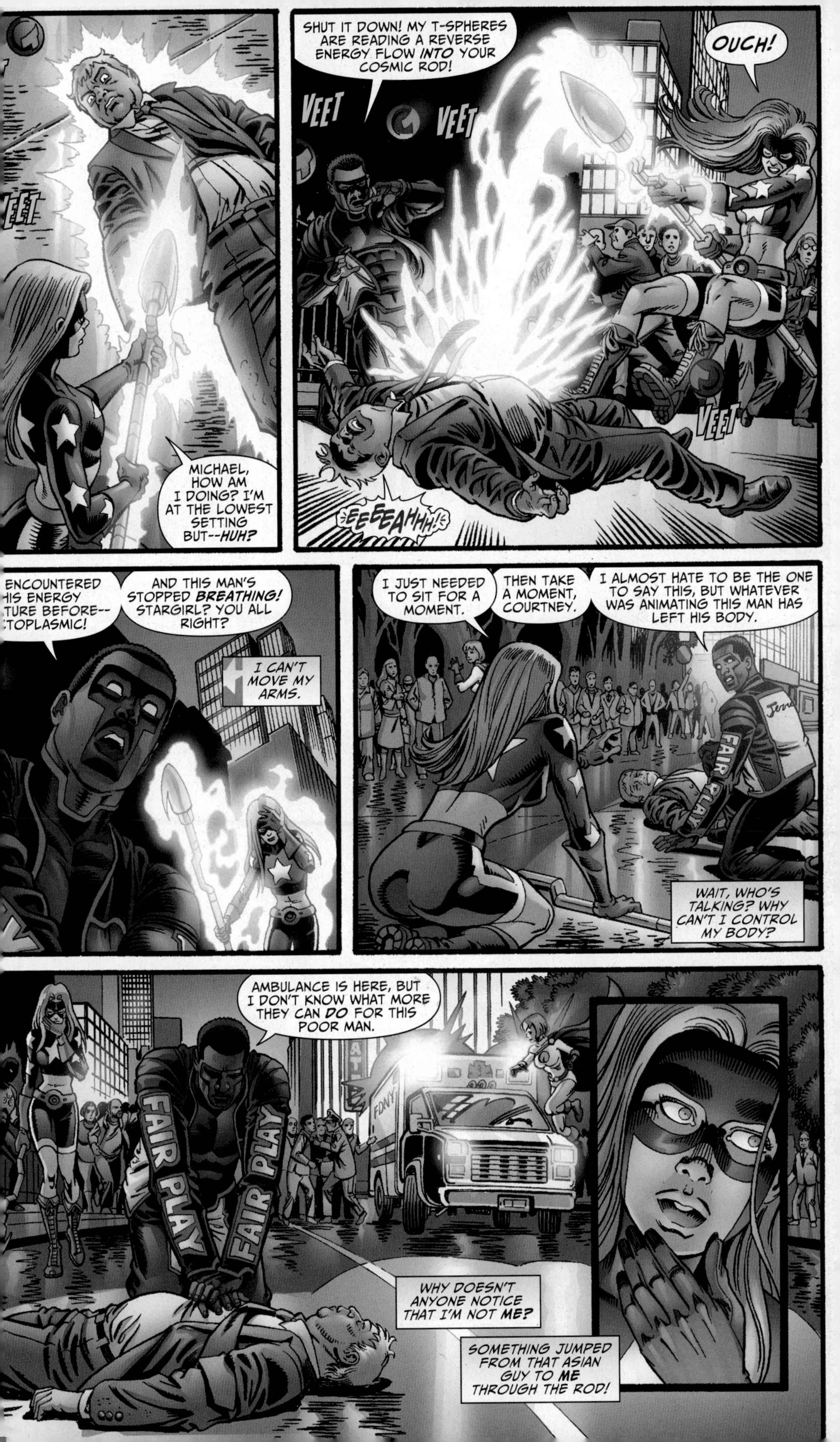
VEET
MICHAEL, HOW AM I DOING? I'M AT THE LOWEST SETTING BUT--HUH?
SHUT IT DOWN! MY T-SPHERES ARE READING A REVERSE ENERGY FLOW INTO YOUR COSMIC ROD!
VEET
VEET
OUCH!
VEET
EEEEAHHH!
ENCOUNTERED HIS ENERGY TURE BEFORE-- TOPLASMIC!
AND THIS MAN'S STOPPED BREATHING! STARGIRL? YOU ALL RIGHT?
I CAN'T MOVE MY ARMS.
I JUST NEEDED TO SIT FOR A MOMENT.
THEN TAKE A MOMENT, COURTNEY.
I ALMOST HATE TO BE THE ONE TO SAY THIS, BUT WHATEVER WAS ANIMATING THIS MAN HAS LEFT HIS BODY.
FAIR PLAY
WAIT, WHO'S TALKING? WHY CAN'T I CONTROL MY BODY?
AMBULANCE IS HERE, BUT I DON'T KNOW WHAT MORE THEY CAN DO FOR THIS POOR MAN.
FAIR PLAY
FAIR PLAY
FDNY
WHY DOESN'T ANYONE NOTICE THAT I'M NOT ME?
SOMETHING JUMPED FROM THAT ASIAN GUY TO ME THROUGH THE ROD!

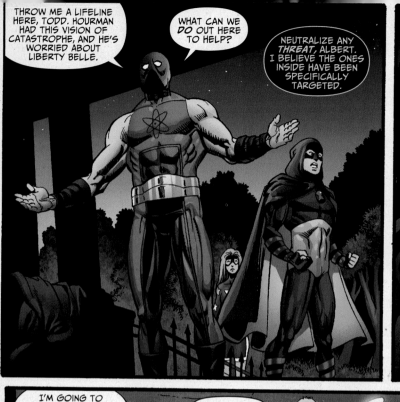

THROW ME A LIFELINE HERE, TODD. HOURMAN HAD THIS VISION OF CATASTROPHE, AND HE'S WORRIED ABOUT LIBERTY BELLE.

WHAT CAN WE *DO* OUT HERE TO HELP?

NEUTRALIZE ANY *THREAT*, ALBERT. I BELIEVE THE ONES INSIDE HAVE BEEN SPECIFICALLY TARGETED.

YEAH, TARGETED BY *YOU*, OBSIDIAN! I CAN'T BELIEVE I'M STANDING HERE ARGUING LIKE THIS!

BOTH OF YOU HAVE LIED TO US IN THE PAST, AND I'M SUPPOSED TO *BELIEVE* YOU NOW?

I'M GOING TO RELUCTANTLY LET THAT COMMENT PASS, BECAUSE I KNOW YOU'RE FLIPPING OUT OVER JESSE, BUT--

--COURTNEY?

LET'S GO, AL--RICK-- CAN'T YOU *TELL* I'M NOT *MYSELF*?

STARGIRL, HELP ME OUT HERE, WILL YOU? OBSIDIAN HASN'T BEEN REMOTELY *HUMAN* LATELY. GOTTA BE SOMETHING WRONG WITH HIM *AGAIN*, RIGHT?

ALBERT! SOMETHING *IS* TERRIBLY WRONG. I CAN *FEEL* THE PRESENCE OF *EVIL* OUTSIDE THE DOOR!

RELAX, IT'S JUST STARGIRL! COURT, PUT TODD AT *EASE* BEFORE THIS ESCALATES INTO SOMETHING.

OH. MY. GOSH. ALBERT, STOP ME!

ARE YOU *DENSE?* I WALKING L A *RUNWA* MODEL, A YOU DON *NOTICE* ANYTHIN *WEIRD?*

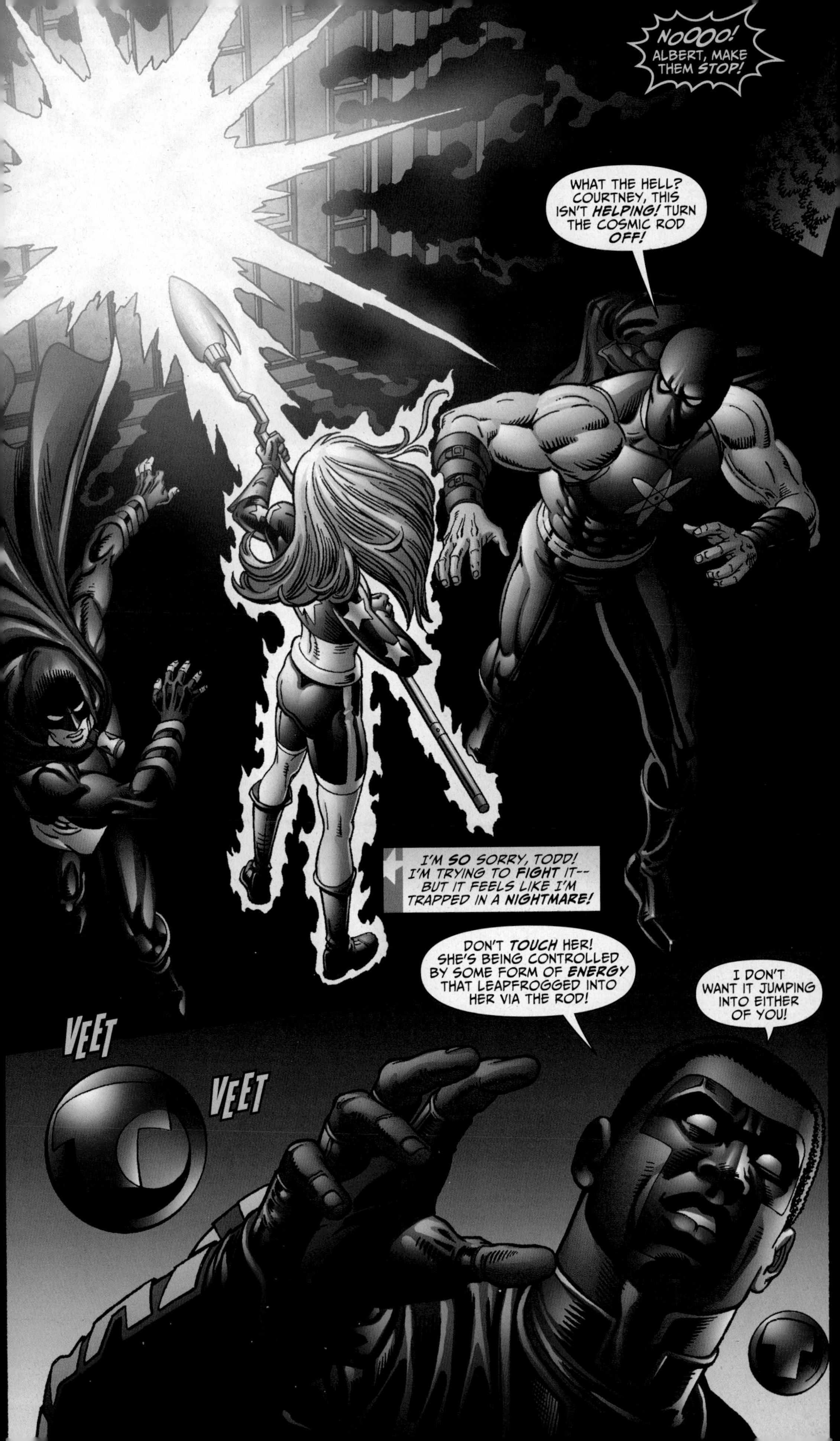
NOOOO! ALBERT, MAKE THEM STOP!
WHAT THE HELL? COURTNEY, THIS ISN'T HELPING! TURN THE COSMIC ROD OFF!
I'M SO SORRY, TODD! I'M TRYING TO FIGHT IT-- BUT IT FEELS LIKE I'M TRAPPED IN A NIGHTMARE!
DON'T TOUCH HER! SHE'S BEING CONTROLLED BY SOME FORM OF ENERGY THAT LEAPFROGGED INTO HER VIA THE ROD!
I DON'T WANT IT JUMPING INTO EITHER OF YOU!
VEET
VEET

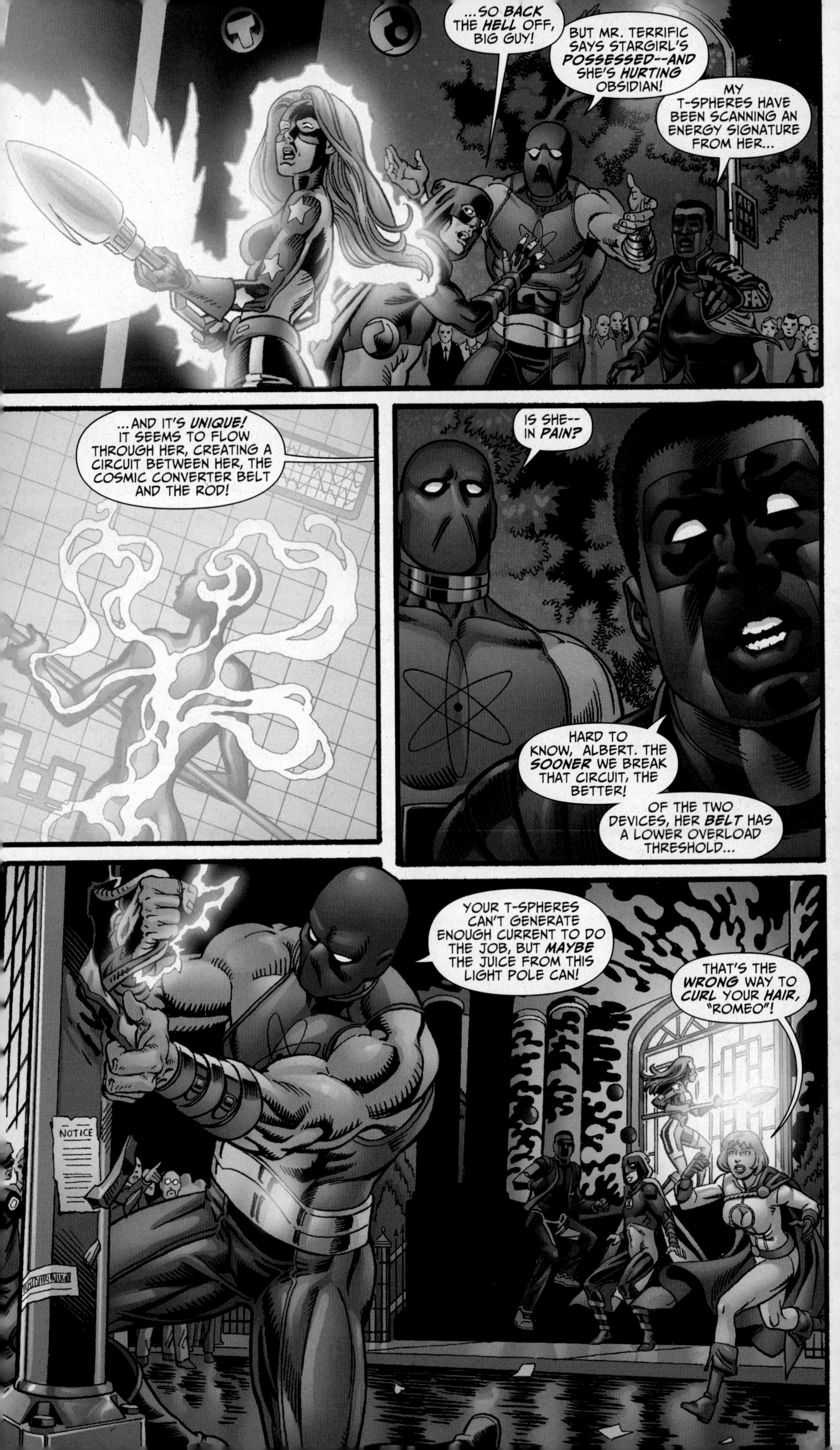
...SO BACK THE HELL OFF, BIG GUY!
BUT MR. TERRIFIC SAYS STARGIRL'S POSSESSED--AND SHE'S HURTING OBSIDIAN!
MY T-SPHERES HAVE BEEN SCANNING AN ENERGY SIGNATURE FROM HER...
...AND IT'S UNIQUE! IT SEEMS TO FLOW THROUGH HER, CREATING A CIRCUIT BETWEEN HER, THE COSMIC CONVERTER BELT AND THE ROD!
IS SHE-- IN PAIN?
HARD TO KNOW, ALBERT. THE SOONER WE BREAK THAT CIRCUIT, THE BETTER!
OF THE TWO DEVICES, HER BELT HAS A LOWER OVERLOAD THRESHOLD...
YOUR T-SPHERES CAN'T GENERATE ENOUGH CURRENT TO DO THE JOB, BUT MAYBE THE JUICE FROM THIS LIGHT POLE CAN!
THAT'S THE WRONG WAY TO CURL YOUR HAIR, "ROMEO"!
NOTICE

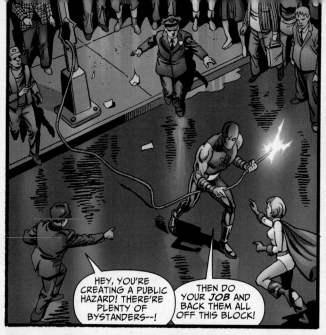

HEY, YOU'RE CREATING A PUBLIC HAZARD! THERE'RE PLENTY OF BYSTANDERS--!

THEN DO YOUR *JOB* AND BACK THEM ALL OFF THIS BLOCK!

AND WHAT'S WITH THE "ROMEO" COMMENT?

I'VE SEEN THE *WAY* YOU TWO *LOOK* AT EACH OTHER, ATOM SMASHER.

I'M BETTER EQUIPP[ED] SURVIVE ELECTROCU[TION] GET READY TO SW[OON] AND CATCH YOU[R] FAIR MAIDEN.

THIS SHOULD TRIP THE CIRCUITS ON THE LIGHT POLE AT THE SAME TIME!

Ohhh!

ZAAMPF

I'VE GOT YOU!

THE COSMIC ROD--?

OH, ALBERT-- IT WAS HORRIBLE-- IT WAS A THOUSAND VOICES SCREAMING FOR VENGEANCE ALL AT ONCE. I WOULD HAVE GONE MAD IF YOU HADN'T STOPPED IT!

WE DID[N'T] STOP I[T]

GET READY TO CATCH IT-- THE ENERGY HAS SPREAD *OUT*, ACROSS THE BUILDING!

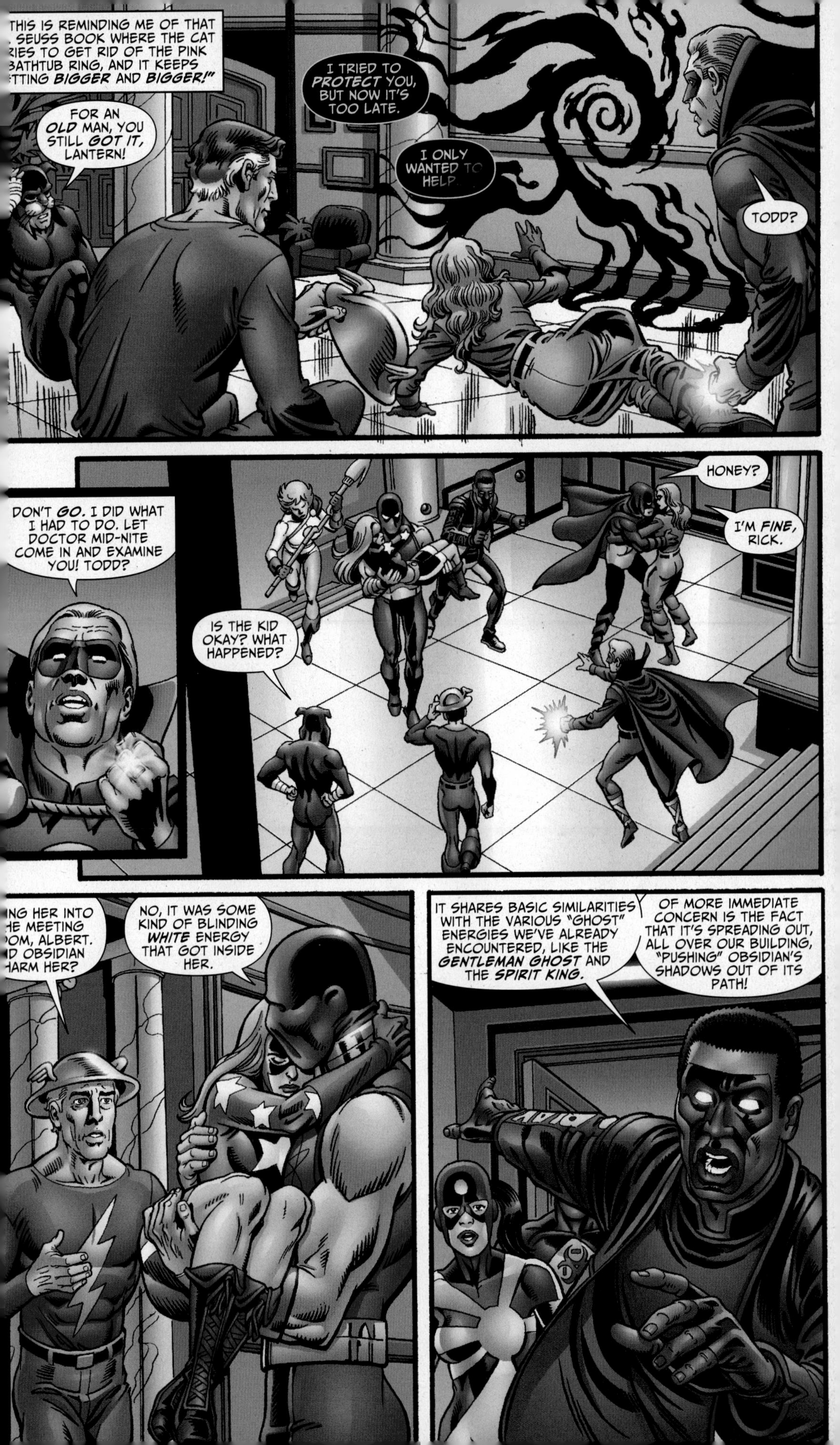
THIS IS REMINDING ME OF THAT . SEUSS BOOK WHERE THE CAT RIES TO GET RID OF THE PINK BATHTUB RING, AND IT KEEPS ETTING BIGGER AND BIGGER!"
FOR AN OLD MAN, YOU STILL GOT IT, LANTERN!
I TRIED TO PROTECT YOU, BUT NOW IT'S TOO LATE.
I ONLY WANTED TO HELP.
TODD?
DON'T GO. I DID WHAT I HAD TO DO. LET DOCTOR MID-NITE COME IN AND EXAMINE YOU! TODD?
HONEY?
I'M FINE, RICK.
IS THE KID OKAY? WHAT HAPPENED?
NG HER INTO HE MEETING OM, ALBERT. D OBSIDIAN HARM HER?
NO, IT WAS SOME KIND OF BLINDING WHITE ENERGY THAT GOT INSIDE HER.
IT SHARES BASIC SIMILARITIES WITH THE VARIOUS "GHOST" ENERGIES WE'VE ALREADY ENCOUNTERED, LIKE THE GENTLEMAN GHOST AND THE SPIRIT KING.
OF MORE IMMEDIATE CONCERN IS THE FACT THAT IT'S SPREADING OUT, ALL OVER OUR BUILDING, "PUSHING" OBSIDIAN'S SHADOWS OUT OF ITS PATH!

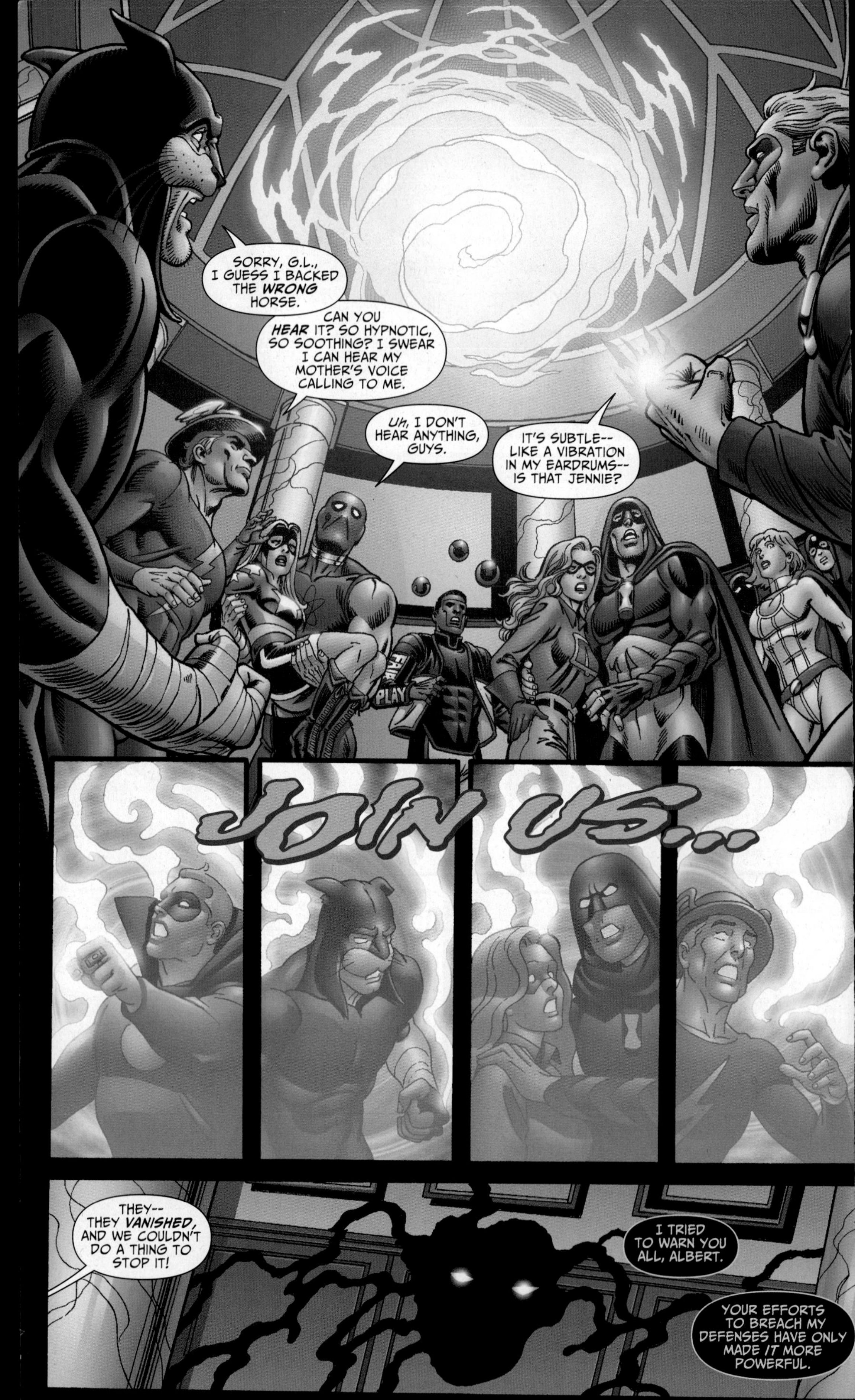
SORRY, G.L., I GUESS I BACKED THE WRONG HORSE.
CAN YOU HEAR IT? SO HYPNOTIC, SO SOOTHING? I SWEAR I CAN HEAR MY MOTHER'S VOICE CALLING TO ME.
Uh, I DON'T HEAR ANYTHING, GUYS.
IT'S SUBTLE-- LIKE A VIBRATION IN MY EARDRUMS-- IS THAT JENNIE?
JOIN US...
THEY-- THEY VANISHED, AND WE COULDN'T DO A THING TO STOP IT!
I TRIED TO WARN YOU ALL, ALBERT.
YOUR EFFORTS TO BREACH MY DEFENSES HAVE ONLY MADE IT MORE POWERFUL.

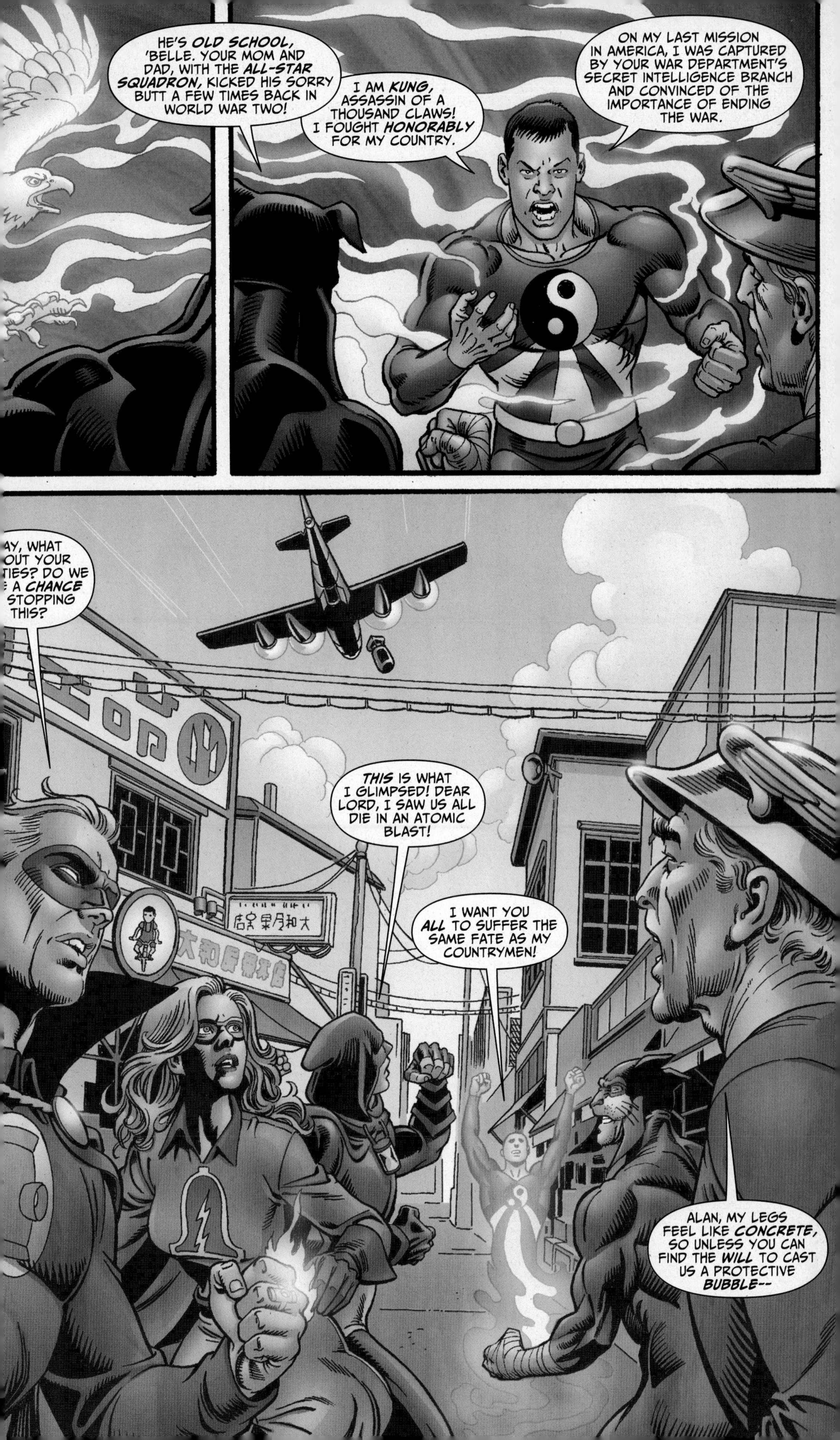
HE'S OLD SCHOOL, 'BELLE. YOUR MOM AND DAD, WITH THE ALL-STAR SQUADRON, KICKED HIS SORRY BUTT A FEW TIMES BACK IN WORLD WAR TWO!
I AM KUNG, ASSASSIN OF A THOUSAND CLAWS! I FOUGHT HONORABLY FOR MY COUNTRY.
ON MY LAST MISSION IN AMERICA, I WAS CAPTURED BY YOUR WAR DEPARTMENT'S SECRET INTELLIGENCE BRANCH AND CONVINCED OF THE IMPORTANCE OF ENDING THE WAR.
AY, WHAT OUT YOUR TIES? DO WE E A CHANCE STOPPING THIS?
THIS IS WHAT I GLIMPSED! DEAR LORD, I SAW US ALL DIE IN AN ATOMIC BLAST!
I WANT YOU ALL TO SUFFER THE SAME FATE AS MY COUNTRYMEN!
ALAN, MY LEGS FEEL LIKE CONCRETE, SO UNLESS YOU CAN FIND THE WILL TO CAST US A PROTECTIVE BUBBLE--

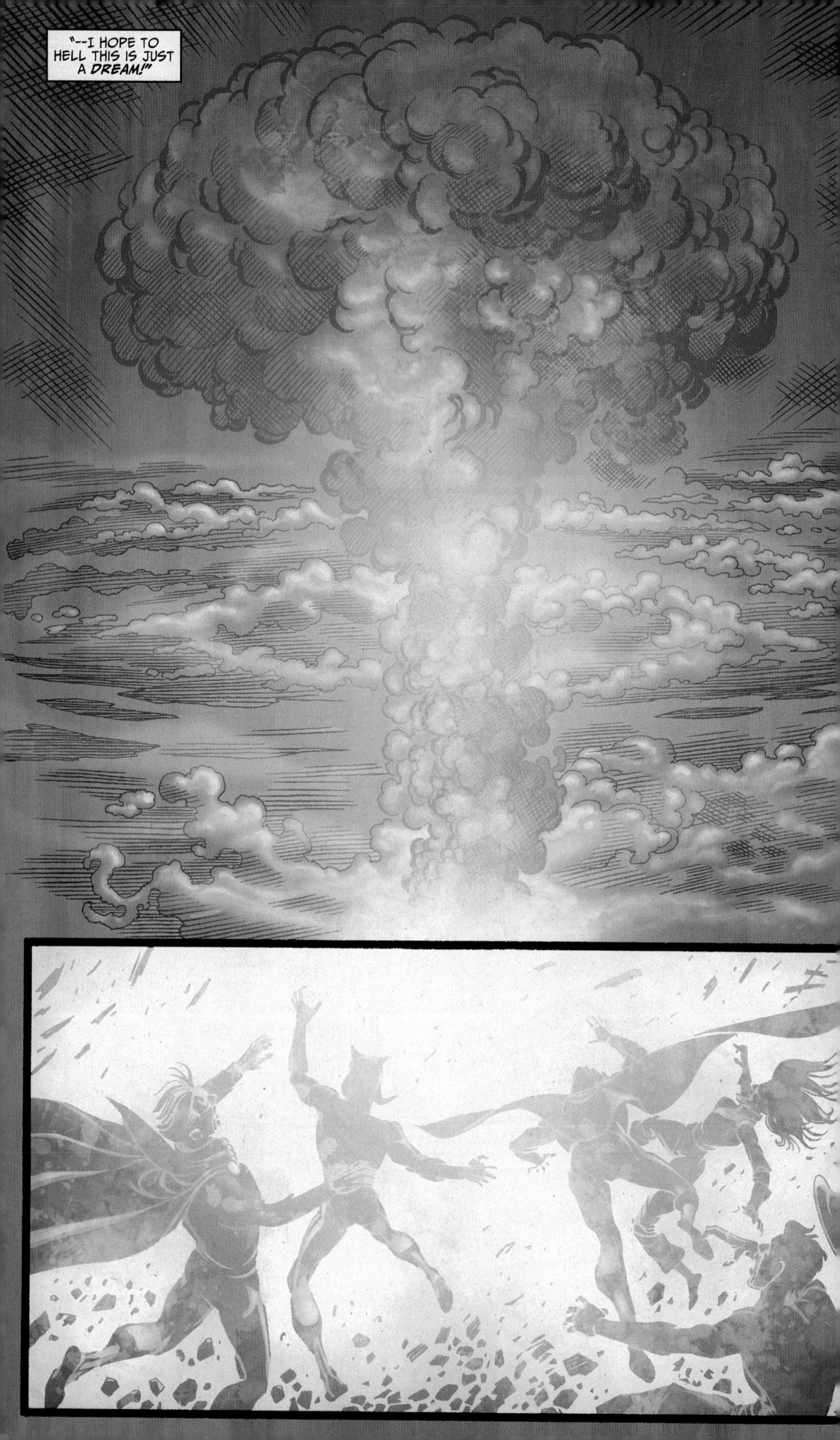
"--I HOPE TO HELL THIS IS JUST A DREAM!"

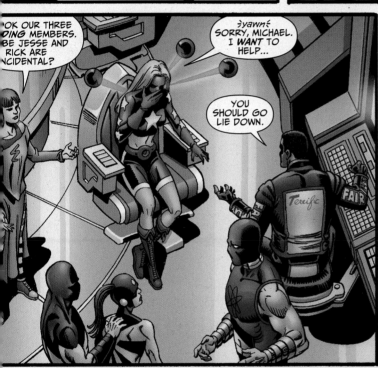

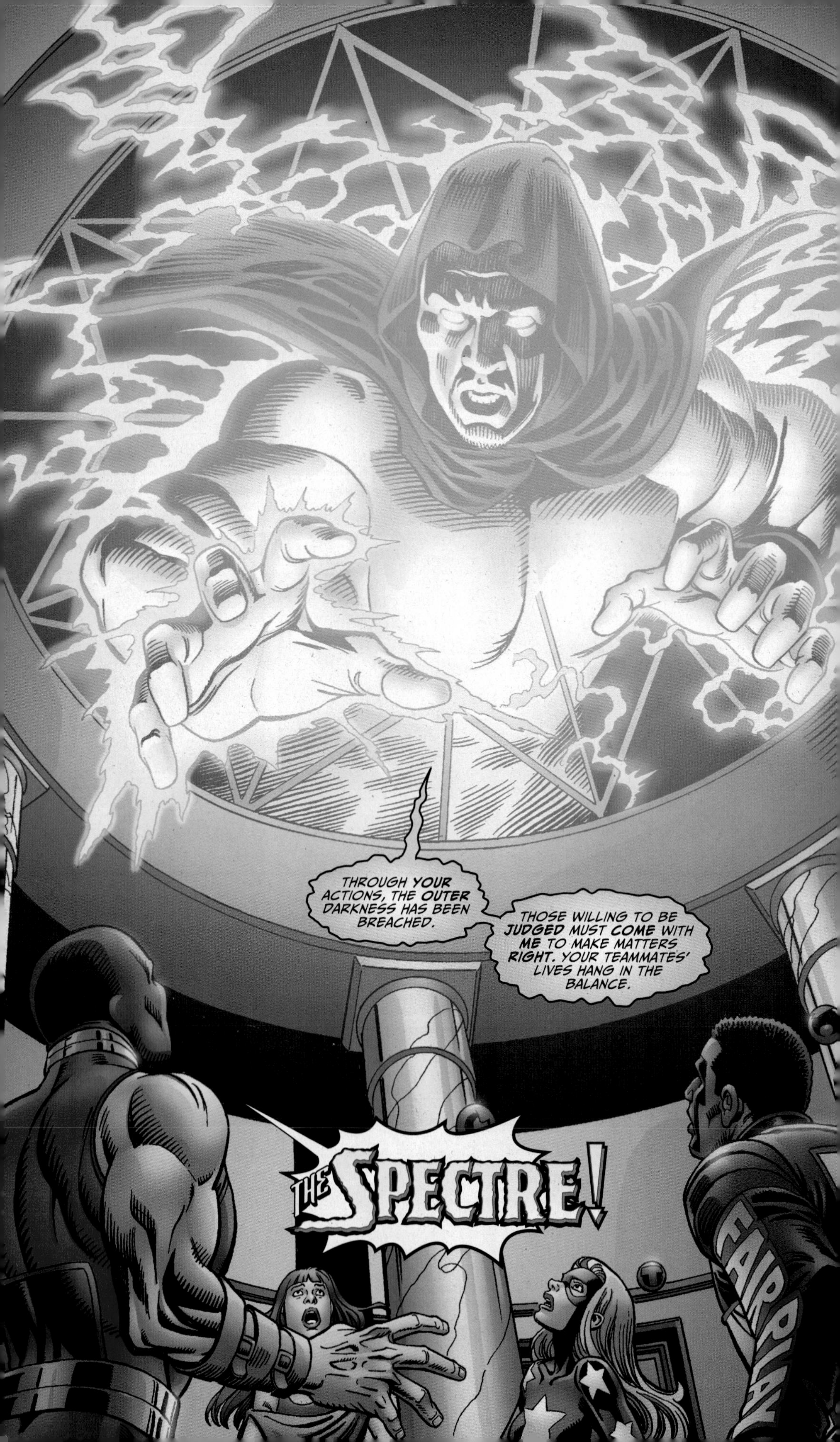
THROUGH YOUR ACTIONS, THE OUTER DARKNESS HAS BEEN BREACHED.
THOSE WILLING TO BE JUDGED MUST COME WITH ME TO MAKE MATTERS RIGHT. YOUR TEAMMATES' LIVES HANG IN THE BALANCE.
THE SPECTRE!
FAIRPLAY

JUSTICE SOCIETY OF AMERICA #28 cover by Jerry Ordway
Interior art by Ordway & Bob Wiacek

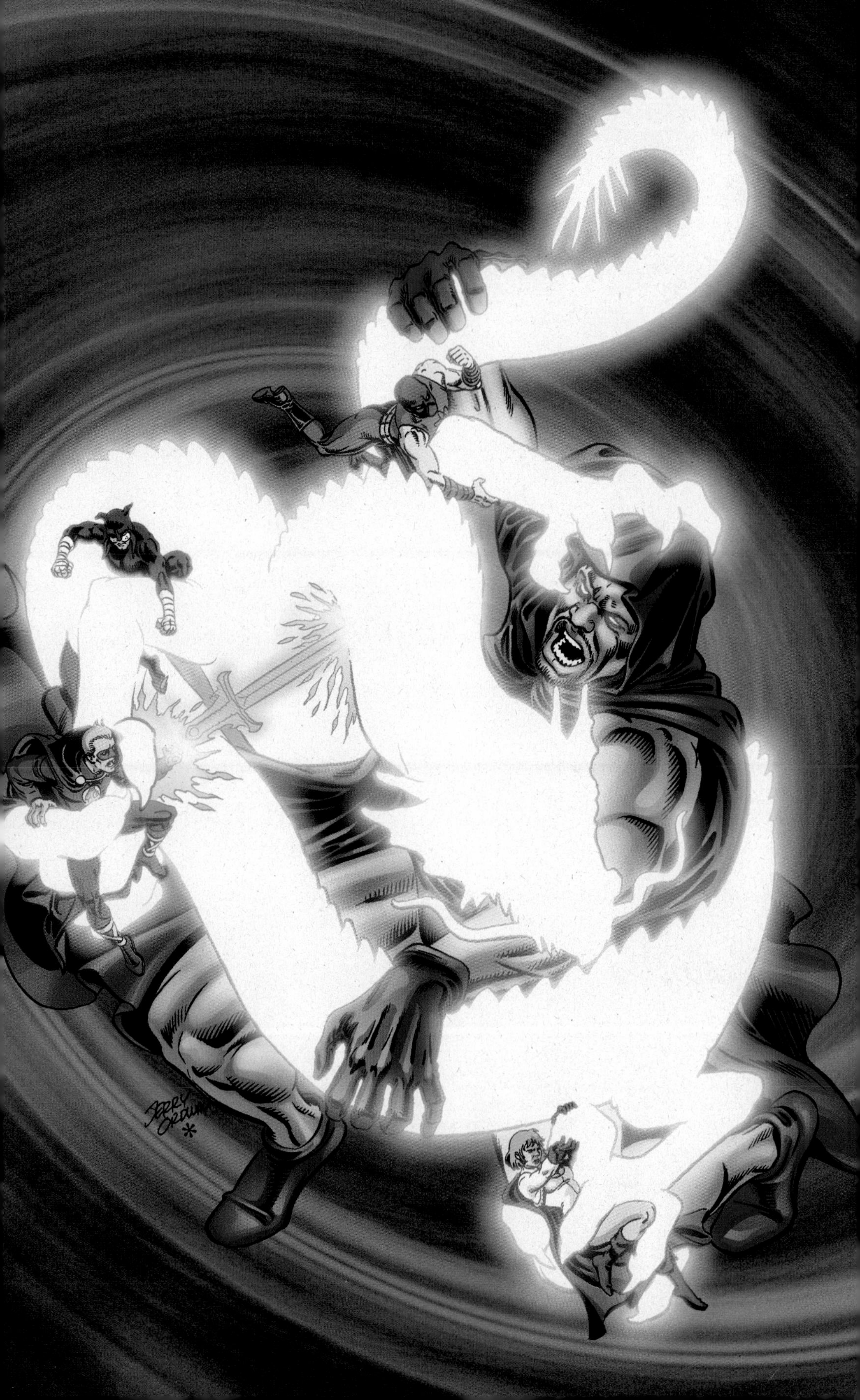
JERRY ORDWAY

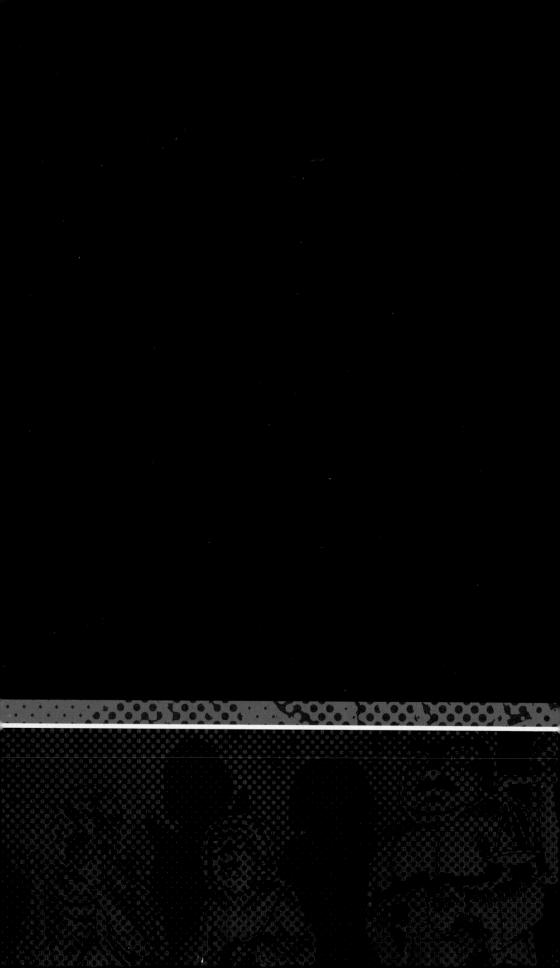

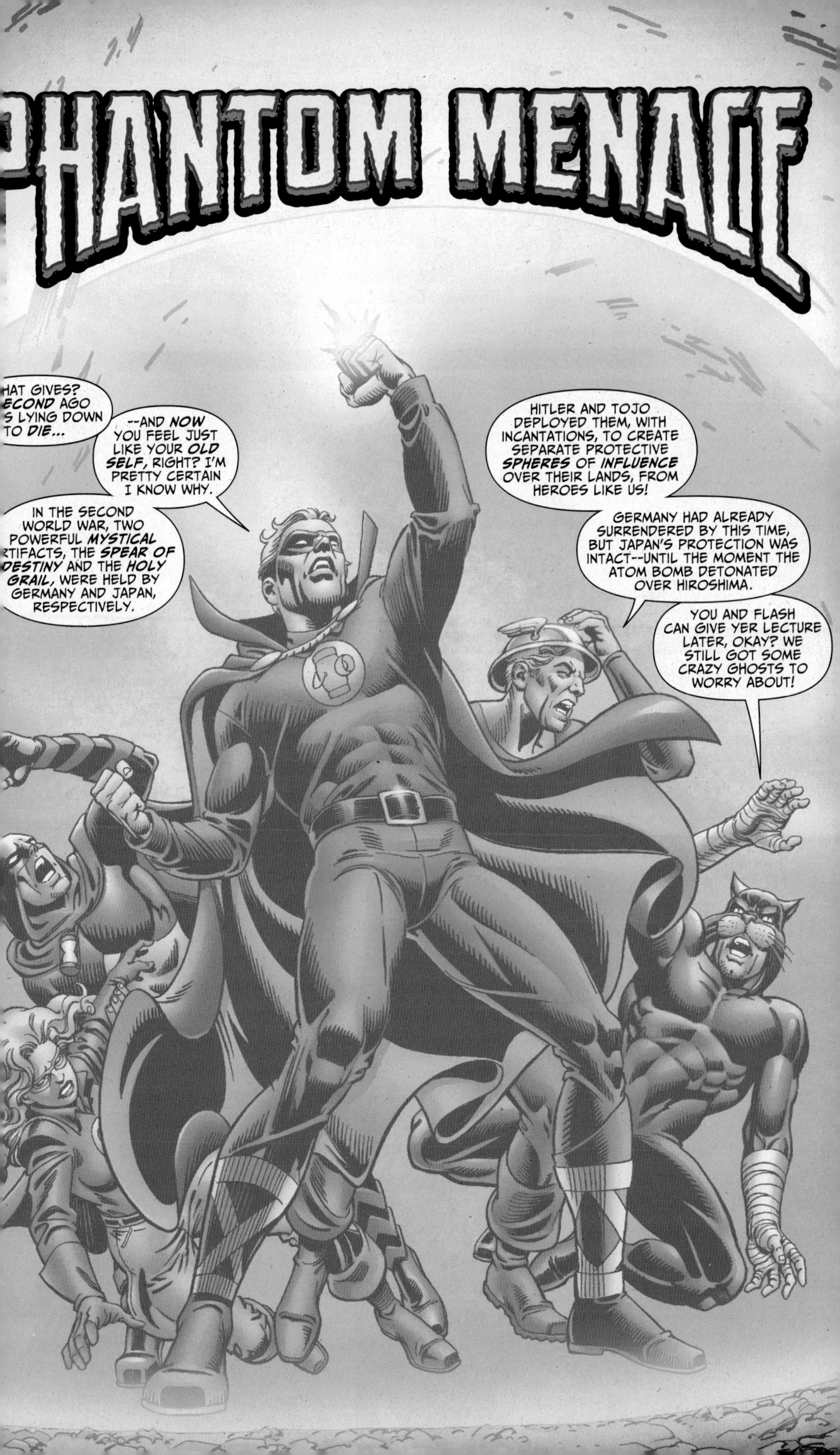
PHANTOM MENACE
HAT GIVES? ECOND AGO S LYING DOWN TO DIE...
--AND NOW YOU FEEL JUST LIKE YOUR OLD SELF, RIGHT? I'M PRETTY CERTAIN I KNOW WHY.
IN THE SECOND WORLD WAR, TWO POWERFUL MYSTICAL RTIFACTS, THE SPEAR OF DESTINY AND THE HOLY GRAIL, WERE HELD BY GERMANY AND JAPAN, RESPECTIVELY.
HITLER AND TOJO DEPLOYED THEM, WITH INCANTATIONS, TO CREATE SEPARATE PROTECTIVE SPHERES OF INFLUENCE OVER THEIR LANDS, FROM HEROES LIKE US!
GERMANY HAD ALREADY SURRENDERED BY THIS TIME, BUT JAPAN'S PROTECTION WAS INTACT--UNTIL THE MOMENT THE ATOM BOMB DETONATED OVER HIROSHIMA.
YOU AND FLASH CAN GIVE YER LECTURE LATER, OKAY? WE STILL GOT SOME CRAZY GHOSTS TO WORRY ABOUT!

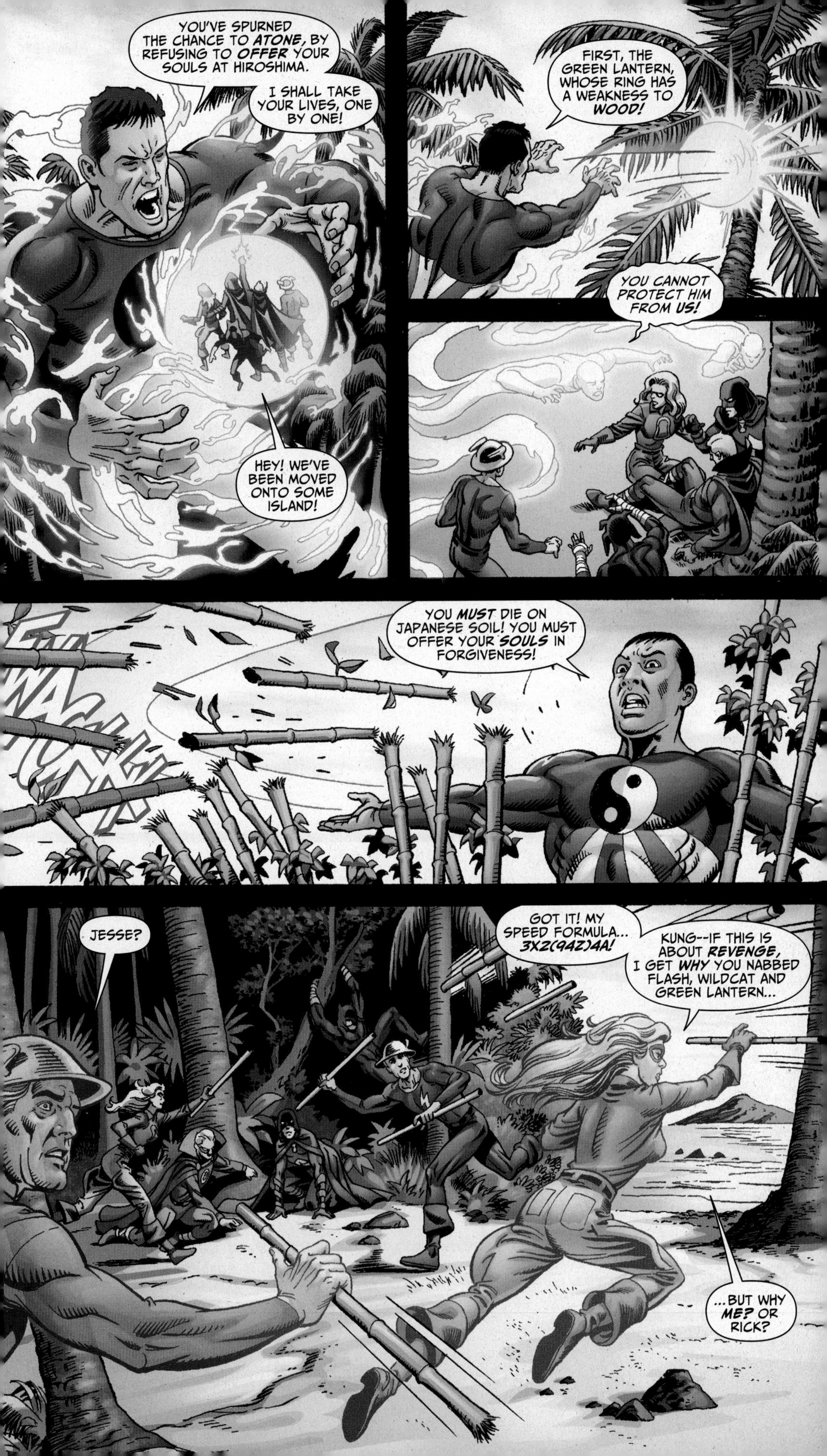
YOU'VE SPURNED THE CHANCE TO ATONE, BY REFUSING TO OFFER YOUR SOULS AT HIROSHIMA.
I SHALL TAKE YOUR LIVES, ONE BY ONE!
HEY! WE'VE BEEN MOVED ONTO SOME ISLAND!
FIRST, THE GREEN LANTERN, WHOSE RING HAS A WEAKNESS TO WOOD!
YOU CANNOT PROTECT HIM FROM US!
YOU MUST DIE ON JAPANESE SOIL! YOU MUST OFFER YOUR SOULS IN FORGIVENESS!
JESSE?
GOT IT! MY SPEED FORMULA... 3X2(9YZ)4A!
KUNG--IF THIS IS ABOUT REVENGE, I GET WHY YOU NABBED FLASH, WILDCAT AND GREEN LANTERN...
...BUT WHY ME? OR RICK?

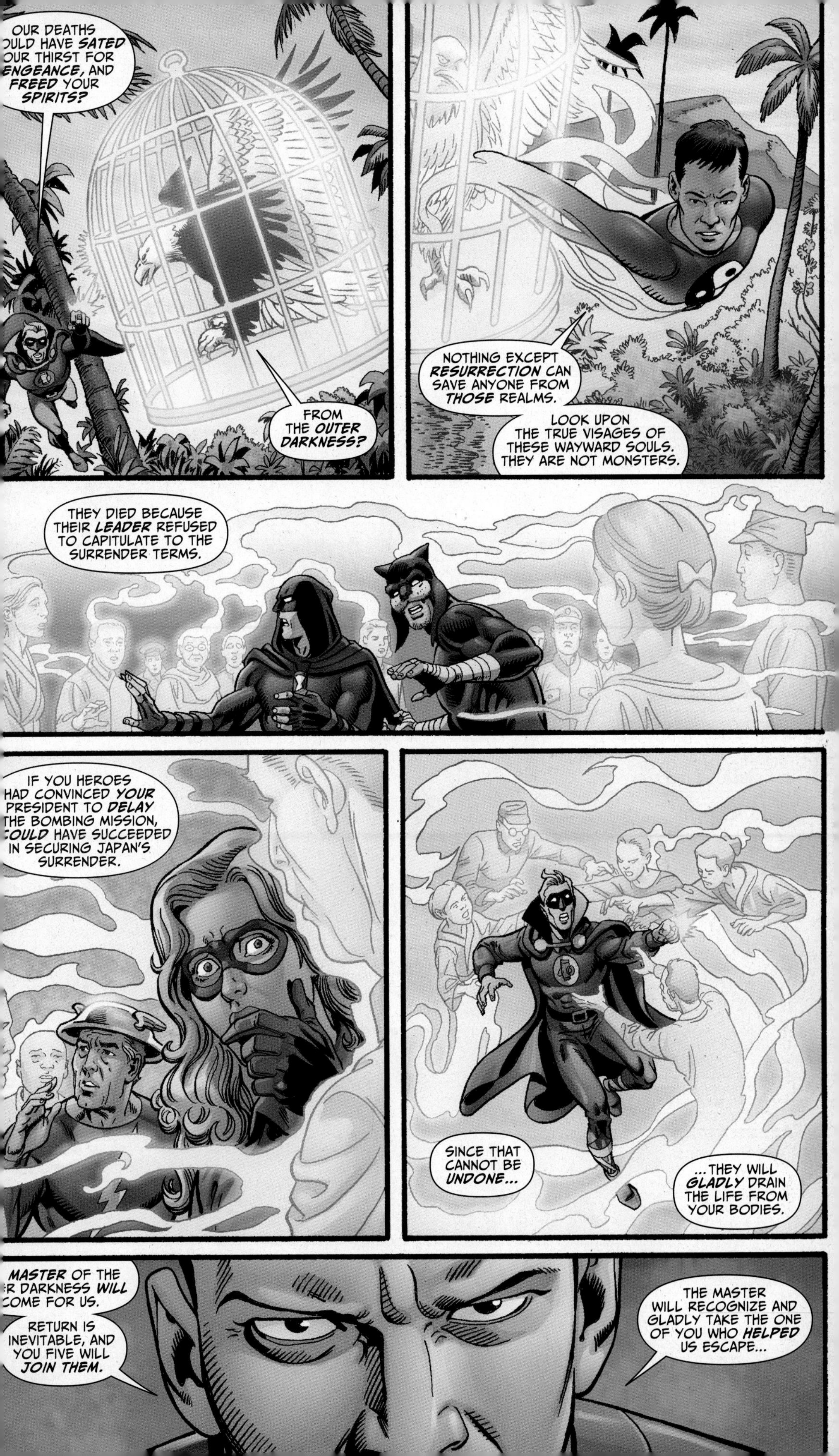

OUR DEATHS OULD HAVE SATED OUR THIRST FOR ENGEANCE, AND FREED YOUR SPIRITS?
FROM THE OUTER DARKNESS?
NOTHING EXCEPT RESURRECTION CAN SAVE ANYONE FROM THOSE REALMS.
LOOK UPON THE TRUE VISAGES OF THESE WAYWARD SOULS. THEY ARE NOT MONSTERS.
THEY DIED BECAUSE THEIR LEADER REFUSED TO CAPITULATE TO THE SURRENDER TERMS.
IF YOU HEROES HAD CONVINCED YOUR PRESIDENT TO DELAY THE BOMBING MISSION, COULD HAVE SUCCEEDED IN SECURING JAPAN'S SURRENDER.
SINCE THAT CANNOT BE UNDONE...
...THEY WILL GLADLY DRAIN THE LIFE FROM YOUR BODIES.
MASTER OF THE R DARKNESS WILL COME FOR US.
RETURN IS INEVITABLE, AND YOU FIVE WILL JOIN THEM.
THE MASTER WILL RECOGNIZE AND GLADLY TAKE THE ONE OF YOU WHO HELPED US ESCAPE...

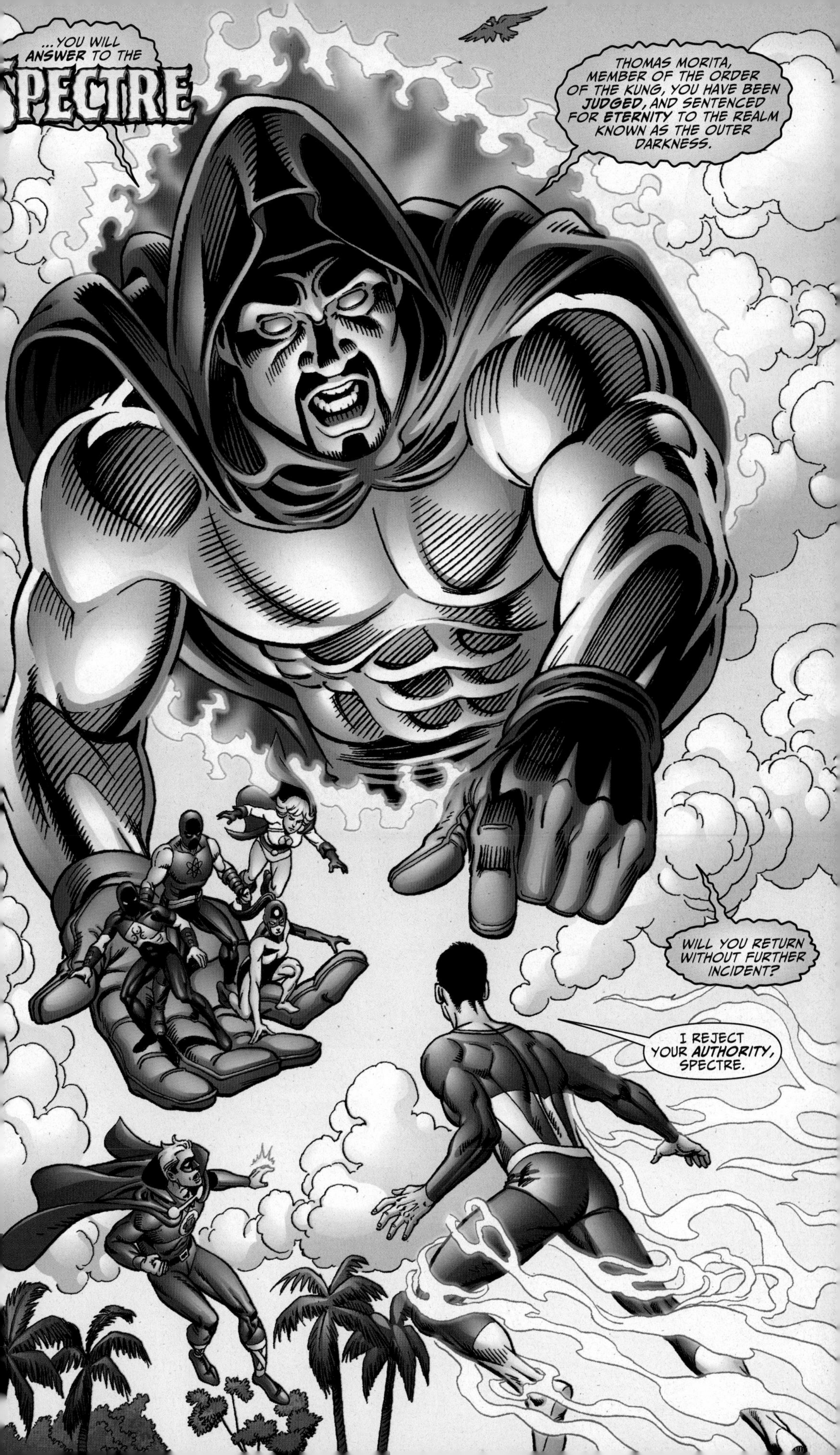
...YOU WILL ANSWER TO THE
SPECTRE
THOMAS MORITA, MEMBER OF THE ORDER OF THE KUNG, YOU HAVE BEEN JUDGED, AND SENTENCED FOR ETERNITY TO THE REALM KNOWN AS THE OUTER DARKNESS.
WILL YOU RETURN WITHOUT FURTHER INCIDENT?
I REJECT YOUR AUTHORITY, SPECTRE.

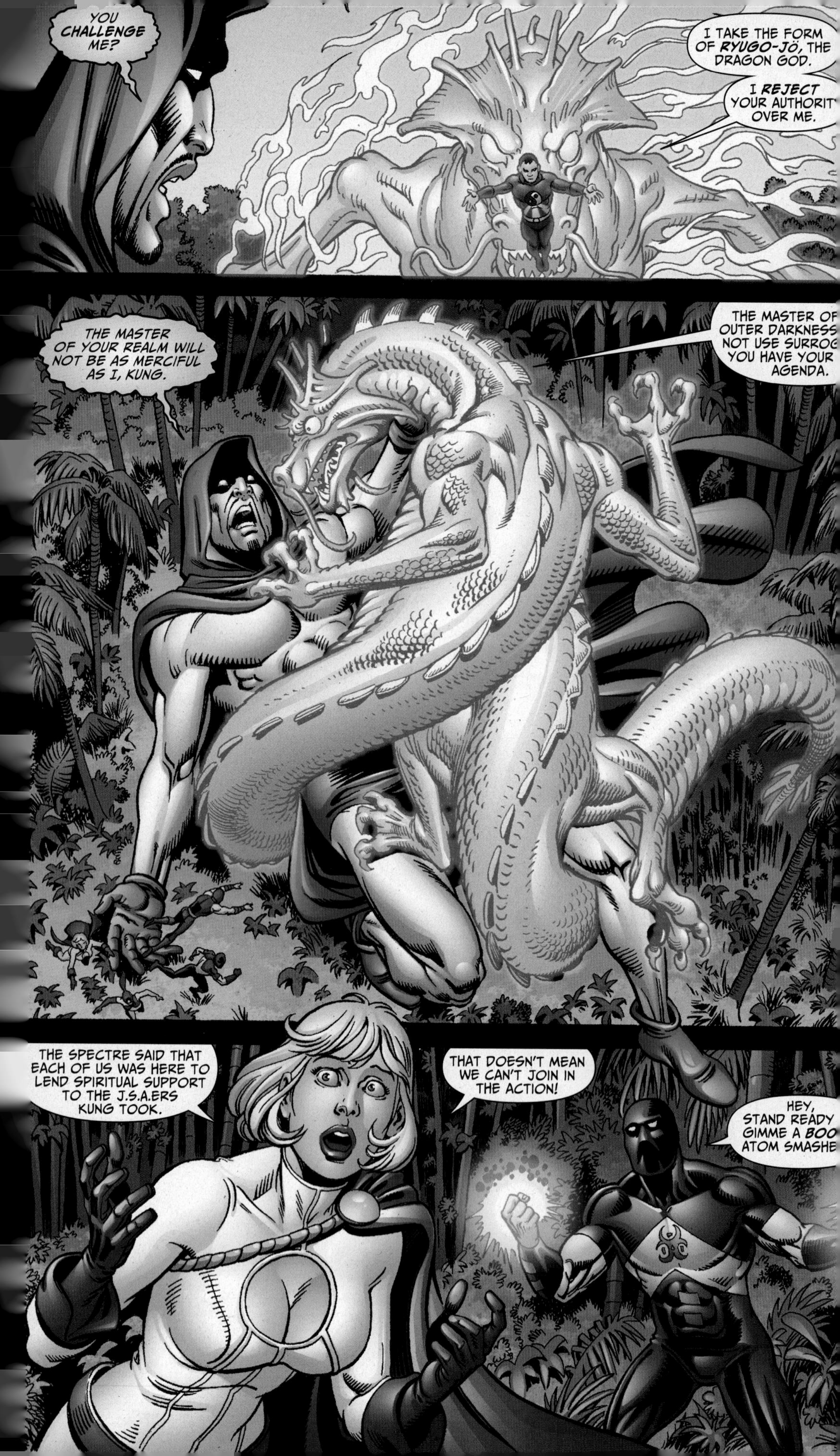
YOU CHALLENGE ME?
I TAKE THE FORM OF RYUGO-JÖ, THE DRAGON GOD.
I REJECT YOUR AUTHORIT OVER ME.
THE MASTER OF YOUR REALM WILL NOT BE AS MERCIFUL AS I, KUNG.
THE MASTER OF OUTER DARKNESS NOT USE SURROG YOU HAVE YOUR AGENDA.
THE SPECTRE SAID THAT EACH OF US WAS HERE TO LEND SPIRITUAL SUPPORT TO THE J.S.A.ERS KUNG TOOK.
THAT DOESN'T MEAN WE CAN'T JOIN IN THE ACTION!
HEY, STAND READY GIMME A BOO ATOM SMASHE

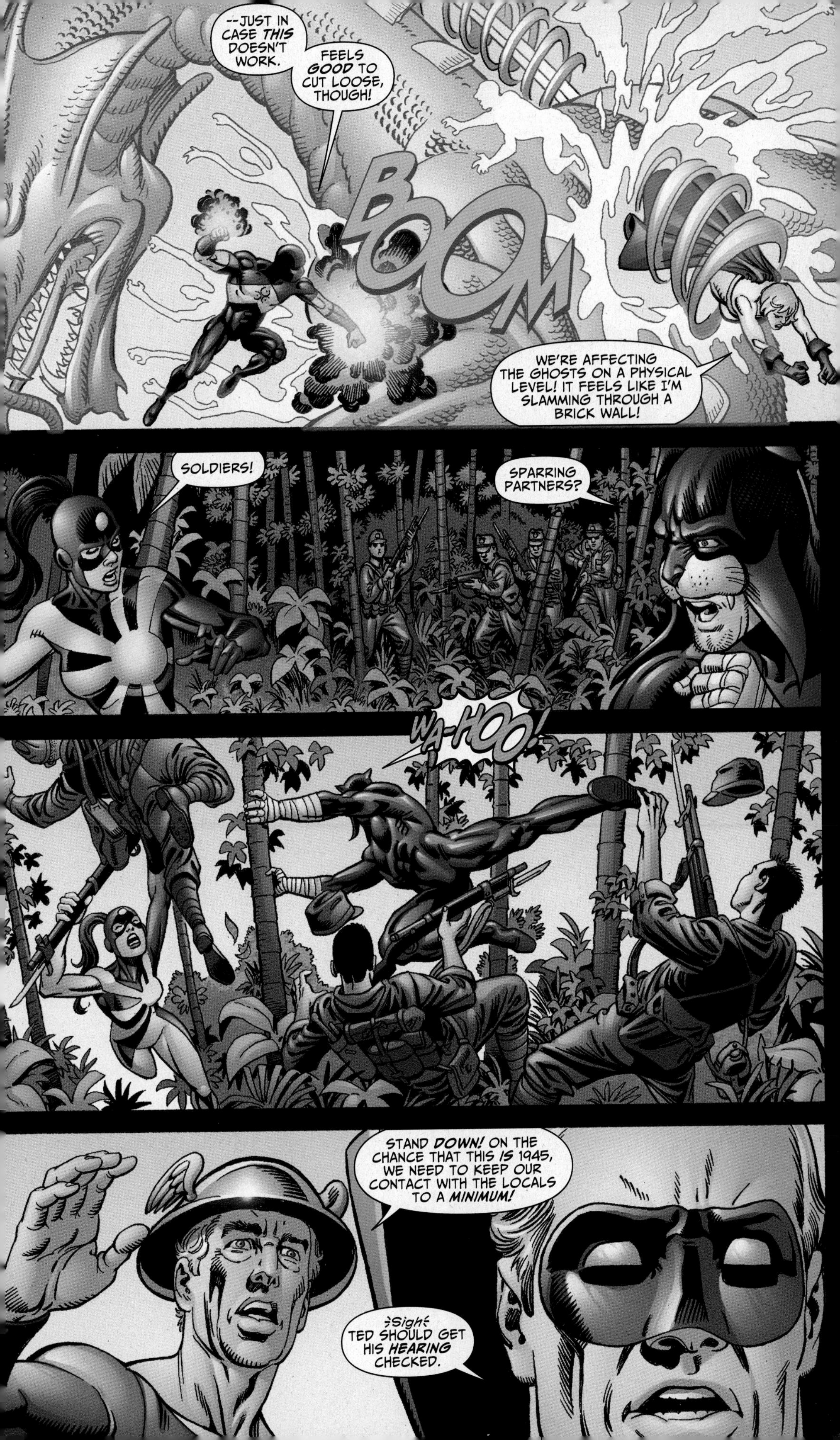
--JUST IN CASE *THIS* DOESN'T WORK.
FEELS *GOOD* TO CUT LOOSE, THOUGH!
BOOM
WE'RE AFFECTING THE GHOSTS ON A PHYSICAL LEVEL! IT FEELS LIKE I'M SLAMMING THROUGH A BRICK WALL!
SOLDIERS!
SPARRING PARTNERS?
WA-HOO!
STAND *DOWN!* ON THE CHANCE THAT THIS *IS* 1945, WE NEED TO KEEP OUR CONTACT WITH THE LOCALS TO A *MINIMUM!*
Sigh TED SHOULD GET HIS *HEARING* CHECKED.

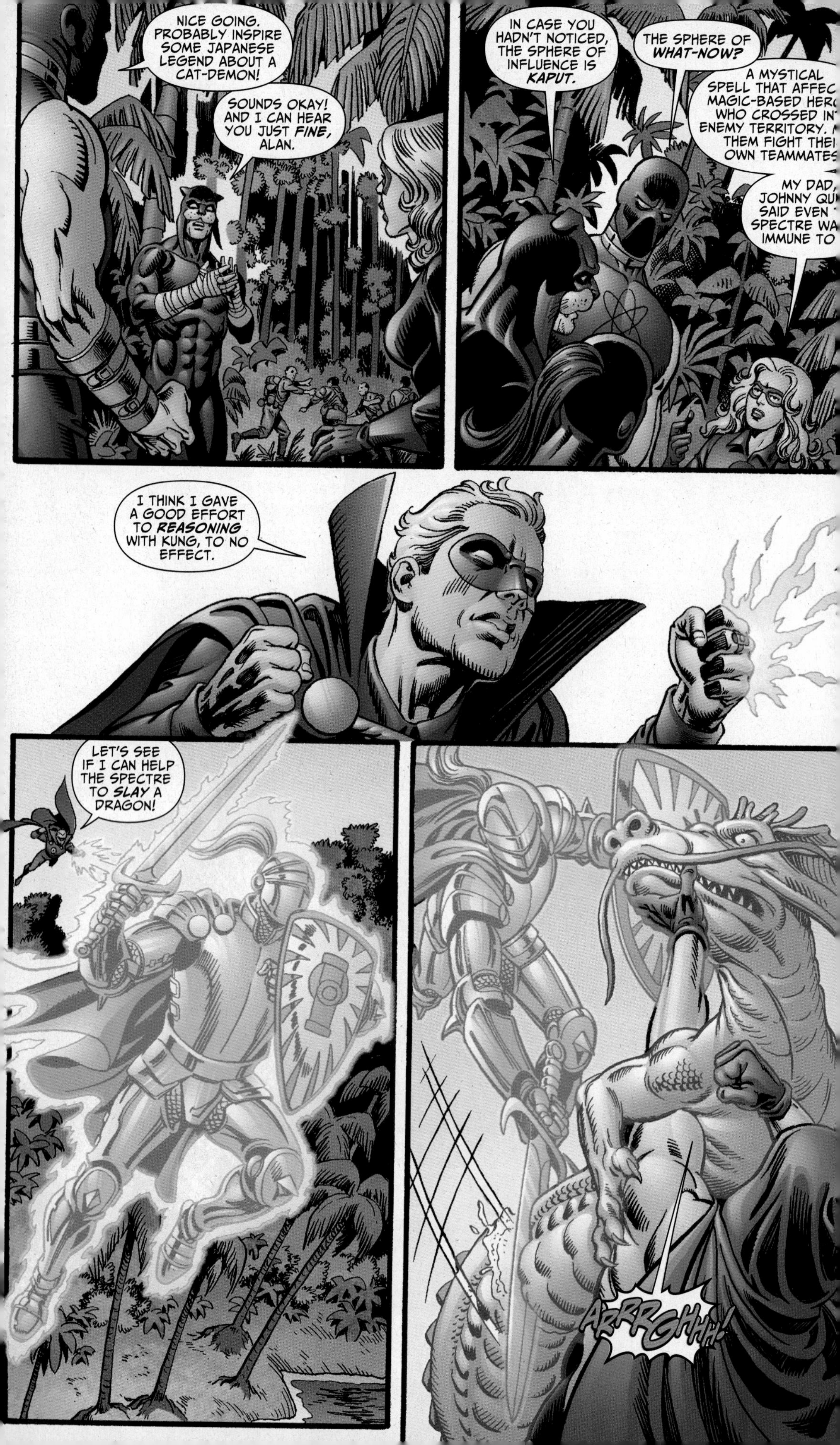

NICE GOING. PROBABLY INSPIRE SOME JAPANESE LEGEND ABOUT A CAT-DEMON!
SOUNDS OKAY! AND I CAN HEAR YOU JUST FINE, ALAN.
IN CASE YOU HADN'T NOTICED, THE SPHERE OF INFLUENCE IS KAPUT.
THE SPHERE OF WHAT-NOW?
A MYSTICAL SPELL THAT AFFEC MAGIC-BASED HERO WHO CROSSED IN ENEMY TERRITORY. A THEM FIGHT THEI OWN TEAMMATES
MY DAD, JOHNNY QU SAID EVEN SPECTRE WA IMMUNE TO
I THINK I GAVE A GOOD EFFORT TO REASONING WITH KUNG, TO NO EFFECT.
LET'S SEE IF I CAN HELP THE SPECTRE TO SLAY A DRAGON!
ARRRGHHH!

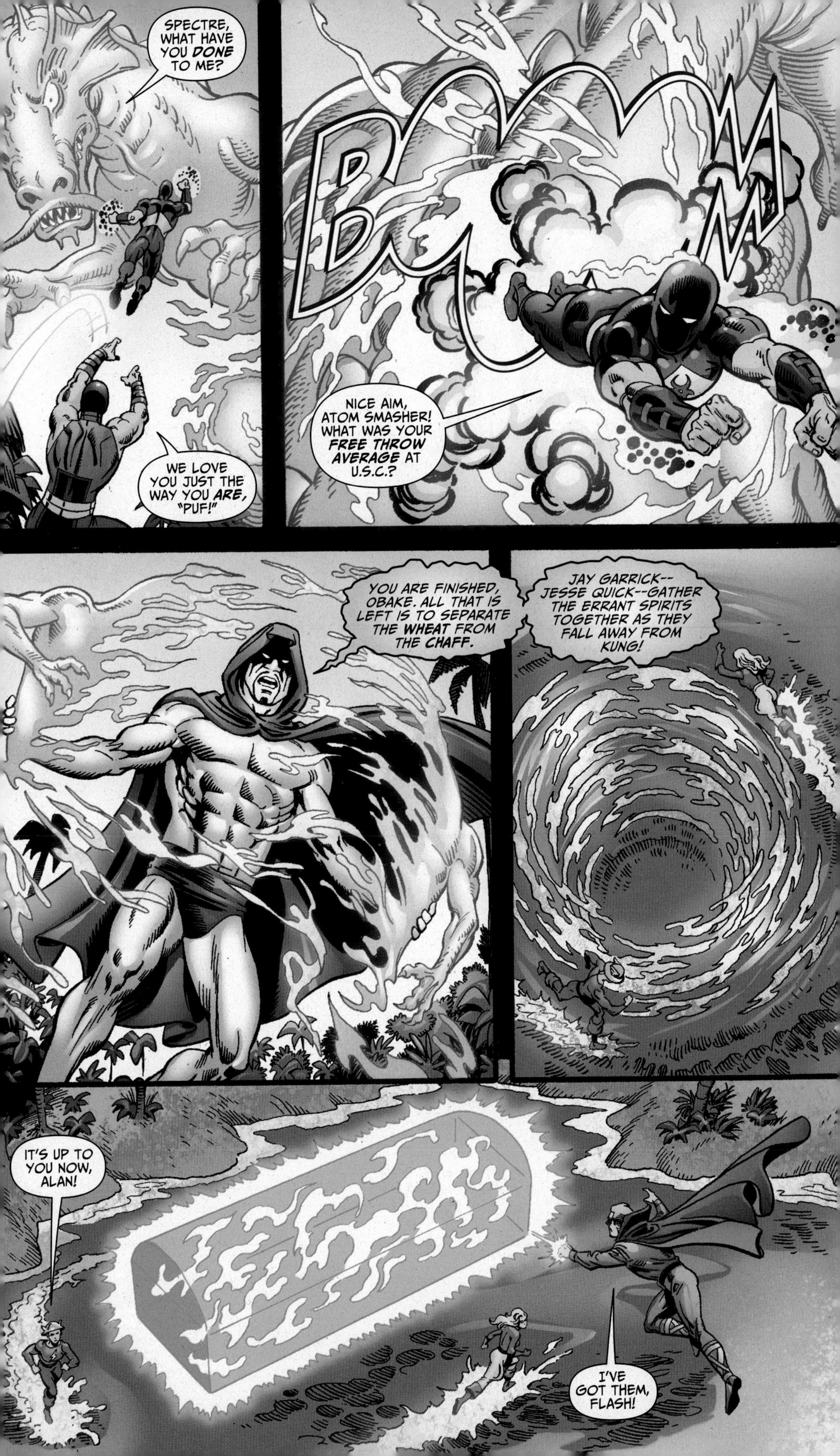
SPECTRE, WHAT HAVE YOU *DONE* TO ME?
WE LOVE YOU JUST THE WAY YOU *ARE*, "PUF!"
BOOM
NICE AIM, ATOM SMASHER! WHAT WAS YOUR *FREE THROW AVERAGE* AT U.S.C.?
YOU ARE FINISHED, OBAKE. ALL THAT IS LEFT IS TO SEPARATE THE *WHEAT* FROM THE *CHAFF.*
JAY GARRICK-- JESSE QUICK--GATHER THE ERRANT SPIRITS TOGETHER AS THEY FALL AWAY FROM KUNG!
IT'S UP TO YOU NOW, ALAN!
I'VE GOT THEM, FLASH!

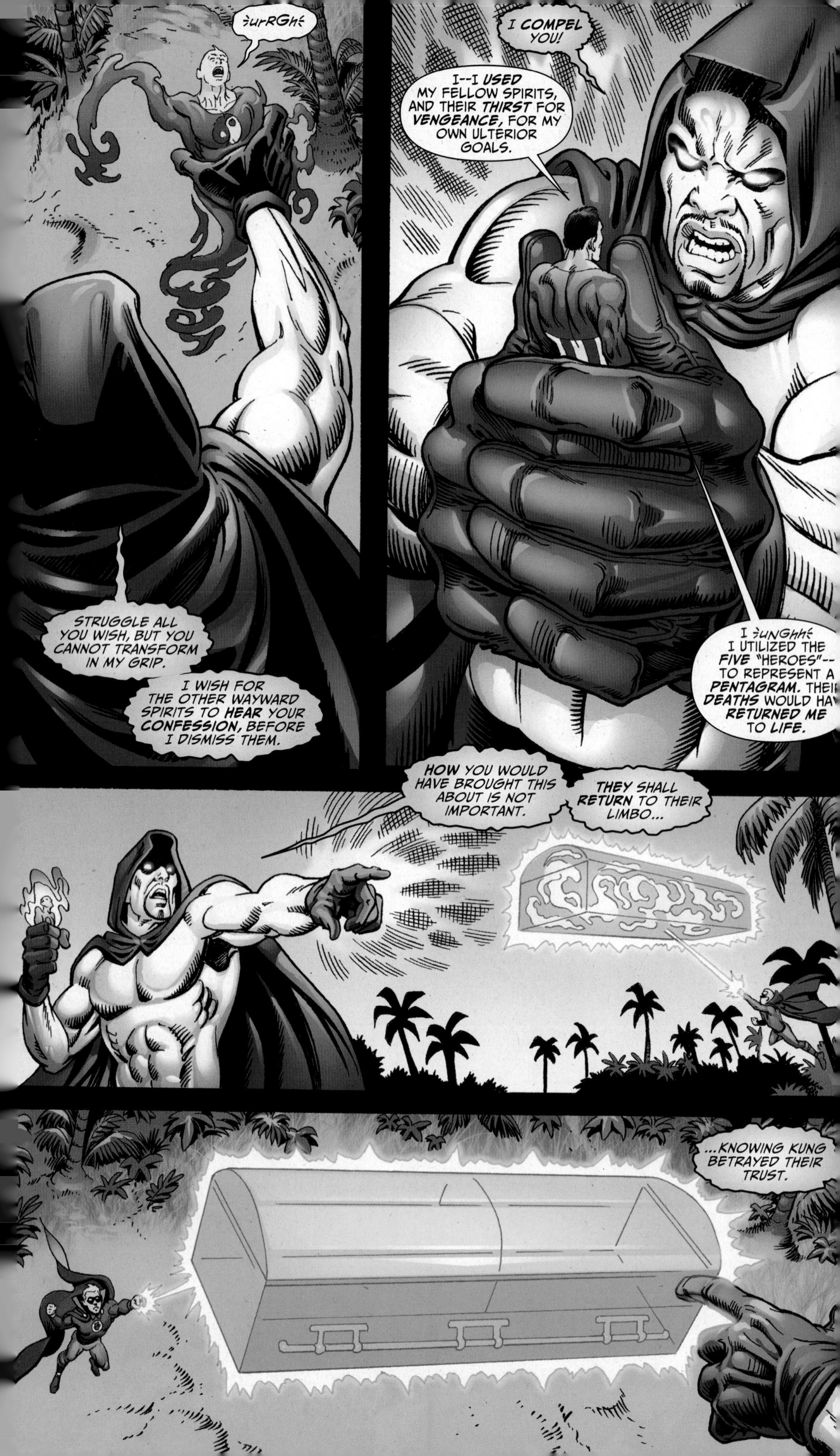

urRGh
STRUGGLE ALL YOU WISH, BUT YOU CANNOT TRANSFORM IN MY GRIP.
I WISH FOR THE OTHER WAYWARD SPIRITS TO HEAR YOUR CONFESSION, BEFORE I DISMISS THEM.
I COMPEL YOU!
I--I USED MY FELLOW SPIRITS, AND THEIR THIRST FOR VENGEANCE, FOR MY OWN ULTERIOR GOALS.
I UNGHH I UTILIZED THE FIVE "HEROES"-- TO REPRESENT A PENTAGRAM. THEI DEATHS WOULD HA RETURNED ME TO LIFE.
HOW YOU WOULD HAVE BROUGHT THIS ABOUT IS NOT IMPORTANT.
THEY SHALL RETURN TO THEIR LIMBO...
...KNOWING KUNG BETRAYED THEIR TRUST.

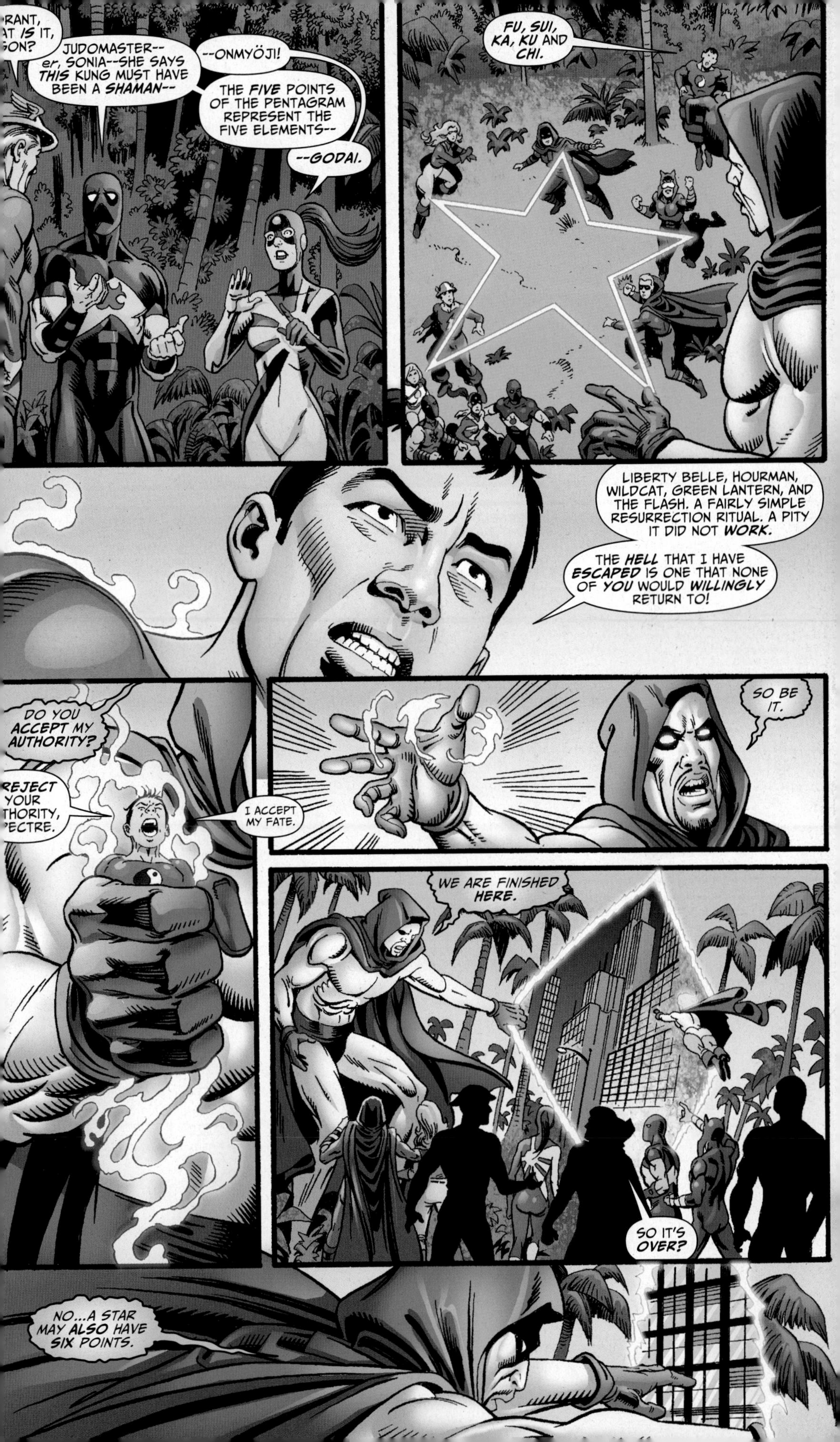

RANT,
AT IS IT,
GON?
JUDOMASTER--
er, SONIA--SHE SAYS THIS KUNG MUST HAVE BEEN A SHAMAN--
--ONMYŌJI!
THE FIVE POINTS OF THE PENTAGRAM REPRESENT THE FIVE ELEMENTS--
--GODAI.
FU, SUI, KA, KU AND CHI.
LIBERTY BELLE, HOURMAN, WILDCAT, GREEN LANTERN, AND THE FLASH. A FAIRLY SIMPLE RESURRECTION RITUAL. A PITY IT DID NOT WORK.
THE HELL THAT I HAVE ESCAPED IS ONE THAT NONE OF YOU WOULD WILLINGLY RETURN TO!
DO YOU ACCEPT MY AUTHORITY?
REJECT YOUR THORITY, PECTRE.
I ACCEPT MY FATE.
SO BE IT.
WE ARE FINISHED HERE.
SO IT'S OVER?
NO...A STAR MAY ALSO HAVE SIX POINTS.

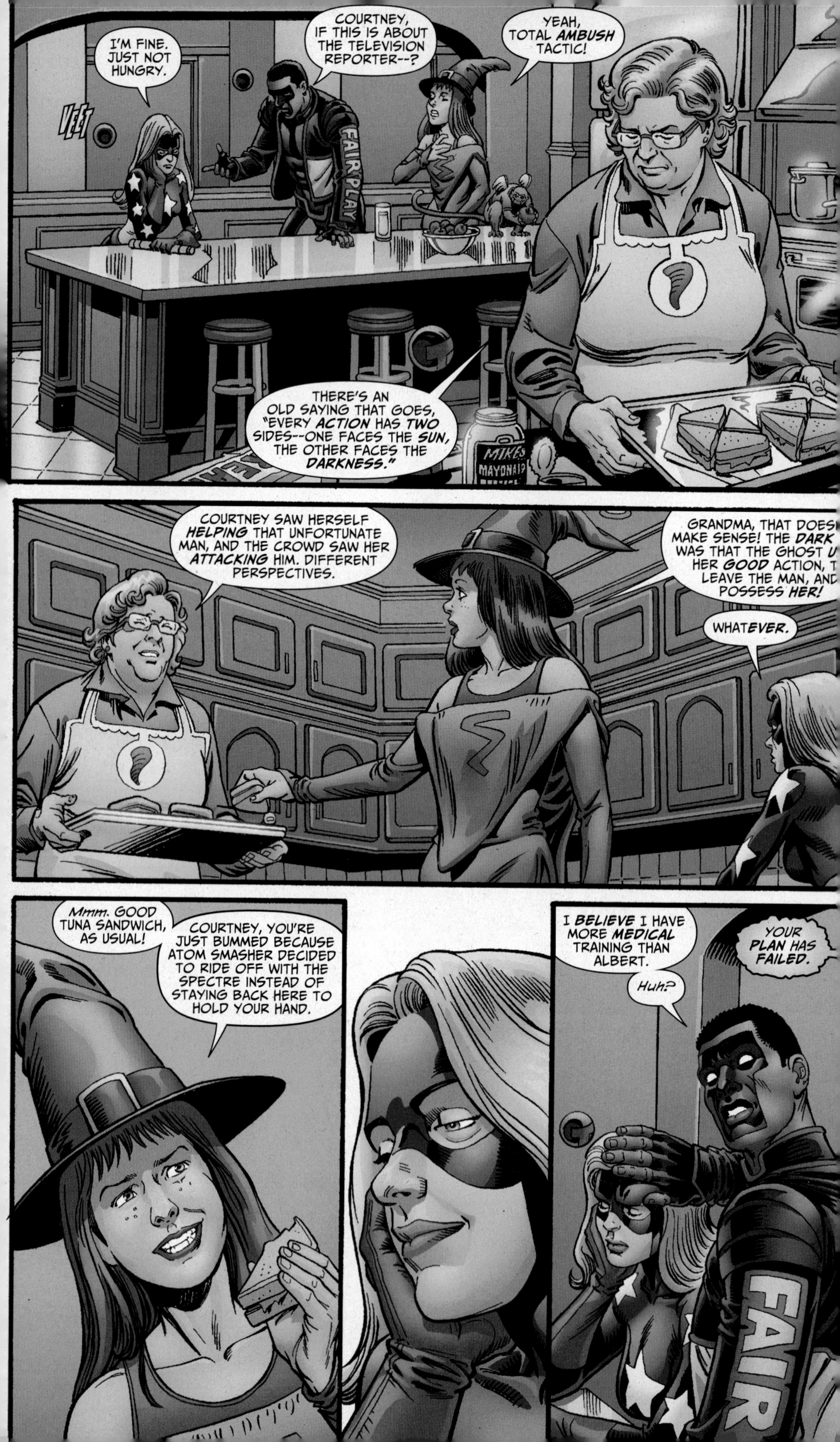
I'M FINE. JUST NOT HUNGRY.
VEET
COURTNEY, IF THIS IS ABOUT THE TELEVISION REPORTER--?
YEAH, TOTAL AMBUSH TACTIC!
FAIRPLAY
THERE'S AN OLD SAYING THAT GOES, "EVERY ACTION HAS TWO SIDES--ONE FACES THE SUN, THE OTHER FACES THE DARKNESS."
COURTNEY SAW HERSELF HELPING THAT UNFORTUNATE MAN, AND THE CROWD SAW HER ATTACKING HIM. DIFFERENT PERSPECTIVES.
WHATEVER.
Mmm. GOOD TUNA SANDWICH, AS USUAL!
COURTNEY, YOU'RE JUST BUMMED BECAUSE ATOM SMASHER DECIDED TO RIDE OFF WITH THE SPECTRE INSTEAD OF STAYING BACK HERE TO HOLD YOUR HAND.
I BELIEVE I HAVE MORE MEDICAL TRAINING THAN ALBERT.
Huh?
YOUR PLAN HAS FAILED.
FAIR

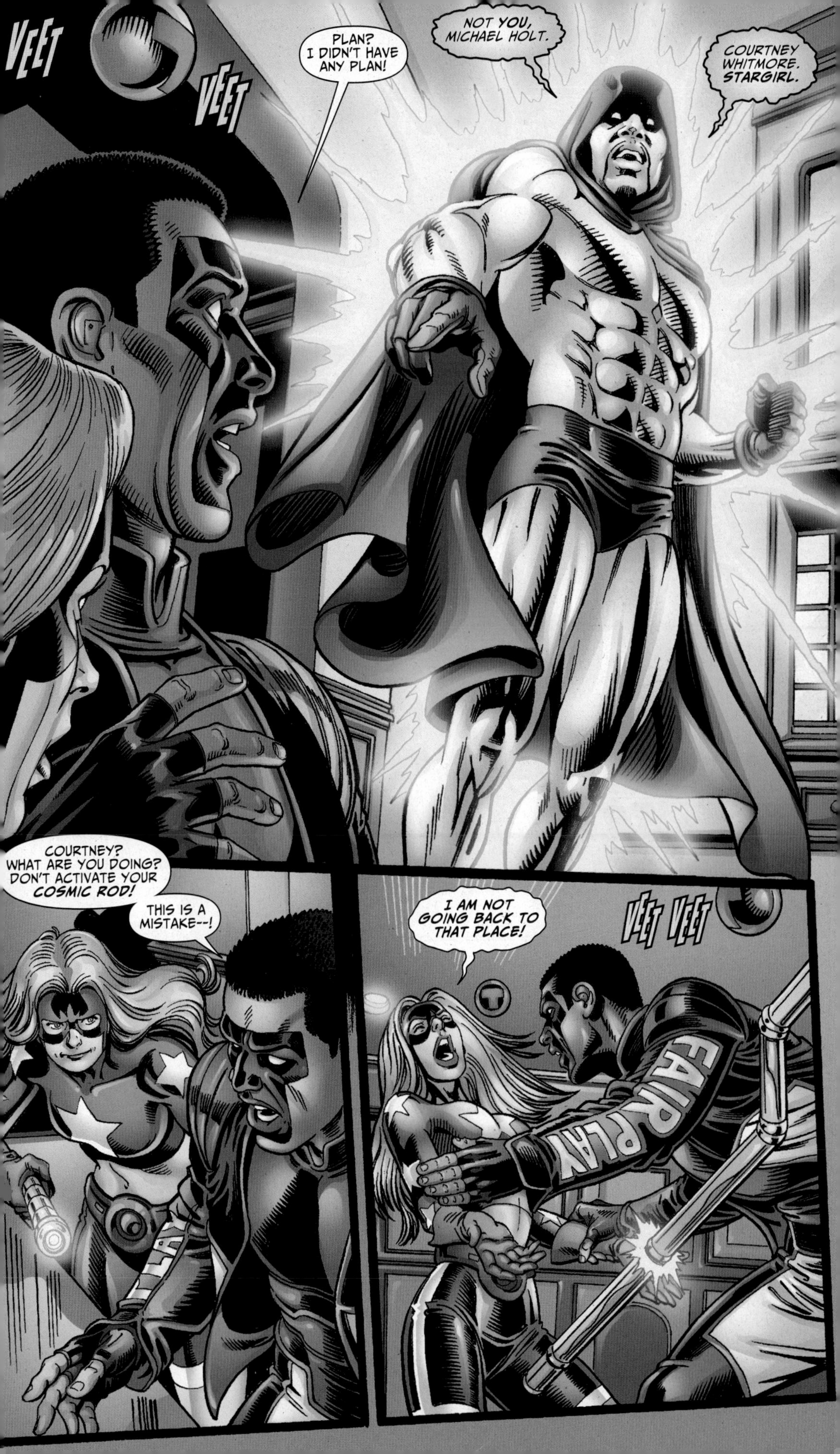
VEET
VEET
PLAN? I DIDN'T HAVE ANY PLAN!
NOT YOU, MICHAEL HOLT.
COURTNEY WHITMORE. STARGIRL.
COURTNEY? WHAT ARE YOU DOING? DON'T ACTIVATE YOUR COSMIC ROD!
THIS IS A MISTAKE--!
I AM NOT GOING BACK TO THAT PLACE!
VEET VEET
FAIR PLAY

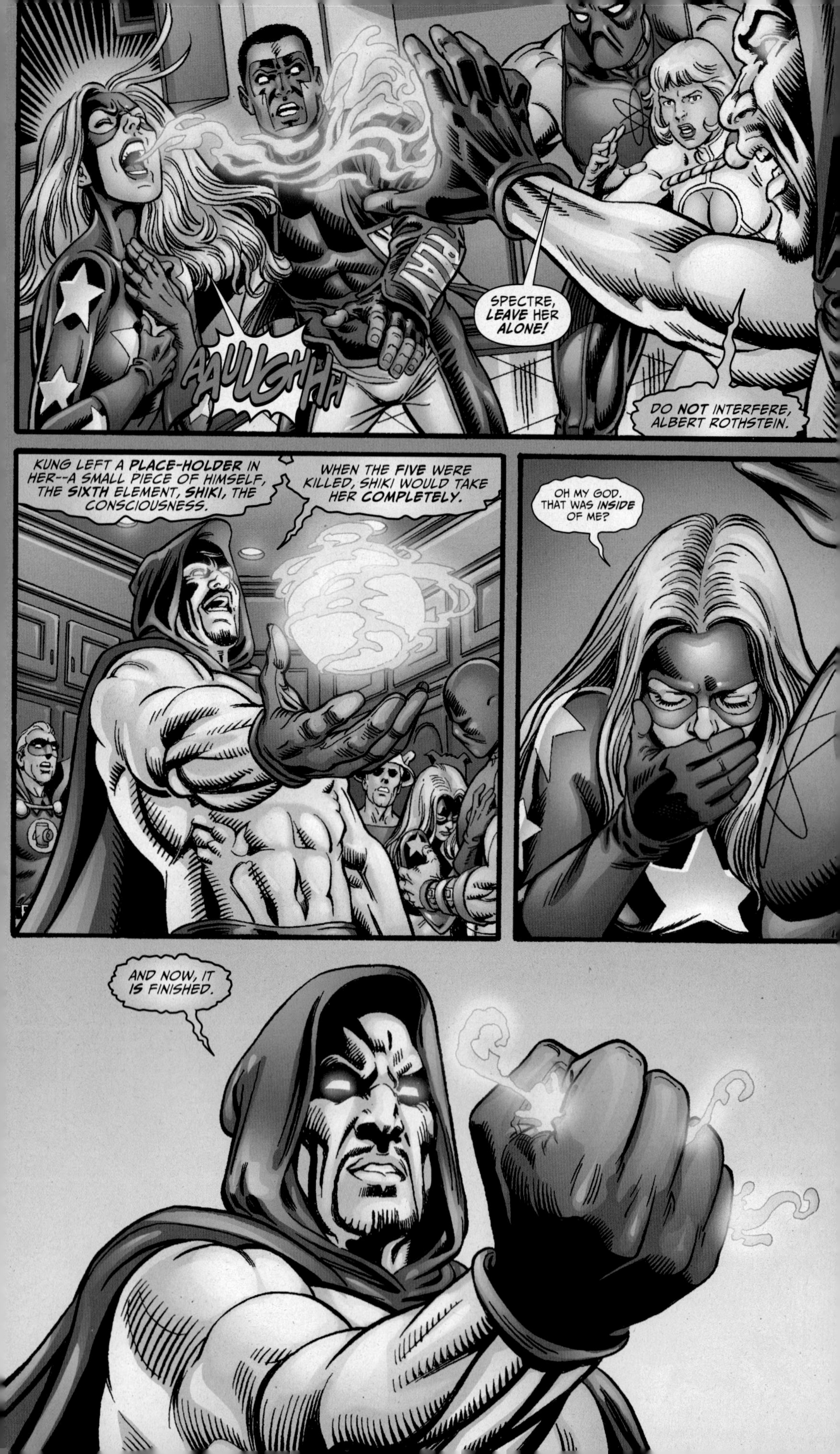
AAUUGHHH
SPECTRE, LEAVE HER ALONE!
DO NOT INTERFERE, ALBERT ROTHSTEIN.
KUNG LEFT A PLACE-HOLDER IN HER--A SMALL PIECE OF HIMSELF, THE SIXTH ELEMENT, SHIKI, THE CONSCIOUSNESS.
WHEN THE FIVE WERE KILLED, SHIKI WOULD TAKE HER COMPLETELY.
OH MY GOD. THAT WAS INSIDE OF ME?
AND NOW, IT IS FINISHED.

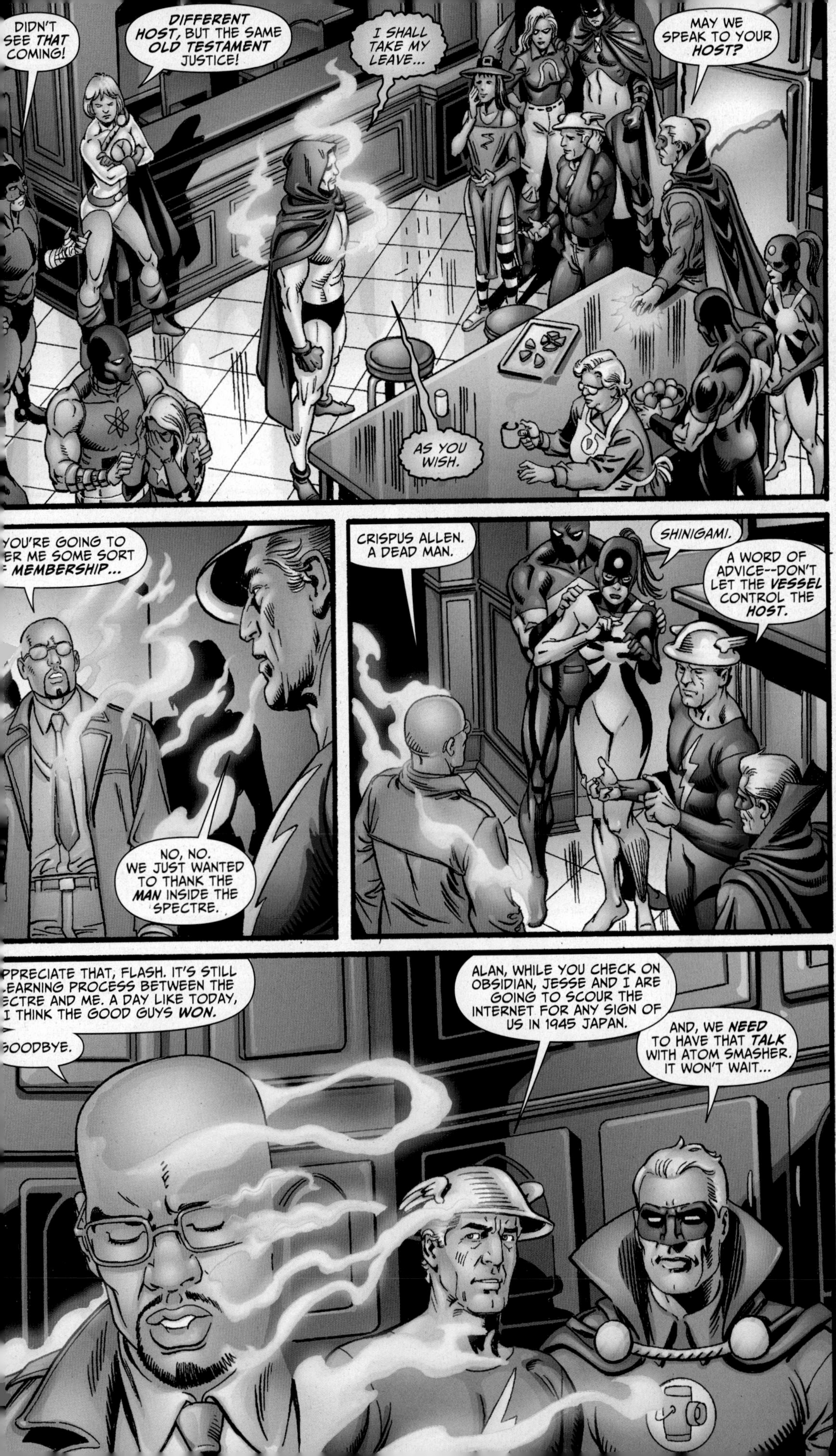
DIDN'T SEE THAT COMING!
DIFFERENT HOST, BUT THE SAME OLD TESTAMENT JUSTICE!
I SHALL TAKE MY LEAVE...
MAY WE SPEAK TO YOUR HOST?
AS YOU WISH.
YOU'RE GOING TO ER ME SOME SORT F MEMBERSHIP...
NO, NO. WE JUST WANTED TO THANK THE MAN INSIDE THE SPECTRE.
CRISPUS ALLEN. A DEAD MAN.
SHINIGAMI.
A WORD OF ADVICE--DON'T LET THE VESSEL CONTROL THE HOST.
PPRECIATE THAT, FLASH. IT'S STILL EARNING PROCESS BETWEEN THE ECTRE AND ME. A DAY LIKE TODAY, I THINK THE GOOD GUYS WON.
OODBYE.
ALAN, WHILE YOU CHECK ON OBSIDIAN, JESSE AND I ARE GOING TO SCOUR THE INTERNET FOR ANY SIGN OF US IN 1945 JAPAN.
AND, WE NEED TO HAVE THAT TALK WITH ATOM SMASHER. IT WON'T WAIT...

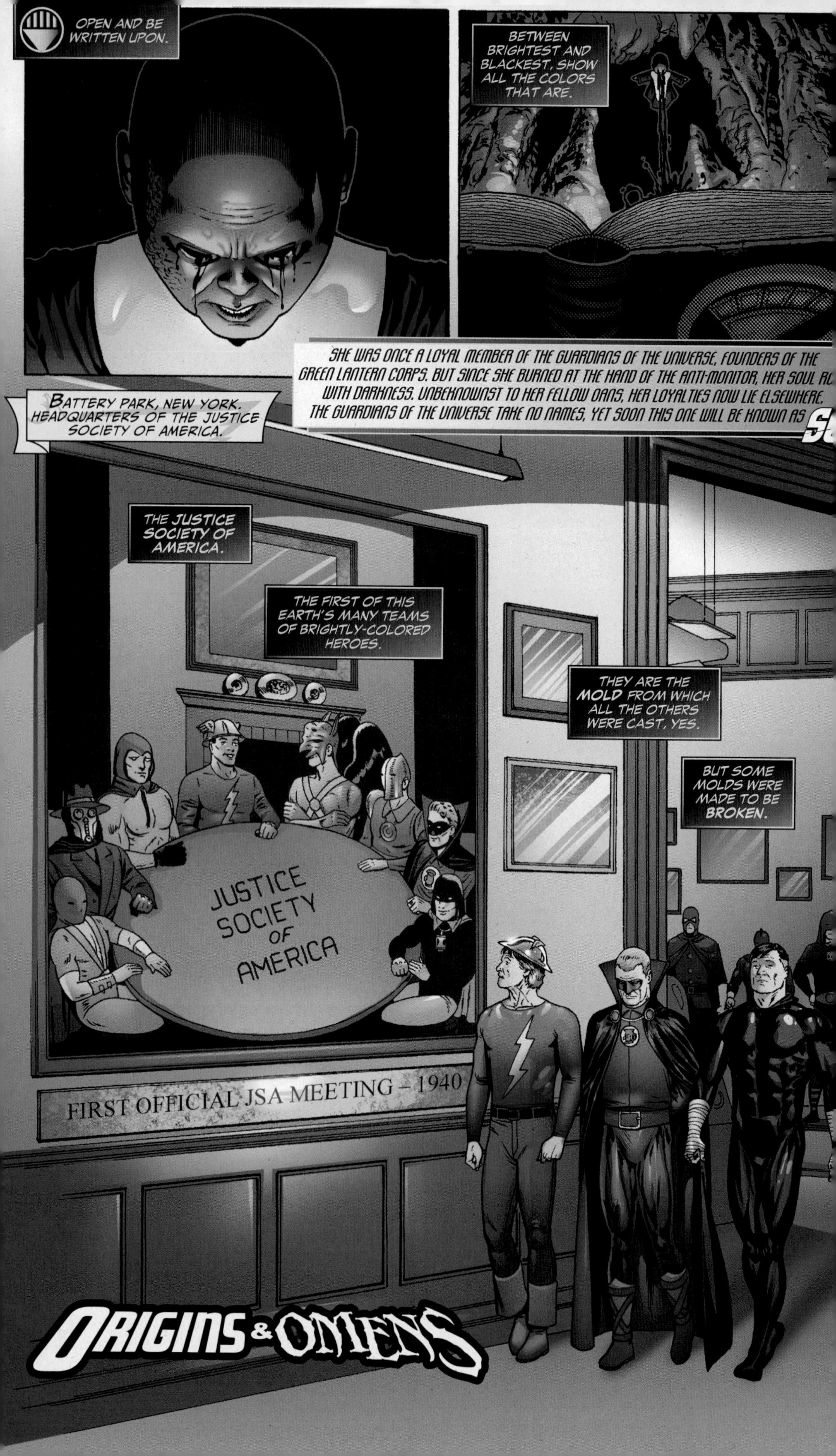
OPEN AND BE WRITTEN UPON.
BETWEEN BRIGHTEST AND BLACKEST, SHOW ALL THE COLORS THAT ARE.
SHE WAS ONCE A LOYAL MEMBER OF THE GUARDIANS OF THE UNIVERSE, FOUNDERS OF THE GREEN LANTERN CORPS. BUT SINCE SHE BURNED AT THE HAND OF THE ANTI-MONITOR, HER SOUL
WITH DARKNESS. UNBEKNOWNST TO HER FELLOW OANS, HER LOYALTIES NOW LIE ELSEWHERE. THE GUARDIANS OF THE UNIVERSE TAKE NO NAMES, YET SOON THIS ONE WILL BE KNOWN AS
BATTERY PARK, NEW YORK. HEADQUARTERS OF THE JUSTICE SOCIETY OF AMERICA.
THE JUSTICE SOCIETY OF AMERICA.
THE FIRST OF THIS EARTH'S MANY TEAMS OF BRIGHTLY-COLORED HEROES.
THEY ARE THE MOLD FROM WHICH ALL THE OTHERS WERE CAST, YES.
BUT SOME MOLDS WERE MADE TO BE BROKEN.
JUSTICE SOCIETY OF AMERICA
FIRST OFFICIAL JSA MEETING – 1940
ORIGINS & OMENS

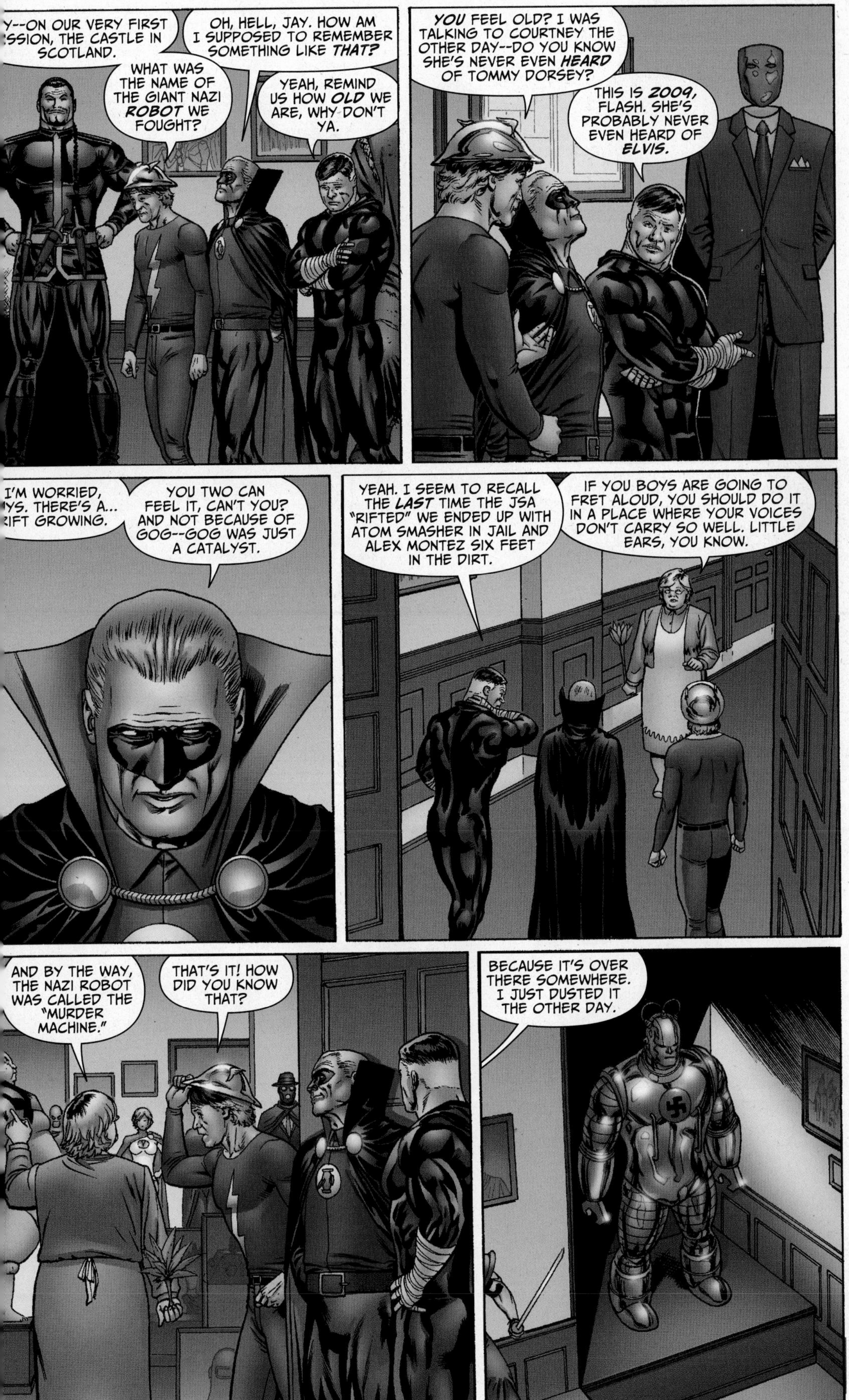
Y--ON OUR VERY FIRST
SSION, THE CASTLE IN SCOTLAND.
WHAT WAS THE NAME OF THE GIANT NAZI ROBOT WE FOUGHT?
OH, HELL, JAY. HOW AM I SUPPOSED TO REMEMBER SOMETHING LIKE THAT?
YEAH, REMIND US HOW OLD WE ARE, WHY DON'T YA.
YOU FEEL OLD? I WAS TALKING TO COURTNEY THE OTHER DAY--DO YOU KNOW SHE'S NEVER EVEN HEARD OF TOMMY DORSEY?
THIS IS 2009, FLASH. SHE'S PROBABLY NEVER EVEN HEARD OF ELVIS.
I'M WORRIED, YS. THERE'S A... RIFT GROWING.
YOU TWO CAN FEEL IT, CAN'T YOU? AND NOT BECAUSE OF GOG--GOG WAS JUST A CATALYST.
YEAH. I SEEM TO RECALL THE LAST TIME THE JSA "RIFTED" WE ENDED UP WITH ATOM SMASHER IN JAIL AND ALEX MONTEZ SIX FEET IN THE DIRT.
IF YOU BOYS ARE GOING TO FRET ALOUD, YOU SHOULD DO IT IN A PLACE WHERE YOUR VOICES DON'T CARRY SO WELL. LITTLE EARS, YOU KNOW.
AND BY THE WAY, THE NAZI ROBOT WAS CALLED THE "MURDER MACHINE."
THAT'S IT! HOW DID YOU KNOW THAT?
BECAUSE IT'S OVER THERE SOMEWHERE. I JUST DUSTED IT THE OTHER DAY.

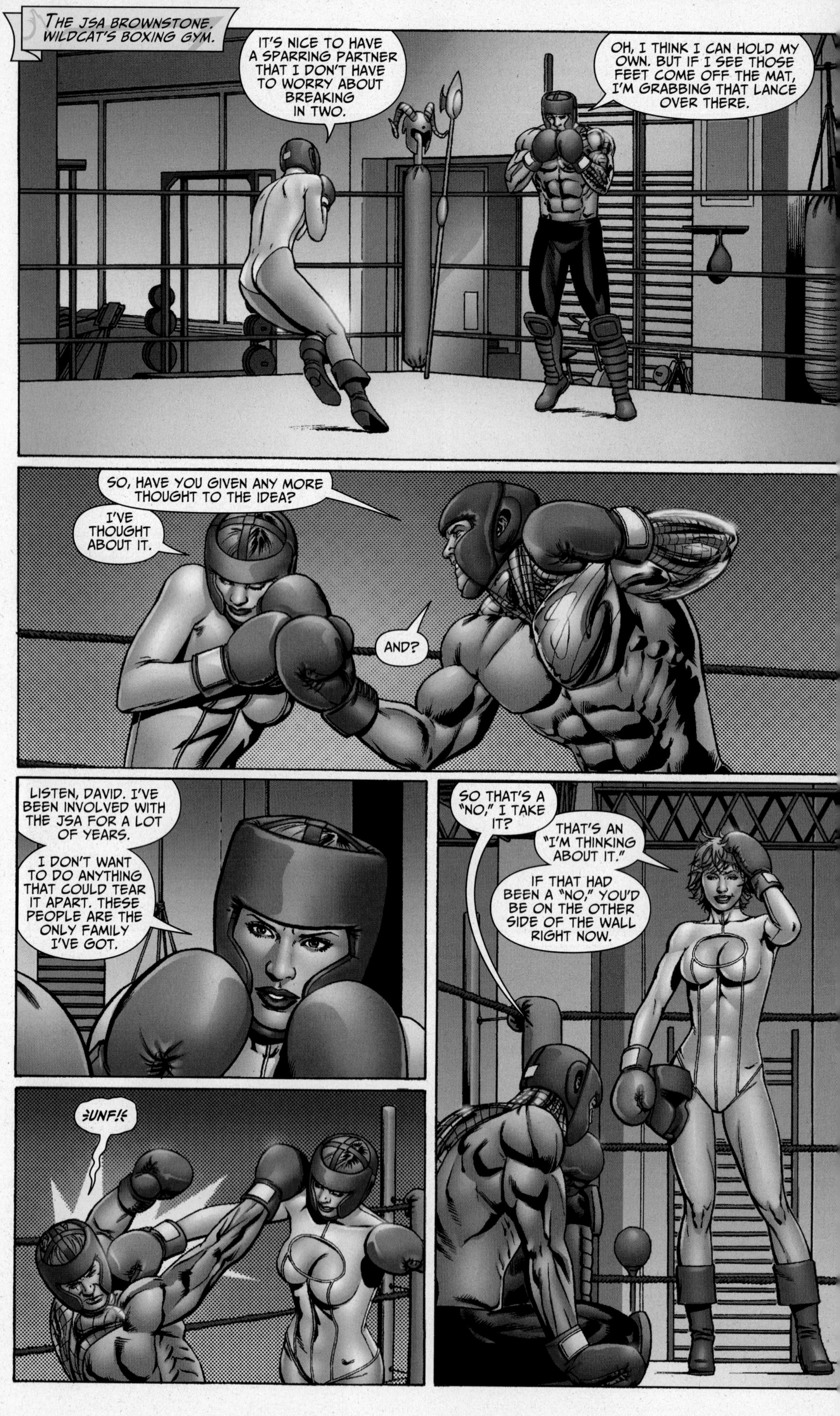
THE JSA BROWNSTONE. WILDCAT'S BOXING GYM.
IT'S NICE TO HAVE A SPARRING PARTNER THAT I DON'T HAVE TO WORRY ABOUT BREAKING IN TWO.
OH, I THINK I CAN HOLD MY OWN. BUT IF I SEE THOSE FEET COME OFF THE MAT, I'M GRABBING THAT LANCE OVER THERE.
SO, HAVE YOU GIVEN ANY MORE THOUGHT TO THE IDEA?
I'VE THOUGHT ABOUT IT.
AND?
LISTEN, DAVID. I'VE BEEN INVOLVED WITH THE JSA FOR A LOT OF YEARS.
I DON'T WANT TO DO ANYTHING THAT COULD TEAR IT APART. THESE PEOPLE ARE THE ONLY FAMILY I'VE GOT.
UNF!
SO THAT'S A "NO," I TAKE IT?
THAT'S AN "I'M THINKING ABOUT IT."
IF THAT HAD BEEN A "NO," YOU'D BE ON THE OTHER SIDE OF THE WALL RIGHT NOW.

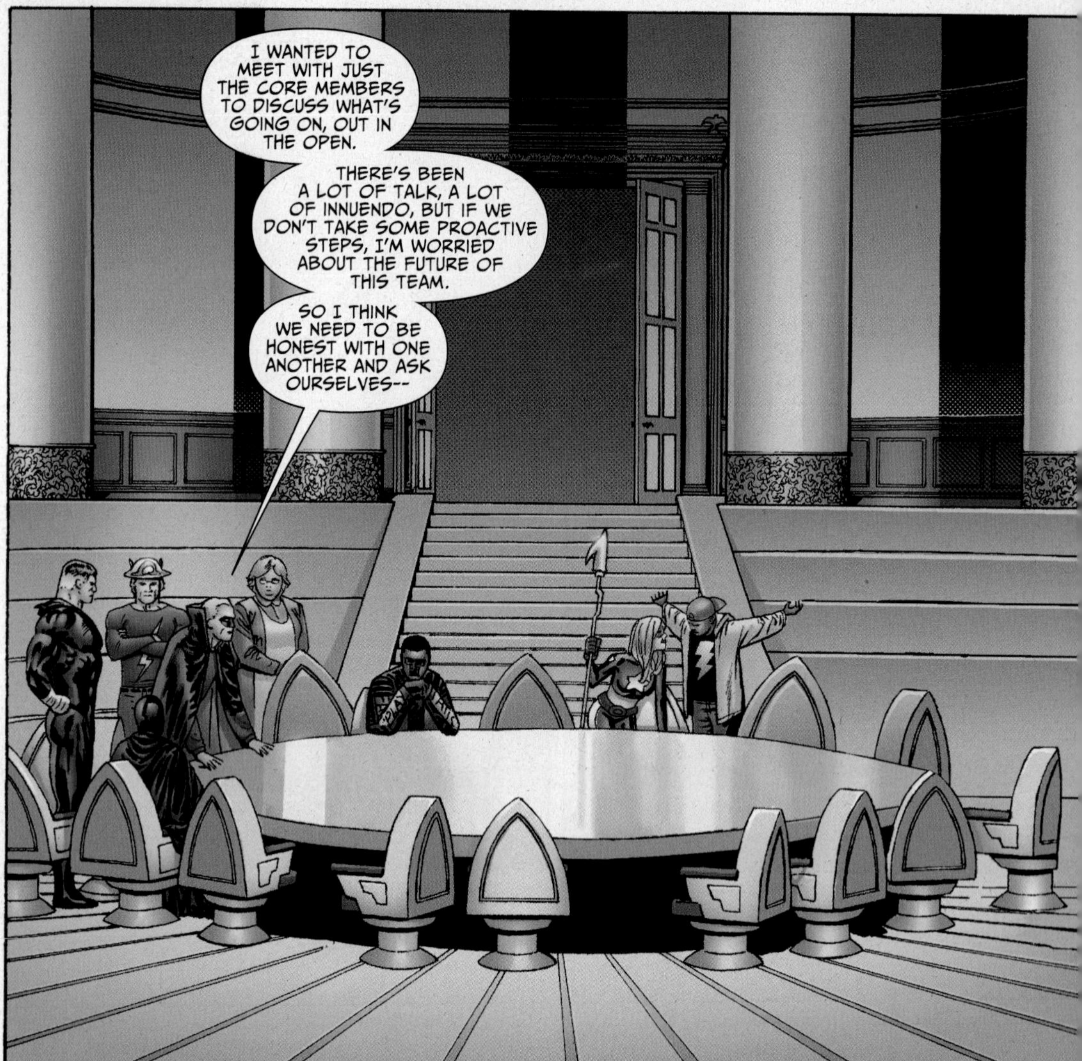
I WANTED TO MEET WITH JUST THE CORE MEMBERS TO DISCUSS WHAT'S GOING ON, OUT IN THE OPEN.
THERE'S BEEN A LOT OF TALK, A LOT OF INNUENDO, BUT IF WE DON'T TAKE SOME PROACTIVE STEPS, I'M WORRIED ABOUT THE FUTURE OF THIS TEAM.
SO I THINK WE NEED TO BE HONEST WITH ONE ANOTHER AND ASK OURSELVES--

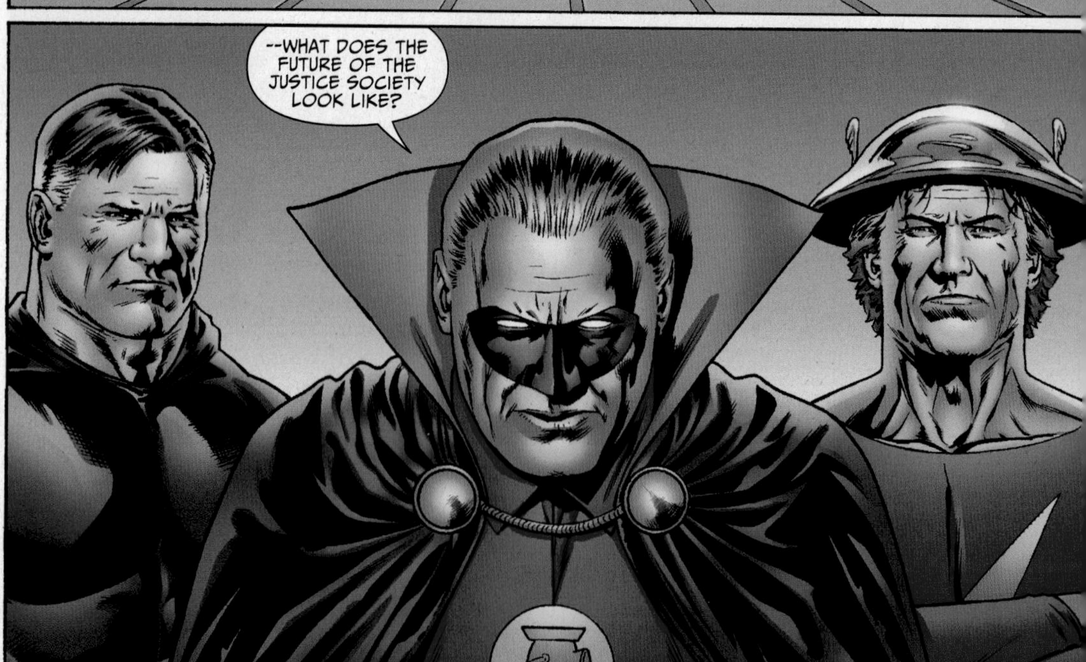
--WHAT DOES THE FUTURE OF THE JUSTICE SOCIETY LOOK LIKE?

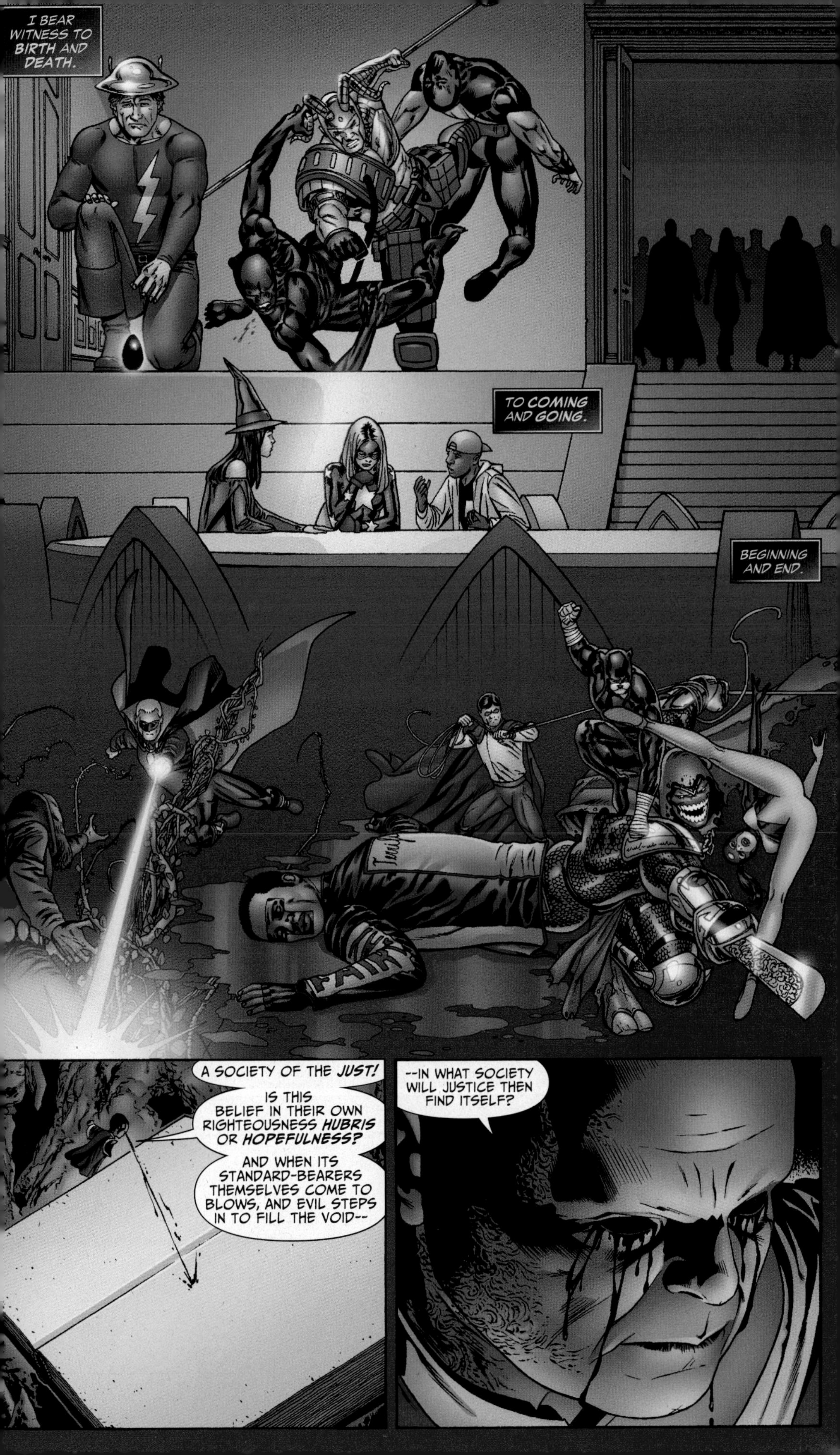
I BEAR WITNESS TO BIRTH AND DEATH.
TO COMING AND GOING.
BEGINNING AND END.
A SOCIETY OF THE JUST!
IS THIS BELIEF IN THEIR OWN RIGHTEOUSNESS HUBRIS OR HOPEFULNESS?
AND WHEN ITS STANDARD-BEARERS THEMSELVES COME TO BLOWS, AND EVIL STEPS IN TO FILL THE VOID--
--IN WHAT SOCIETY WILL JUSTICE THEN FIND ITSELF?

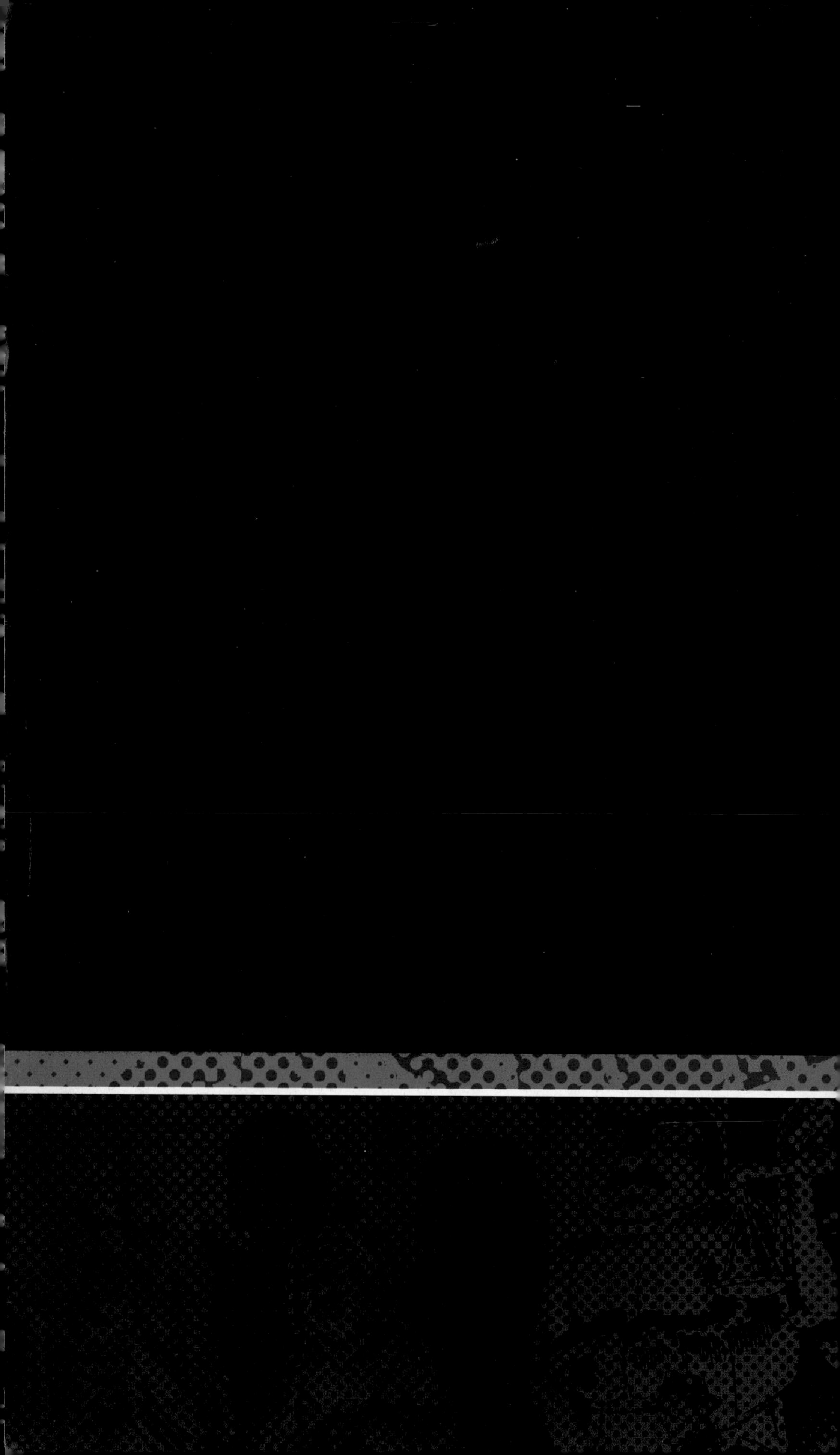

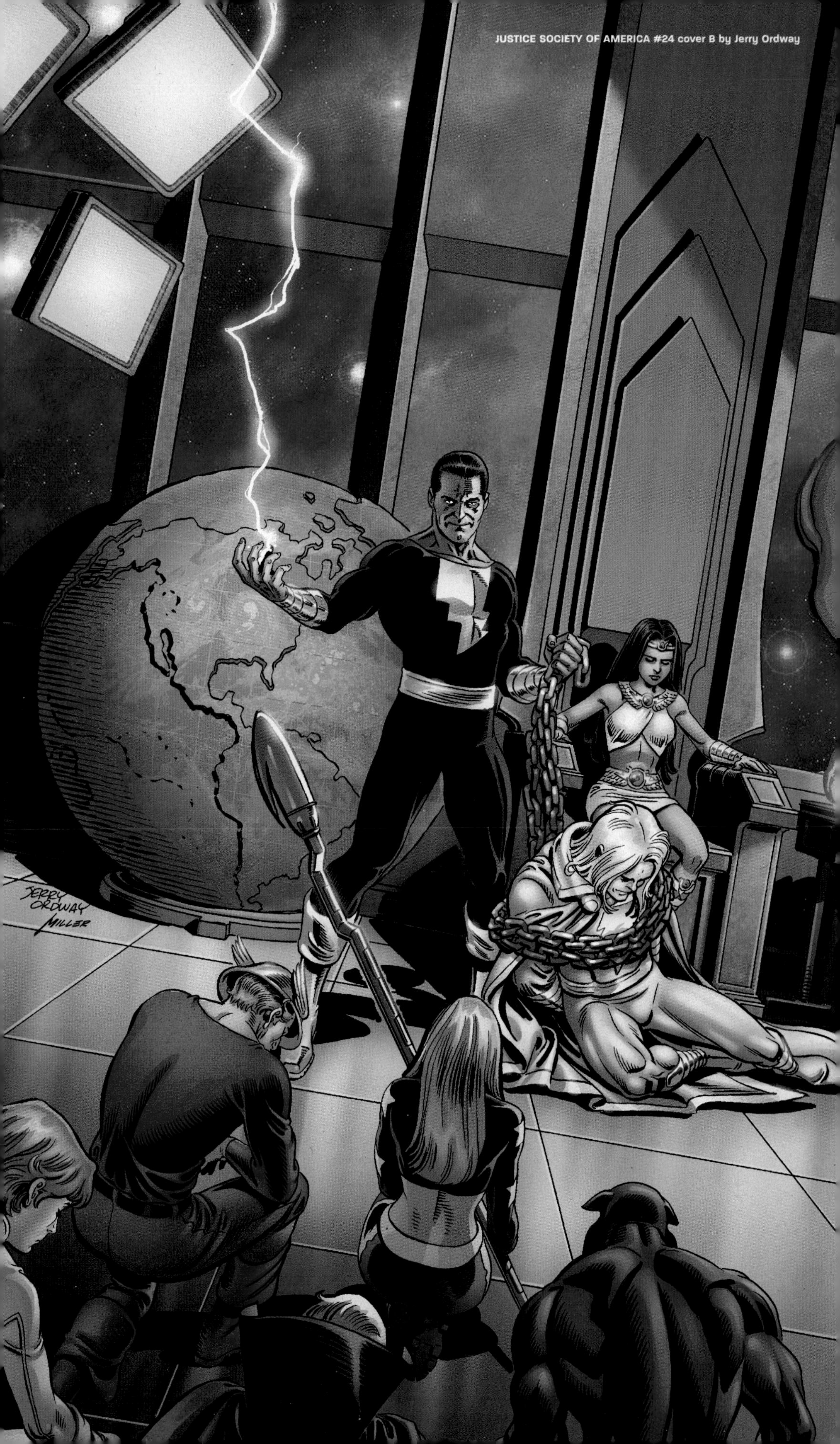
JERRY ORDWAY
MILLER
JUSTICE SOCIETY OF AMERICA #24 cover B by Jerry Ordway

JUSTICE SOCIETY OF AMERICA #25 cover B by Jerry Ordway

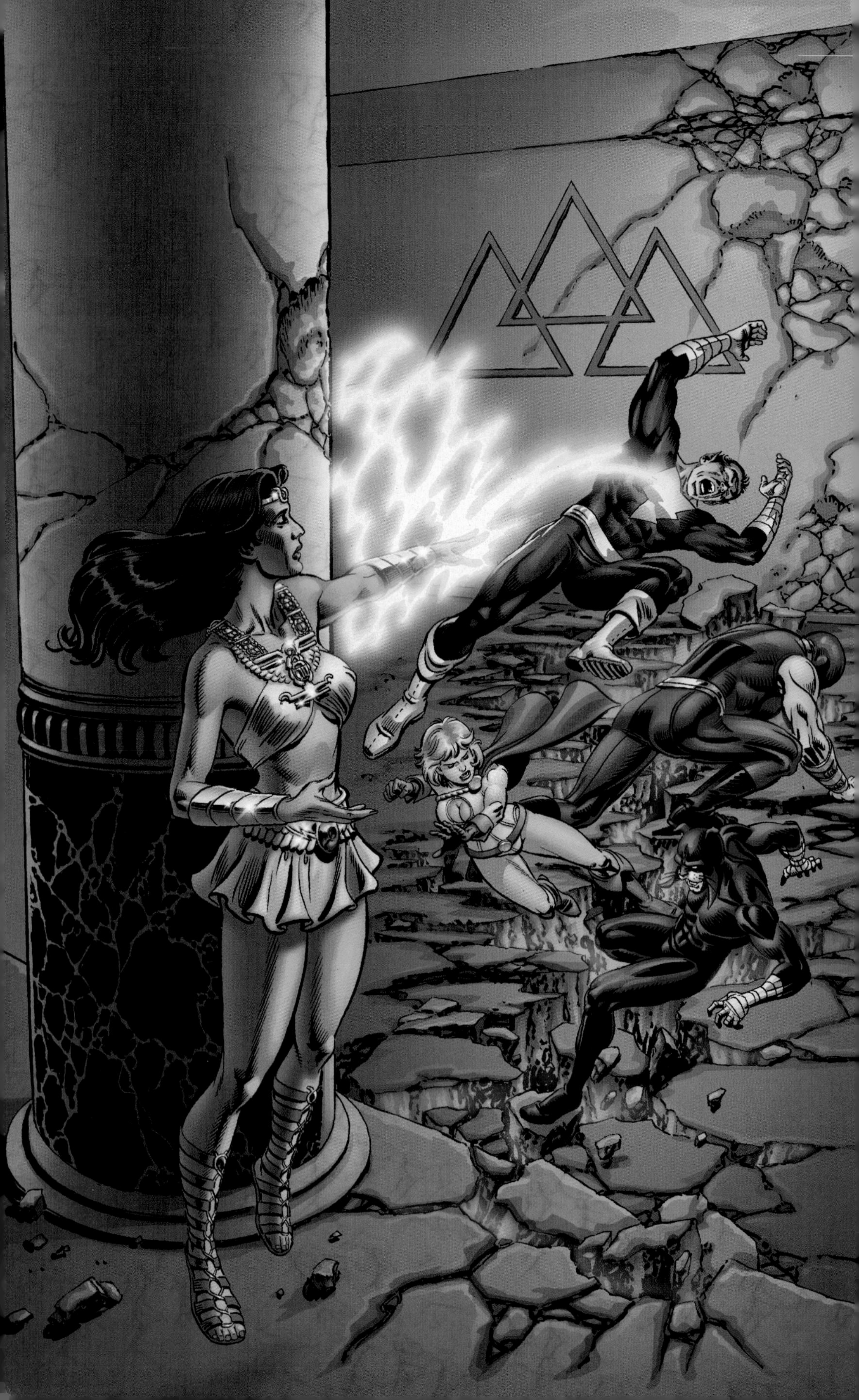

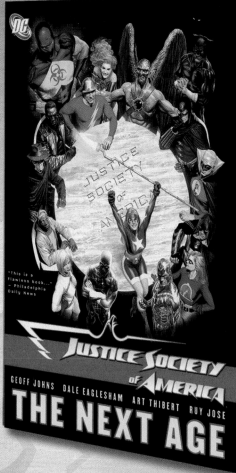

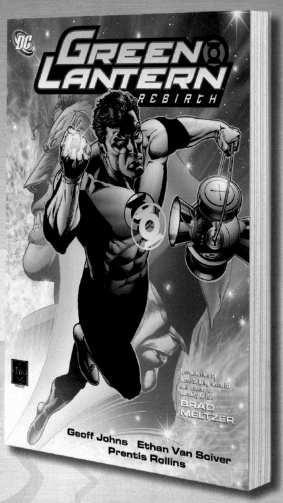

FROM THE WRITER OF
GREEN LANTERN *AND* JSA

GEOFF JOHNS

Witness the gathering of a new team of Teen Titans and their initial battle against an old, familiar foe: the most lethal mercenary on earth, Deathstroke!

with MIKE McKONE

VOL. 1: A KID'S GAME
VOL. 2: FAMILY LOST
VOL. 3: BEAST BOYS AND GIRLS
VOL. 4: THE FUTURE IS NOW
VOL. 5: LIFE AND DEATH
VOL. 6: TITANS AROUND THE WORLD
TEEN TITANS / OUTSIDERS: THE INSIDERS

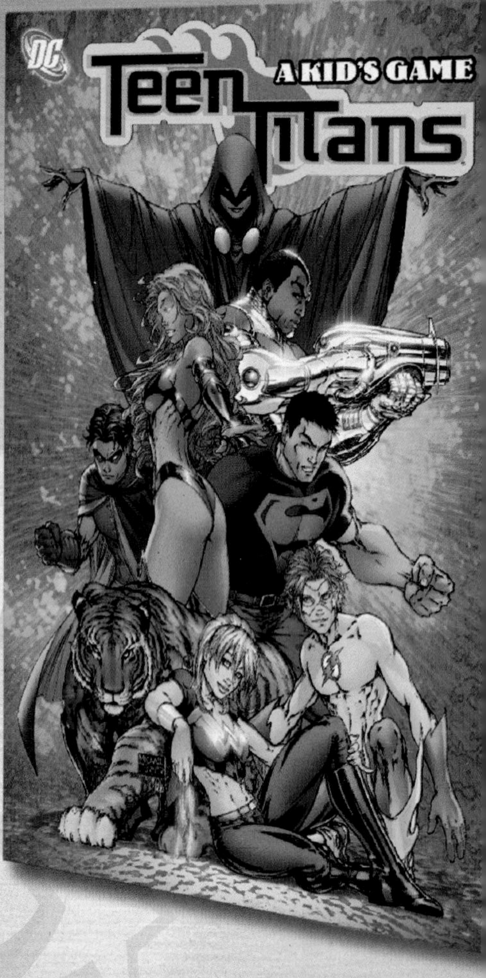
DC
Teen Titans
A KID'S GAME

TEEN TITANS VOL. 2:
FAMILY LOST

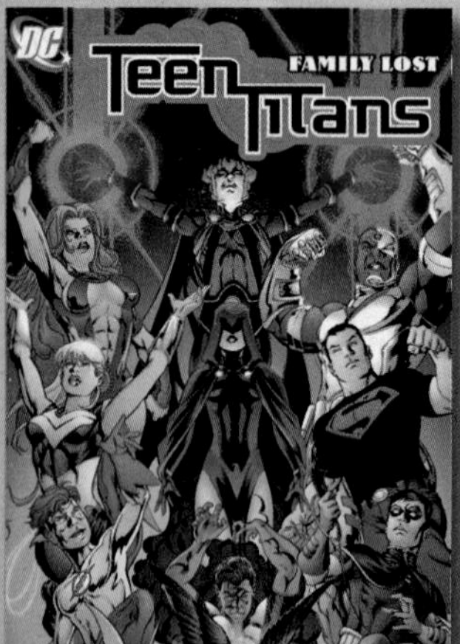
DC
Teen Titans
FAMILY LOST

with
MIKE McKONE

TEEN TITANS VOL. 4:
THE FUTURE IS NOW

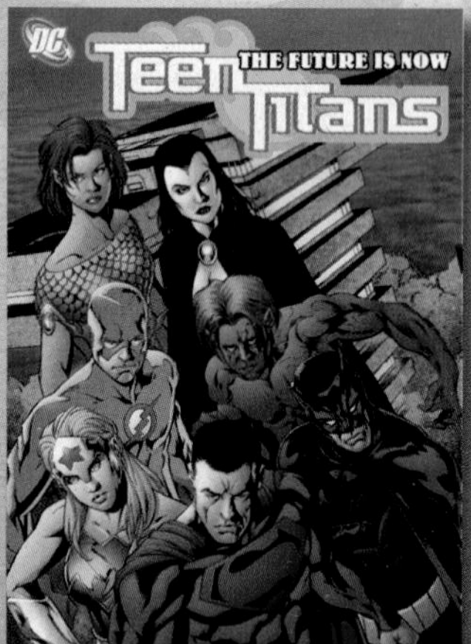
DC
Teen Titans
THE FUTURE IS NOW

with
MIKE McKONE

TEEN TITANS VOL. 5
LIFE AND DEATH

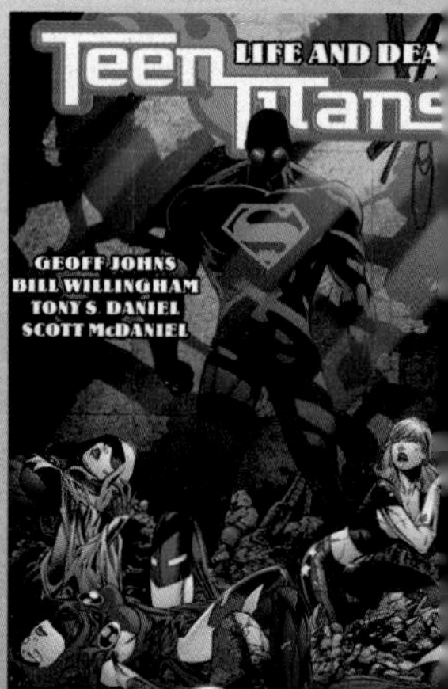
GEOFF JOHNS
BILL WILLINGHAM
TONY S DANIEL
SCOTT McDANIEL

with
VARIOUS ARTISTS

SEARCH THE GRAPHIC NOVELS SECTION OF
DCCOMICS.COM
FOR ART AND INFORMATION ON ALL OF OUR BOOKS!